Islam: America's Trojan Horse!

A Christian Looks at Islam

Don Boys, Ph.D.

Ellen Boys, Editor

Freedom Publications

P. O. Box 944

Ringgold, GA 30736

ISLAM: America's Trojan Horse!

ISBN 1-879805-05-7

First Edition 2003

Library of Congress Card Catalog Number 2003090599

Note: If you would like to have Dr. Boys speak to your organization, write Cornerstone Communications, P.O. Box 944, Ringgold, GA 30736 or e-mail him at cstinfo@aol.com.

Cover art by Doug Heckaman, Jr. of Louisville, KY

All Scripture quotes are from the King James Version.

Dedication

To my wife Ellen, who made this book possible.

About the Author

The author was born in West Virginia where he received his early training. After his conversion as a teen, he was educated at Moody Bible Institute, Tennessee Temple College, Immanuel College, Freedom University and received his Ph.D. from Heritage Baptist University.

Boys served in the Indiana House of Representatives and while in the House, the media identified him as "the most conservative voice in the General Assembly." He authored legislation to require the public schools to teach scientific creation on an equal basis with evolution; life in prison for rape; prison for sodomy; reinstatement of the death penalty and other conservative measures.

Dr. Boys has authored 12 other books: *Liberalism: A Rope of Sand*; *How to Feel Better, Look Younger, Live Longer*; *A Time to Laugh*; *Pilgrims, Puritans and Patriots*; *Is God a Right-Winger?*; *Christian Resistance: An Idea Whose Time Has Come—Again!*; *Pioneers, Preachers and Politicians: The True Story of America*; *Boys' Big Book of Humor*; *AIDS: Silent Killer*; *Evolution: Fact, Fraud or Faith?*; and *Y2K*.

Boys has written many feature articles that have appeared in major journals and from 1985 to 1993 wrote columns for *USA Today*. He has been interviewed by scores of magazines, journals and newspapers and is contacted from time to time by major magazines and newspapers as a fact checker, especially relating to fundamental and evangelical Christianity.

His writing has resulted in his appearing on many of the major talk shows, such as CNN's "Crossfire"; "Sally Jesse Raphael Show" (twice); "Jerry Springer Show" (three times); "NBC Nightly News"; "CBS Morning News"; and many others. He has also been on many of the major radio talk shows.

Dr. Boys and his wife, Ellen, spend much of their time doing Christian Couples' Conferences, Child Rearing Conferences, Creation Conferences, revival meetings, etc., in churches throughout North America, Australia, Africa and Europe. They live in North Georgia and can be reached at P.O. Box 944, Ringgold, GA 30736. His website is cstnews.com (stands for common sense today).

Table of Contents

Acknowledgments

Well, my book is finished and it is time to give credit where credit is due. This, I am pleased to do. It is normal procedure to praise the spouse at times like this, and this is no exception. In fact, it is required since my wife Ellen has been invaluable during this process of research, interviews, writing, re-writing, and re-writing. She has been my editor and made me focus on what I was trying to communicate to others. She found many typos, ambiguities, dangling participles (I have a tendency to let them dangle), and inconsistencies. Her editorial expertise is exceptional. It is interesting that my book published in March of 1999 was sent back to us by my publisher with only one correction to be made. When Ellen looked at it, the correction was wrong! The publisher agreed with her conclusion. Anyway, keep in mind that a superb editor makes a good book, a better book. Thanks sweetheart.

I am also grateful to Dr. Pat Taylor, a long time friend living in North Georgia, for her work in proofreading my manuscript. Pat has taught at two colleges (one Christian and the other a state school). Her comments, criticisms, and smiley faces were invaluable to this work. Thanks Pat.

Then there is my old, college friend, Dr. Harold Willmington of Liberty University in Lynchburg, Virginia. I thought Harold might write me thusly: Dear Don: I just finished reading your manuscript, *Islam: America's Trojan Horse!* and while it is good and original, the part that is good is not original and the part that is original is not good. Your Friend, Harold. Well, he did not do that so I can rest easy. He said, "In my opinion this is the most concise, yet complete overview of the evils of the Muslim faith in print today. It is a book that must be read by every American." Thanks friend!

The cover art by my good friend, Doug Heckaman, Jr., of Louisville, KY adds much to the book. It epitomizes the whole book. Thanks for a great job, Doug.

Of course any errors or omissions are my own and will be corrected in the second edition. Any suggestions or corrections can be sent to cstinfo@aol.com or to P.O. Box 944, Ringgold, GA 30736.

Foreword

Watch Out for Snakes!

There are over 2,000 Muslim mosques in America with others planned. In fact, Muslims plan to conquer America. Well, that's not exactly true; they plan to take over the world! And that statement is easily proved, as you will soon see. We are facing the greatest challenge to our nation that we have ever faced. That includes the War Between the States (or as some call it, "Lincoln's War of Northern Aggression") and our 70-year conflict with Communism. The enemy is already among us: Muslim extremists.

Every Muslim is not a terrorist and all Muslims do not encourage terrorism, but a large number of them do. Many were trained that way from infancy. There is a Trojan Horse already **within** our walls. Muslim extremists are the ones that I am concerned about, not those Muslims who are peaceful, kind, law-abiding, and lovers of freedom.

TRAGEDY OF TROY

Homer told of the tragedy of Troy in the legend, *The Odyssey*. Troy was taken by stealth, not sword, and America may be taken the same way if the Muslims persist and Americans drift off to sleep watching "I love Lucy" for the 17th time.

Troy was a magnificent city with high, thick walls and massive gates ably defended by the most courageous soldiers. They were sure their city would live forever, somewhat like super-confident Americans believe.

Paris, a Trojan prince, stole Helen, the world's most beautiful woman, away from her husband, Menelaus, a king of the Greeks. For two years the Greeks prepared for war; and, with Ulysses, they set sail in a thousand ships to avenge the King's honor.

The battle lasted for nine years and numerous heroes were slain on both sides. Finally, Ulysses contrived a plan to take the city; this plan required brains, not battles. He instructed his men to build a huge wooden horse that would hold a hundred men. One night, he and his armed men climbed into the horse, and the cleverly concealed door was closed.

That night, the Greeks boarded their ships and sailed away;

the last of them were seen sailing out of sight by the early risers of Troy. But the Greeks only sailed behind a distant island and waited for a time to strike. The next day not a Greek tent could be seen on the plain, only the wooden horse with soldiers of death inside. The trap was set. The people of Troy were elated with their "victory" and were enthralled with the token of victory, the wooden horse. Some wanted to take it into the city as a war trophy, while others were afraid of it.

Laocoon, the priest, loudly warned against the horse saying, "I fear the Greeks even when they bear gifts." During this time, a Greek soldier, Sinon by name, was found who pretended to be a deserter from the Greeks. Ulysses planned that Sinon should convince the people to take the horse inside the city. Sinon told them that Troy would never be destroyed if the horse were inside its walls. He also promised the favor and protection of the goddess, Athene. With the horse, they would have happiness and prosperity forever. (Sound familiar? "We must learn to accept everyone's religion and culture as equal to ours; it is narrow and bigoted to think otherwise. Why, what would world opinion be if we thought America should always be first in our minds?")

Again, the priest warned, "beware, beware of the treacherous Greek. Cast the horse into the sea, or burn it, for it will bring you only misery and ruin." Obviously, the priest was prejudiced and bigoted, a nationalist who wrapped himself in the Trojan flag yelling, "Troy first!" The Liberals in the government were probably already planning to send foreign aid to the Greeks to "shore up world opinion," and to show that the Trojans were willing to "forgive and forget" to maintain world peace (and profitable trade with the Greeks).

The militant priest (who was a member of the Religious Right?) frustratingly, although bravely, threw his spear at the wooden horse, resulting in a hollow clang of the armor. But alas, the brave priest was not long for this world, for out of the sea slithered two immense serpents with eyes and tongues flashing flames of fire. They snaked through the terrified crowd, oblivious to everyone except the priest and his two right-wing sons. To the horror and delight of the crowd, the serpents entwined the priest and his sons and crushed them to death—their conservative, obstructionist voices stilled forever. The serpents, their job done, slithered through the crowd and back into the sea.

Of course, uninformed people, following the hysterical cries of liberal leaders, interpreted the episode as a vindication of their permissive philosophy and demanded that the horse be brought into the city, ere they get a federal judge to **require** it. And so it was done. They even tore down a portion of their defense system, their walls, to get the horse into the city, but after all, they were now safe. Had not the authorities told them so?

For the first time in nine years, the city was unguarded, but there was no need to spend money on defense. (Spend it on illegal immigrants instead?) While the unguarded city slept, Sinon released Ulysses and his men from the bowels of the horse. A beacon signaled the Greeks, and soon the streets of Troy were swarming with thousands of enemy soldiers. The Trojans were awakened from their sweet dreams of peace, prosperity, and pleasure by the sounds of battle.

The King was slain, along with his noble soldiers, and while peoples' arms and legs were shackled, they watched their proud city on the shores of the Aegean Sea burn to the very foundations. As the Greek ships sailed from the harbor, gorged with all the wealth of the great, grand, and glorious Troy, the people rattled their chains in the stinking ships' holds and remembered the words of their faithful priest: "Beware of the treacherous Greeks…. [I]t will bring you only misery and ruin." Troy was gone forever because the people refused to listen to words of warning.[1]

AMERICA LAST

Alas, our nation is being lulled to sleep by leaders whose motto is "America last," and they have permitted a wooden horse to be dragged inside our walls. Is the day coming when our glorious Republic will only be remembered as a "noble experiment" between the great oceans? In kindness we have permitted aliens inside our nation who have no intention of being absorbed into our "melting pot." They believe in the "salad bowl" theory. Muslims will not adopt our ways and be assimilated into our culture. They are determined to change our culture, laws, and religion as they have in England, France, and other nations.

I have a question for those who think I am too hard, harsh, or even hateful: What if terrorists drop a nuclear bomb over one of

11

our major cities resulting in the deaths of 100,000 Americans from the blast with another 300,000 dying of radiation; plunging the stock market to the basement; devastating our economy for a generation; putting millions of people out of work; producing fear and anxiety up and down every street in the nation; would you still think me to be too harsh? Many national leaders think the above could happen, or we might have millions infected by a biological or chemical weapon. Keep my question in mind as you read this book. The extremists are here, today!

Arnaud de Borchgrave reported that Islamists in Pakistan expect that "in the next 10 years, Americans will wake up to the existence of an Islamic army in their midst–an army of jihadis who will **force** [my emphasis] America to abandon imperialism and listen to the voice of Allah." (*NewsMax.com* web site, 8-21-02.) Most sleeping Americans are not aware of the danger. I hope to awaken them, anger them, and alarm them with this message: There is a Trojan Horse in America filled with the enemy.

I have cast my spear at the side of the wooden horse. Those who believe in unlimited immigration and multiculturalism will not cast a spear (except in the direction of Conservatives). They, in fact, tell us to throw down our weapons and to help them drag a strange wooden horse even deeper inside our land. Meanwhile, Christian Conservatives had better watch for snakes in our midst.

1.   Cited by Don Boys in *Is God a Right-Winger?*, Goodhope Press, Indianapolis, 1984, p. 71-74.

Introduction

Stepping on Your Face

Our war with terrorism is rooted in the early days of mankind, in the tent of Abraham when he refused to wait for God's promise to provide him a son! At his wife's suggestion (and in keeping with the pagan practice of Sarai's homeland), Abraham took Hagar to bed rather than wait for God's promise to be fulfilled. The result was the birth of Ishmael who, according to Genesis 16:12, would become "a wild man; his hand will be against every man...." This seems to have been played out in history and maybe in the acts of terror perpetrated by Muslim terrorists in recent years and sadly on September 11, 2001.

ISLAM IS LEGAL IN U.S.

Muslims have a legal right to live in America and to practice their religion (even a perverted religion), and they have a right to think that all other religions are wrong. This is America where First Amendment rights are precious to all of us. I don't want to see anyone's rights abused or denied. After all, if it can happen to you, it can happen to me. Muslims and Methodists, Buddhists and Baptists have a right to believe what they want to believe. If they believe error, then there will be eternal consequences for that error. Of course, that would also be true of me. So be it.

I don't hate Muslims (or anyone else) and I wish them no harm. In fact, I love them as I do all people. I read Islam as **I** Sincerely **L**ove **A**ll **M**uslims, and will try to show them by telling them the truth in this book. I have no reason to believe they are not sincere. I am sure many of them want to serve Allah and to be faithful to their "holy" book, as I want to serve Christ and be faithful to the Bible. You see, my convictions are as precious and important to me as theirs are to them. This is America where we can have honest disagreements without being disagreeable. We can contend without being contentious. However, you will discover on these pages that there are many sharp points of disagreement, and I plan to write **bluntly** to make my point.

It is interesting that the Muslim countries do not have freedom of speech, religion, assembly, and press; furthermore, their "moderate" leaders in those nations have not demanded such freedom since the September 11 attack on America! Why are all the "moderates" so quiet on this subject? And why haven't American Muslims demanded freedom in Islamic nations? Is it because they are not moderates? You will be surprised with my exclusive interviews with Muslim leaders that are reported in this book.

RADICAL ISLAM

President Bush told Americans that we are at war. He is correct. It is called *jihad*: a holy war that all Muslims know they are obligated to support, and that war is against Israel and America. This war is the most unusual one we have ever fought. The enemy is not associated with one aggressive nation located on a fixed spot on earth. It is also true that Congress must declare war, and they have not done so. That is a mistake and major miscalculation on the part of the administration. The enemy is radical Islam who wants to destroy the U.S., and while we are not at war with all Muslims, we must be aware that many of them are our sworn enemies.

If I see Muslims (or anyone else) being mistreated, I will come to their defense. No one should be harassed, intimidated, or punished for what he believes. There are many Muslims who are horrified at what happened on September 11. I accept their word that they are sincere. However, out of the estimated two million (**not** 11 million) Muslims in America, many **do** believe in terror and **do** believe they will go to Paradise as their body bomb goes off or their hijacked plane explodes against a building, killing thousands of "infidels."

Some of our politicians, preachers, and pundits are telling us that there are no differences in religions. One is as good as another. We are told that Islam is a religion of peace. I think those uninformed or dishonest people should stay in their own fields and not pretend to be theologians. Those people have a right to say what they want; however, I reject many of them, and I am compelled to rebuke them as Paul commands in II Timothy 4:2. Christians should be outraged when the pompous pundits equate Allah with the God of the Bible! Since the politicians work for me (I pay their salaries), I demand that they speak the truth or keep quiet on the subject.

ALL TERRORISTS HAVE BEEN MUSLIMS

I shall be accused of being a hater and bigot, but that doesn't negate my major premise that Islam is a Trojan Horse in America. Muslim clerics will scream at me for being so intolerant; however, I insist that they point out my errors! They will say that I am slandering their religion, but if so, I am "slandering" it with truth and truth is far more important than political correctness. I would like for a Muslim leader to tell me why he has the right to offend me with lies about Christ's deity, death, and resurrection and I am supposed to sit there and smile like an idiot, but I cannot point out the incredible contradictions, mistakes, and absurdities in the religion of Islam without being called a hater.

America opened her doors to Arabs and Muslims, and with the good guys have come the scum (we know that scum comes to the top as does cream). While all Muslims are not terrorists, **all the terrorists have been Muslims!** Our open doors and acceptance of Muslims have kicked us in the face. Some of our guests have repaid good with evil.

Folks, there isn't much anyone can do if there are dedicated, sincere, and fearless Muslims who have decided that we are their enemy. No amount of security measures will ever protect us against terrorist attacks. Those politicians who say we can **ever** be free of terror are dishonest or uninformed or very naïve. Whatever the reason, they should run, not walk, to hand in their resignations. To say that we will eradicate evil is a silly, nonsensical statement.

U. S. RESPONSE

There is evidence that our government knew of Muslim terrorists many years ago but did nothing about it. We must hold politicians and bureaucrats accountable for their actions and inaction. Don't listen to their rhetoric but **watch** the reality. Public rhetoric since the terrorist attack attempts to assure Americans that Islam is a religion of peace, and many Americans have adopted that mantra since we **want** to believe it. However, after further attacks, killing thousands or maybe hundreds of thousands, the unwisely adopted mantra that Islam is peaceful will be discarded as quickly as a low-rated television show by network executives.

In this book I will deal with the Massacre, the Myths, the Monsters, the Movement (Islam), the Mavericks, the Mistakes (in their "holy" book, the Koran), the Motives, the Menace, and the Message. You will be shocked that many Muslim children are trained from infancy to become killers of "infidels," at the pugnacious policies of Muslim leaders, at the numerous mistakes in their holy book, at the root cause of Muslims' hatred, at the very real nuclear, chemical, and biological threat to millions of Americans, at how we may respond to major disasters, and finally, at what our response should be to the Muslims and the world.

It is Christ who sets men free, and if we fail to liberate Muslims from Islam, they will be stepping on your face in a very few years. I think you will find this book shocking but informative so that you can make decisions about your own security and response. Read on.

Chapter One

The Massacre

Suicidal Slaves to Islam

It was the best of times; it was the worst of times. History will record that in the summer of 2001, America was in clover. There was high employment, and while the stock market was slipping, few people thought it would hit bottom. Things were looking good for America. We had elected as President a professing Christian who wasn't ashamed of his faith in Christ. All of us received a tax refund with promises of more tax cuts. While there were indications that jobs were going south, we were still the financial power of the earth. And no informed person questioned our military superiority.

Then on September 11, 2001, the world changed forever when 19 Muslim terrorists from Egypt and Saudi Arabia flew two planes into the twin towers of the World Trade Center in Manhattan and one into the Pentagon in Washington causing over 3000 deaths. Another plane was crashed in Pennsylvania before it reached Washington. It is not incidental that those two targets represented America's perceived strength: commerce and military. They hit us where we were the strongest. And they made us bleed.

Americans watched in horror as the two massive towers fell, trapping thousands of innocent people inside. There were many acts of courage and some of infamy: police and fire fighters rushed into the burning buildings to save lives and later scabs on society robbed the dead and used stolen credit cards to plunder victims' bank accounts. An article in many national papers (8-6-02) revealed: "4,000 use ATMs to steal $15 million."

PREACHERS: CHEERLEADERS OF DESTRUCTION

Since the attack, many blinded eyes have miraculously received sight concerning incompetent government and irrational religion, but until I'm proved wrong, I still believe most Americans are using a white-tipped cane as they walk the streets. Before the dust and smoke cleared from the attacks, religious leaders stumbled over each other to get to television cameras to absolve Islam from any guilt. In doing so, they displayed political correctness and personal cowardice. They will be recognized as cheerleaders for our destruction. Those sickly, smiling clergymen wearing panty hose, silk shorts, lace around their shirts, and sniffing French perfume from frilly handkerchiefs made me ashamed to be an American, let alone a preacher. Most Americans want leaders with hair on their chests, bone in their backs, and a brain in their heads. Many clergymen lack all three. Leaders who are afraid of adverse public opinion and being labeled "conservative" (gasp!) or "Fundamentalist" (gasp! gasp!) are moral cripples who are not aware of their limp and crooked walk. Such leaders, in crises, are as useless as a milking stool under a bull. When courageous leaders such as Franklin Graham, Jerry Falwell, Jerry Vines, Pat Robertson, and others spoke the truth about Islam, unprincipled politicians, preachers, and pundits fled from them like the mythical vampire flees the rising sun. Soft religious leaders are now "building bridges" (of mist) between Christianity and Islam, and the uninformed who cross that "bridge" of mist will fall into a noxious swamp of unbelief.

It is astounding that religious leaders would come to the defense of a religion that produced such a massacre of innocent people, but men such as television preacher Robert Schuller did. He even had a Muslim imam (cleric) on his television show! (Many thinking people consider Schuller as the biggest phony in America.) Another soft, "sensitive," servile preacher is Bill Hybels of Willow Creek Community Church in Illinois, and I think he is President of the League of the Willfully Blind! According to Voice of the Martyrs web site, Hybels also had a Muslim leader in his pulpit on October 7, 2001. Faisal Hammouda said, "We believe in Jesus more than you do, in fact." Did Bill correct him with the truth that Muslims do not believe Christ is divine or that he died for our sins? No, Bill Hybels wants everyone to feel warm and fuzzy. He may think he is showing love, but love is not love without truth. Without that truth his love would encourage Muslims in their unbelief. Our concern should not be inter-religious tolerance but regeneration of the lost. Maybe he should try to "build bridges" between Islam and the thousands of widows and orphans of those who died in the September attacks.

TERRORISTS ARE NOT COWARDS

Many pundits, politicians, and preachers called the killers cowardly, but they were hardly that. These assassins were dedicated to their cause and their cause was Islam. It does take some courage to follow a plan from which one knows there is no hope of escape. To steer a plane into a building is criminal. It is atrocious; it is hideous, but it is not cowardly. They were sadistic, suicidal slaves to Islam. They were inside America's Trojan Horse.

Those Islamic killers were not cowardly nor were they deranged. It was murder but not madness. They were all educated young men who worked diligently to complete a dastardly task: to murder innocent people and to spread fear down every street, from the hovels of Appalachia to the palatial mansions of Beverly Hills. They succeeded in accomplishing the worst terrorist attack upon America, but it was not, as some have said, the first terrorist attack upon our nation. Before, during, and after the terrorist attacks on America, there were some strange things that happened that most Americans don't know. I will try to bring it all together in this book.

ISLAMIC TERRORISTS AND OKLAHOMA CITY
BOMBING

To lay a foundation, we must go back to the first bombing of the World Trade Center in 1993 and to the Oklahoma City bombing. Yes, there is a connection, but you won't hear that from the FBI or national politicians. Both the first World Trade Center bombing and the Oklahoma City bombing are classic examples of the incompetence of our security people and a super-sensitive spirit of multiculturalism, not wanting to hurt the feelings of a large host of Muslims. I wish the government were as concerned every now and then about how born-again Christians feel.

Geoff Metcalf reported in a column in *WorldNetDaily*[1] and on his radio show that Jayna Davis, a reporter for the NBC affiliate in Oklahoma City, had astounding evidence about Middle East terrorists' involvement with the Oklahoma City bombing and the 1993

World Trade Center attack! After the Oklahoma City bombing, Jayna wrote a letter to David Schippers, a lifetime Chicago Democrat who was the impeachment attorney for the House of Representatives Clinton impeachment proceedings. (He did a good job but was frustrated by the Republican leadership.) Investigative reporter Davis wrote him: "I have information about the Oklahoma City bombing and a Middle Eastern connection." She sent him a packet of material and asked him to read it and to call her. He did and she said, "You've just seen the tip of the iceberg. I have a lot more. Would you be interested in looking at it?" He asked her, "Why don't you go to the FBI or to the people who are interested?" She replied, "I went to the FBI with everything I have here, and they refused to take it." This was **before** the McVeigh Trial, and they weren't interested in pertinent evidence!

Schippers said, "I saw evidence that there were nine security cameras that picked up the people running from the place **before** the bombing. I found out that the FBI had seized all those films, and no one has ever seen them." Could the federal authorities not want those tapes seen because they show Middle Eastern men running away before the bombing?

Davis and her husband flew into Chicago and brought three large binders and a tape of all her material that she had aired during the course of her investigation. Enclosed were affidavits from people warning that a terrorist attack was coming. (This was a warning concerning the Oklahoma City bombing.) From her information, Schippers became convinced that there was a Middle Eastern connection in the Oklahoma City bombing. The following incredible statement seems to prove a connection of bin Laden to the Oklahoma City bombing: "Mr. Bodansky [author of *Bin Laden: The Man Who Declared War on America*] talked to Jayna Davis. He was one of the people behind the warning that came out Feb. 19, 1995, and this was the warning that I saw: that there was going to be an attack on the United States by bin Laden's people, that the original target–and this is the way it reads–the original target was supposed to be the White House and the Capitol building, and they were going to use commercial airliners as bombs."

In July of 2001, Schippers made contact with a U. S. Deputy Attorney General and told him of his information and he replied, "I'll have somebody get back to you right away." He still has not heard from him!

About a month and a half **before** Sept. 11 Schippers had incredible information but nobody wanted to see it! He said, "The Jayna Davis material and the Oklahoma City bombing are just a part of the stuff I've got. I have information indicating there was going to be a massive attack in lower Manhattan. I couldn't get anybody to listen to me." Schippers said, "Jayna received a call–I think she said 15 minutes **before** the first plane hit the tower. She received a call from an individual she described as having a Middle Eastern accent, and all he said was, "Turn on your television." She did and saw the twin towers come down! Note that the call came just **before** the first plane hit the tower! Mrs. Davis then received a call from a friend who is in naval intelligence. This guy called her from overseas, and he said to her, "The same people did this (the towers) that did Oklahoma City," and then he said, "Get out of the house. You are in danger."

We all know that John Doe number two was reported to have had a Middle Eastern appearance and there are signed affidavits swearing that a Middle Eastern man was seen running from the Murray Building just before the bomb (or more correctly, **bombs)** went off. But our employees at the FBI were not interested in the information! Interestingly, we know that they have been following thousands of leads since September 11, even rather silly ones, but are not interested in what evidence two very reputable people tried to give them!

Only minutes after the Oklahoma City blast, an APB (All Points Bulletin) went out to all law officers in the state to be on the lookout for Middle Eastern men who were seen speeding from the crime scene in a brown Chevy pickup. Furthermore, motel clerks in a downtown motel reported that Tim McVeigh was seen with an unknown number of Middle Eastern men only weeks before the blast. A total of eight Middle Eastern men were identified by 24 witnesses as being seen with McVeigh and Nichols before the bombing and most were former Iraqi soldiers! Yes, there was a Middle East connection.

Joseph Farah reported further about Jayna Davis and the Oklahoma City bombing: "Davis, now represented by former House impeachment counsel David Schippers, presented Nichols' defense with the names of more than two dozen witnesses who identified several Arab men tied to various stages of the Oklahoma bombing plot. Included in that package were 200 pages of police and court records along with statements by law enforcement and intelligence sources that corroborated aspects of the eyewitness testimony."[2]

FBI KNEW ABOUT THE PLOT

Could it be that the government does not want to know about a Middle East connection to the Oklahoma City bombing? After all, they went on record telling us that there was no such connection even though they knew in February of 1995 that Middle East terrorists were operating in Oklahoma City. The FBI has been less than candid about the bombing of the Murrah Building. Now we have discovered that the FBI's top counter-terrorist expert, Danny Coulson, checked into an Oklahoma City motel nine hours **before** the bomb exploded killing 168 people. In his book, published in 1999, Coulson claimed to be in Fort Worth at the time of the bombing. However, a receipt from Embassy Suites proves he was in Oklahoma City.[3] This seems to support the many claims that the explosion was part of a Federal sting operation that went awry. The sting allegedly involved white supremacists, religious nuts, and Middle East terrorists. Why has our government been involved in so many dastardly deeds, then been "forced" to cover the posterior portions of their anatomy?

Although Federal officials deny it, the evidence keeps stacking up providing very convincing proof of a Middle East (Iraqi) connection, running from the 1993 World Trade Center bombing, to the Oklahoma City bombing, to the September 11 attacks! The most recent evidence turned up in late June of 2002, revealing that a contact in the Saudi government warned the FBI on **April 19, 1995,** of the pending Oklahoma City bombing! Mike Johnston, attorney with Judicial Watch, reported: "Vincent Canastraro, who is the former chief of counter-terrorism for the CIA ... called Special Agent Kevin L. Foust and informed him that one of his best sources from Saudi Arabian intelligence specifically advised him that there was a squad of people currently in the United States, very possibly Iraqi, who, and I'm quoting, 'have been tasked with carrying out terrorist acts against the United States.'"[4]

Johnston added that the Saudi informant told Federal officials that he had seen the list of possible targets of terror and "first on the list was the federal building in Oklahoma City, Oklahoma."

Johnston told the radio audience that there "was some evidence suggesting that Khalid Shaikh Mohammed–a top al-Qaida lieutenant whom federal authorities believe may have masterminded the Sept. 11 attacks–trained Nichols for the OKC bombing in the Philippines." It is known that Mohammed was in the Philippians the same time Terry Nichols made his last of many trips there just before the Oklahoma City bombing. We now know that Mohammed was in control of the terrorist cell and its many nefarious activities in the Philippines.

WARNING FROM THE PHILIPPINES

Mohammed, born in Kuwait, put his co-conspirators in a one-room Manila apartment (with their explosives!) while he lived in a swanky apartment across town. On January 6, 1995, the small apartment caught fire (from the explosive chemicals) resulting in an investigation that probably saved thousands of lives! Mohammed, along with others, conspired to bomb twelve U.S. passenger planes during a two-day period in January of 1995. For this conspiracy, he was indicted in the Southern District of New York in January of 1996. Evidence also suggests that the conspirators may have been planning to kill President Bill Clinton and Pope John Paul during visits to the Philippines in late 1994 and early 1995. The conspirators' alternative plan was to use airplanes as missiles by flying them into U.S. Federal buildings! Note this was 1995! Why are officials saying the thought of flying planes into buildings was unthinkable at September 11?

It is believed by some authorities that Mohammed was a co-conspirator with Ramzi Yousef (an Iraqi now serving a life sentence in a Federal prison and Mohammed's nephew) to bomb the World Trade Center in 1993, blow 12 airplanes out of the sky (and/or kill Clinton and the Pope), and attack the Trade Center and the Pentagon on September 11. Mohammed is one of the baddest of the bad and was captured March 1, 2003 in Islamabad, Pakistan.

Now, why did U.S. authorities not put the dots together? The World Trade Center bombing in 1993, the 1995 bombing in Oklahoma City, and the 1995 plot in the Philippians to blow up 12 airplanes **or fly one or more into Federal buildings** all involved Muslim terrorists! The Feds knew that many Muslim men were training to be pilots, and some only wanted to steer planes. And no one thought: "Hey, maybe we should look into this thing."

Edwin Angeles was a mysterious Filipino government agent who penetrated the terrorist Abu Sayyaf group (who recently killed American missionary Martin Burnham), but Angeles, whose Muslim name was Ibrahim Yakub, became a leader in the terrorist group! He hatched the plot to fund their terrorist cause by kidnapping innocent people. He ended up dying in his wife's arms, after having been shot leaving a mosque in the southern Philippines. Angeles signed a handwritten statement admitting that he knew Terry Nichols and that Nichols had also met with Ramzi Yousef in the Philippines in November of 1991 for bomb making, firearms training, handling explosives, etc. We also know that Abdul Hakim Murrad was held in New York City by the Feds for allegedly plotting to blow up airplanes, and he told his keepers and the FBI that the Oklahoma City bombing had been orchestrated by Ramzi Yousef, his former roommate in the Philippines. And the FBI still denies any Islamic, Middle East connection with the Oklahoma City bombing!

One of the major investigators in the Philippine case, General Avelino "Sonny" Razon, said, "We told the Americans about the plan to turn planes into flying bombs as far back as 1995. Why didn't they pay attention?"[5] Yes, indeed. Why?

The thread of terror stretches from many Middle East countries to many U.S. states, and the terror would not have happened if the U.S. had been alert and taken various warnings seriously. We did not, and thousands of innocent citizens are dead.

TRAIL OF TERROR

There have been numerous acts of horror perpetrated upon men. In fact, it is one of the great questions of life: how can sane people do such wicked, harmful things to fellow humans? When men don't believe in God, the God of the Bible, they are capable of **anything**.

Even respectable people have defended terror when it was a handy tool for them to use! Former Israeli Prime Minister Yitzhak Shamir opined that the Jews used justified terror while the Palestinians are unjustified in its use. He said that Jews were without a state and had no choice but terror while the Palestinians are "fighting for land that is not theirs...."[6] The fact is that terror is never justified however noble the cause.

Men have committed great atrocities under the guise of politics, government, and religion while others have done so for their own cause, whatever that might be. Communist China (Red China) has killed an estimated 60 million of its own people since 1949, and Soviet Russia killed about 40 million. Then Hitler slaughtered about 10 million. (I have never received an answer as to why leftists in the world wax eloquently with indignation about Hitler's slaughter but are strangely silent about the genocide in China and in the old Soviet Union. Anyone want to try?)

Communists have always used terror as an orchestra leader uses his wand: to get what he wants from his orchestra. Lenin introduced the terror concept as a strategy when he declared that "we can achieve nothing unless we use terror." The Communists became masters of terror throughout the world. Terror could be felt in the streets and back alleys of the Soviet Union. Lenin issued the following to his secret police as reported in *Pravda*.[7] "We are not waging war against separate individuals; we are exterminating the bourgeoisie as a class....Do not ask for incriminating evidence to prove that the prisoner opposed the Soviet Government either by arms or word. Your first duty is to ask him what class he belongs to, what were his origin, education, and occupation. Those questions should decide the fate of the prisoner. This is the meaning and essence of Red Terror."

We see Lenin's terror concept as we face incredible Muslim ingenuity to terrorize. They are not thieves; they are on a mission to spread terror throughout our nation and the world. It is a battle between Islam and Christianity (even a perverted Christianity, i.e., those who are Christian in name only or "Christianized"). It is a battle between Islam and the entire non-Islamic world.

JAPANESE TERROR

Militarist Japan deftly used terror to keep people in line during the 1930s and 1940s. Japanese troops invaded Shanghai in November of 1937, and by the middle of December, they moved on to Nanking, the capital city of Nationalist China. The Chinese army surrendered, but the Japanese High Command ordered their execution. The cold-blooded order arrived: "All prisoners of war are to be executed." In one day, 14,777 Chinese soldiers were tied up, then machine-gunned, after which each soldier was bayoneted.

But the butchers weren't finished and a planned time of terror was initiated against the civilian population. Very old and very young females were repeatedly raped, then shot. Officers competed with each other to see which one could behead more Chinese people! Each soldier managed to behead about 150 people for the "crime" of being Chinese. For seven weeks the Japanese performed atrocities in public for the purpose of terror. They buried people alive, permitted wild dogs to rip people apart, used live people for bayonet practice and generally terrorized everyone in the city. Eventually more than 300,000 citizens of Nanking were murdered, all following the surrender and slaughter of the Chinese soldiers![8] Terrorists (as opposed to freedom fighters) do not restrict their activities to the military. Innocent, helpless civilians are often their targets. Muslim terrorists have read the same book as the Japanese.

TERROR IN ARMENIA

One of the worst cases of terror and death took place in Armenia in 1915 when Muslims tried to deport and destroy the Christian Armenians. This tragic event is hardly known by the rest of the world. On May 27, 1915, the Turkish government, an ally of Germany against Russia, alleging Armenian disloyalty during the First World War, decided to deport the whole Armenian population to Syria and Mesopotamia. Out of the total Armenian population (about 1,800,000), one-third escaped deportation, one-third was deported, and one-third was massacred. Muslims have been at this terror business for a long time. They learned it from Mohammed; however, terror had been around long before Mohammed threw stones in the desert.

JIHAD IS HOLY WAR

The leading Muslim mullahs have clearly endorsed war with the non-Muslim world. Every healthy, adult Muslim is obligated to help conquer every country so the Koran (Muslims' holy book along with the Hadith) can be implemented in that society. The *Dictionary of Islam* clearly defines *jihad* as "a religious war with those who are unbelievers in the mission of Muhammad. It is an incumbent religious duty, established in the Quran [Koran] and in the Traditions as a divine institution, enjoined specially for the purpose of advancing Islam and of repelling evil from Muslims."[9] The purpose of "repelling evil from Muslims" compels Islam to change all societies, which requires forced conversion. It is disingenuous for Muslim clerics to say otherwise. Muslims insist on change of life whether or not there is a change of heart. Christians have no such mandate.

Muslims quickly tell all who will listen that *jihad* means struggle, inner struggle, but history clearly proves that it means struggle against the non-Muslim world! "*Jihad*, or holy war, means an active struggle, using armed force whenever necessary. The object of *jihad* is not the conversion of individuals to Islam but rather the gaining of political control over the collective affairs of societies to run them in accordance with the principles of Islam. Individual conversions occur as a by-product of this process when the power structure passes into the hands of the Muslim community."[10] The *Encyclopedia Britannica* admitted in their Ready Reference computer edition: "Muslims are enjoined to defend Islam against unbelievers through jihad."

So it is no surprise that Muslims have deftly welded the sword across the Arabian Peninsula, around North Africa and Europe, leaving a prodigious amount of human skulls in their wake. No surprise that the butchery is still taking place. It's what all Muslims are taught from birth as they memorize the Koran and hear their Islamic clerics belch out vile, vicious, and vitriolic hatred against all "unbelievers," especially Jews and Christians.[11]

Yasser Arafat bellowed: "We know but one word: struggle, struggle. *Jihad, Jihad, Jihad*. When we stop our *intifada,* when we stop our revolution, we go to the greater *Jihad*, the *Jihad* of the independent Palestinian state with its capital Jerusalem." Peace maker? I think not. George Will quoted Arafat's Palestinian television station as it gave the following instructions: "All weapons must be aimed at the Jews...whom the Koran describes as monkeys and pigs....We will enter Jerusalem as conquerors....Blessings to he who shot a bullet into the head of a Jew."[12] That doesn't sound like "inner struggle" but inner hatred.

Abdallah al-Shami, Muslim terrorist, said "We want this successful operation to prove to the terrorist (Israel Prime Minister, Ariel Sharon) that we can, and we will continue to get him and his fellow pigs and monkeys where it hurts the most."[13] Al-Shami is a senior Islamic Jihad official.

TERROR IS RELIGIOUS DUTY

The poster boy of terror, Osama bin Laden, put a fine point

on terror when he, along with other terrorist leaders, issued this *fatwa* against all Americans: "The ruling to kill the Americans and their allies–civilians and military–is an individual duty for every Muslim who can do it in any country in which it is possible to do it, in order to liberate the al-Aqsa Mosque [of Jerusalem] and the Holy Mosque [of Mecca] from their grip, and in order for their Armies to remove out of all the lands of Islam....We–with God's help–call on every Muslim who believes in God and wishes to be rewarded to comply with God's order to kill the Americans and plunder their money wherever and whenever they find it."[14]

With a history of terror and blood shedding and major charismatic leaders preaching *jihad*, it is no surprise that "lesser lights" in the Islamic world are parroting the same message. A Muslim sheikh in London praised young boys who are learning to fire Kalashnikovs rifles. On tapes sold in London bookstores Abdullah el-Faisal calls for Muslims to kill "filthy Jews" because they are "evil to the core."[15] This Apostle of Violence has made two tapes since September 11 calling for all males to train to kill infidels. The bum should be bounced from London, but then I must not suggest that our culture is superior to their seventh-century, desert culture. The sheikh is getting money from the European Development Fund, when I think he should be dropped (by parachute, of course) from a plane onto the Arabian desert. These zealots are as mean as a menopausal pit bull.

Mohammed made it very clear in the Hadith to the most dense Muslim that *jihad* was normal for Islamic followers. Mohammed once was asked: what is the best deed for the Muslim next to believing in Allah and His Apostle? His answer was to "participate in Jihad in Allah's cause" (Al Bukhari vol. 1, book 2, no. 25). Mohammed was quoted as saying: "I have been ordered to fight with the people till they say, none has the right to be worshipped but Allah" (Al Bukhari vol. 4, book 52, no. 196).

Mohammed also said, "The person who participates in (Holy Battles) in Allah's cause and nothing compels him to do so except belief in Allah and His Apostle, will be recompensed by Allah either with a reward, or booty (if he survives) or will be admitted to paradise (if he is killed)" (Al Bukhari vol. 1, book 2, no. 35).

FOOLS AND FANATICS FUND TERROR

It is bad enough to be attacked by foreign terrorists, but it is even worse to finance their evil work! Yes, the free world is funding their cause when tax dollars go to finance Arafat's organization. When Israeli soldiers broke into Yasser Arafat's Ramallah headquarters of his presidential guard (known as Force 17) on Oct. 22, 2001, they found evidence that Arafat was funding the Tanzim-Fatah terrorists out of his presidential budget. Well, **he** isn't funding them. He is only the conduit. European taxpayers are funding them with generous payments to Arafat each year! And American taxpayers have been supporting him for years by our inept international welfare program.

According to *DEBKA-Net-Weekly*, the Middle-East intelligence news service, all of the 10,000 Tanzim Activists were paid in new Israeli shekels for their terrorist activities! Arafat personally directed that each of the terror masters be paid $22,000 to help create the terror group known as Tanzim. He signed the directive three weeks before the outbreak of the *intifada*! The top terrorist leaders were listed in a document that gave specific directions about how Arafat's office was to transfer the Tanzim payroll to the Ramallah office, which would then distribute the funds.

European taxpayers have been "contributing" about $2,190,000 per month to keep that one terrorist organization operating. That's about $57,000,000.00 since September of 2000. There's a lot of money in terror. It is believed that bin Laden spends about the same for his terrorist activities.[16]

The royal family in Saudi Arabia has been pumping billions of dollars into extremist Islam **while** they talk about supporting U. S. efforts to wipe out terror. The Saudi royal family not only sees both sides of the issue, they **take** both sides! Of course, much of that money comes from America through purchase of oil. At least the royal family is diversified, since they fund many facets of Islam. They have supported the infamous al-Qaeda network inside the kingdom as well as in the Balkans, Afghanistan, and Somalia. The pitch from analysts is that the royal family doesn't really want to support the terrorists, but since they must live with them, it is only safe to do so. In other words, it is protection money to keep the royal family alive and on the throne.

The Saudis support over 200 Islamic centers, more than 1500 mosques, over 200 colleges, and almost 2,000 schools throughout the world. They have established chairs in various U.S. colleges such as University of California Santa Barbara, Harvard (five million), as well as University of London, University of Moscow, and others. Schools such as Duke University, Johns Hopkins University, Syracuse University, and Howard University have had "research institutes" set up.[17] Question: Would any of those prestigious schools permit the KKK to establish a chair on "Issues of Race"? No, then you must believe those educators are sanctimonious hypocrites!

President Bush has stated that the U.S. is not only going after the actual terrorists but those who aid and abet them in their terrorism. That includes the nations that sponsor, harbor, or fund them. Does he really mean that? If so, why is he snuggling up to the Saudi leaders? Could it be, dare I say it? Oil?

It is easy to demonize the terrorists in Iraq, Iran, Turkmenistan, Uzbekistan, and all the other "stans," but what about the big oil producers? What about the big boys in China, North Korea, and others? Some of the nations that are supposed to be supporting our war are helping our enemies! Americans should demand consistency from politicians.

CHINESE TERRORISTS

Some will say that we have received support from China for our war on terrorism, but "support" is only "talk" with many U.S. supporters. A column on October 7, 2001, reported that there were long convoys of "Chinese Muslim servicemen" traveling through remote northwest China into Afghanistan to "support the Taliban militia...." The first contingent of Chinese troops crossed the border on October 5 and numbered between 5,000 and 15,000 men.[18] What will our government do about China? You can bet the farm that China will not be treated the way Iraq and other nations are treated. In fact, China recently received full trading rights with the U.S.! Well, none may call it treason, but it is at least "nuts." You don't feed and pamper a buzzard when it has plans to pick out your eyes!

Following the massacre on September 11, a large amount of Chinese ammo was found in al-Qaeda hideouts. It was revealed that large amounts of Chinese-manufactured ammunition were found in the Tora Bora caves of Afghanistan. They found Chinese anti-tank rockets, mortar shells, automatic rifles, and machine guns that had been left by the al-Qaeda soldiers.[19] Can you comprehend that China is supporting the Taliban with men and materiel? Yes, China, our new friend and trading partner, had men fighting with the Taliban! Thus far, the U.S. has refused to return prisoners to China. Sky Television reported that Chinese troops were fighting alongside the Taliban and al-Qaeda in Northern Afghanistan. There were also reports that Chinese troops were killed in the early phase of the Afghanistan war.

We know now that Iraqi President Saddam Hussein is paying relatives of homicidal bombers $25,00.00,[20] and Iran has increased its support of these bombers by 70%! Saudi Arabia has jumped into the act and is also paying family members. Will we have homicidal bombers in America? Probably so, since such activities are easy and inexpensive, and one does not need to be very bright to do it. More alarming is the fact that it is impossible to prevent.

All right, what does the U.S. do now? We are hypocrites and worse if we only attack the smaller nations and leave the big boys alone. No, we don't want a shooting war with China, but do we have to pretend that they are recognized as civilized people? Must we continue to fund their war machine with our trade policies? It's time to take an honest, consistent look at our war on terrorism before there are more massive massacres.

CAN WE TRUST OUR GOVERNMENT?

There are myths that revolve around Muslim terrorists, Islam, and U.S. activities; thinking people must look with a critical eye to arrive at the truth. We can disagree with our government without questioning its legitimacy, and one can love his country yet fear his government. Can we always trust government? Ask an American Indian. It must also be understood that it is reasonable, not treasonable, to question government. Maybe, if more patriotic Americans questioned the authorities, those authorities might not question us. Only fools accept everything they are told. God tells us in I Thessalonians 5:21 to "prove all things." The following two chapters will help you distinguish myth from reality.

1. George Metcalf, *WorldNetDaily,* 10-21-01.

2. Joseph Farah, *WorldNetDaily,* 11-12-01.

3. *WorldNetDaily,* 1-19-02.

4. Jon Dougherty, *WorldNetDaily,* "Saudis warned FBI about OKC bombing?" 6-22-02.

5. William F. Jasper, *New American,* "Terror Trail: WTC, OKC, 9-11"; July 1, 2002.

6. Quoted in *The American Council for Judaism,* October, 1991.

7. *Pravda,* 12-25-18.

8. Don Boys, *Y2K,* Huntington House Publishers, 1999, pp. 71, 72.

9. Quoted by Ibn Warraq in *Why I Am Not a Muslim,* Prometheus Books, Amherst, NY, 1995, p. 12.

10. *The New Encyclopedia Britannica,* Edition 15, vol. 22, p. 8.

11. *The Philadelphia Trumpet,* vol. 12, no. 7, August 2001. p. 5.

12. Quoted by George Will in syndicated column 8-18-01.

13. *USA Today,* 8-10-01.

14. *The Banner,* Michigan Conservative Union, Fall, 2001.

15. *The American Spectator,* "Watch Your Tongue," March/April 2002.

16. *WorldNetDaily,* 10-30-01.

17. *WorldNetDaily,* "Royals pump billions into global Islam," 3-29-02.

18. *WorldNetDaily,* 10-7-01.

19. *WorldNetDaily,* 12-20-01.

20. *CBS.com,* 4-4-02.

Chapter Two

The Myths, I

Did God Cause the Terror Attacks?

Some have suggested that God caused the Muslim terrorist attack on America as His judgment upon us for our national sins. So, God is to blame for the terror! Others tell us that if God exists He would never bring judgment upon a nation. Still others tell us that God is too puny to intercede on man's behalf or doesn't care what happens to men. What is the fact and what is fallacy? What are some myths being promoted today as they relate to the attack on September 11, and can those myths be dangerous to you and America?

God is **never** the author of evil, so He did not cause the attack on America. God does permit evil to happen for the present time, but He is never the author of evil. Evil happens because God gave each person a will to decide between right and wrong. When a person chooses wrong, God has no pleasure in his wickedness. God will not forbid a person to take the wrong path, and a person is free to do atrocious acts, but of course, at the end of the chosen path is judgment. All of us will be accountable for our decisions.

We know that God does not tempt any person, but men are tempted and led astray by the evil one. Men do evil things, such as killing innocent people, because they are of their father the devil. John 8:44 reveals, "Ye are of your father the devil, and the lusts of your father ye will do. He was a murderer from the beginning, and abode not in the truth, because there is no truth in him. When he speaketh a lie, he speaketh of his own: for he is a liar, and the father of it."

Men take over planes and steer them into buildings because their father (Satan) was a murderer from the beginning. Men do wicked things because they have wicked hearts and out of the heart

33

come the issues of life. Proverbs 4:23 reminds us: "Keep thy heart with all diligence; for out of it are the issues of life." These lost, depraved Muslims are only doing the work of their father. They, like all men, do evil because they think evil, and they think evil because they **are** evil. Proverbs 23:7, "For as he thinketh in his heart, so is he."

My talk show opponents have said that God does not exist or if He does, he is a puny, impotent God not deserving of worship and obedience. After all, an all powerful, all knowing, and all loving God would never permit babies to be born blind, crippled, or dead or permit millions to starve in slum conditions. However, they are wrong and Darwin, Voltaire, and thousands of others have "gone down with that ship." They indicted God when He was not guilty.

NOT PUPPETS

Yes, God knew that terrorists were going to kill thousands of innocent people, but He did not create men to be puppets. We each have the ability to choose. The Muslim terrorists chose death for themselves and others. That was not God's choice. God loves mankind, but loving requires a choice or it isn't love. True love, human or divine, can never be forced. Who would want a love that was coerced, even if that were possible? When we have a choice, it can not simply be a choice of good. Evil must be an option; the terrorists **chose** evil. John 3:19 tells us: "And this is the condemnation, that light is come into the world, and men loved darkness rather than light, because their deeds were evil."

God could have created us as puppets or robots that can not know love or fellowship or make choices. However, since we were created for fellowship with a sovereign God, we must have the ability to refuse love and fellowship and choose between right and wrong. The will to do wrong must be as equally available as the will to do right. Terrorists choose to do wrong, and to fault a sovereign God for man's decision to do evil is unfair, unreasonable, and unscriptural.

The many laws of nature were established and men must live by those laws. If a person jumps or falls from a building, he will fall because the law of gravity demands it. God is not to be blamed. We are all aware of the possibility of falling, so we are careful when we are at high places. God could follow every person around and keep him from falling when he stubs his toe, but that was not part of the original plan. We are free to fall and to fail.

What kind of existence would we have if we were forced to love, give, and obey, and if there were no possibility of doing wrong because we had been created as fleshly robots? If we never made a mistake? If we always did the right thing because it was impossible to do the wrong thing? We would love God because it would be impossible not to love Him? God chose not to design us that way. He gave us a will to choose, and He longs to have us choose to love and fellowship with Him.

SOCIETY IS NOT CHRISTIAN

In reading the Koran, I have found no place where a person is commanded to love another! The closest I found was sura 76:8 "And they give food out of **love** for Him to the poor and the orphan and the captive." Love is mentioned 83 times in the Koran and frequently it is used to inform us what Allah does not love. He does not love the proud, the boastful, the unbeliever, etc.

No, God did not stop the terrorist attacks. And that was **not** because He was helpless or wanted them to occur. Those men chose to attack because of their sinful condition. God only permitted them to exercise their free will. If something or someone much higher than himself does not guide man, he will often do wrong and he will be held accountable.

If a person is a Muslim, he will act like a Muslim and will attempt to follow the tenets of the Koran and the Hadith. It will not be surprising if that person is violent. If a person is a Christian, he will attempt to follow the principles of the Bible. He will realize that he is a new creature in Christ and is expected to live Christ-like. He will want to do right and not wrong. He will want to love and not hate. He will want to give rather than take. He will want to forgive rather than hold a grudge. In this day when old truths have been ridiculed, revised, and rejected, the Bible stands as it has for centuries as a trustworthy guide to the lost, as encouragement to the lonely, and as an indictment of the liberal and a map for the pilgrim.

Our society is not Christian, but it has been "Christianized." Men have an imperfect view of the Bible, self, Christ, life, death, etc., but there are flashes, from time to time, of awesome Bible truth and Christian living. Muslims have little conception of Bible principles and Godly living. That is why many Muslims are not appalled at beheadings, chopping off limbs, yanking out tongues, and prying out eyes. They have known that as standard operating procedure, so they shrug their shoulders and walk away.

So it is a myth to think that God caused the terrorist attacks; or that He was too weak to do anything about it; or that if He exists, He would have forbidden it to happen.

ARE ALL RELIGIONS EQUAL?

Another myth is that one religion is as good as another, that all are equal. What they really mean is that truth doesn't matter, and in fact, religion doesn't matter. Follow any religion you want and if you are sincere, then truth is totally irrelevant. That sounds so tolerant, so broadminded, and so kind; however, it is so untrue. If there is a sovereign God (and there is), then He is concerned with truth and wants His creatures to know the truth. He surely does not want us to be involved with error. Truth sets us free. It's God's heaven and He can tell us the prerequisite to enter.

The perpetrators of the above myth want us to believe that the religion of a small Amazon tribe that worships the gods of the air, river, snakes, etc., and who at times, eat their fellow men, is just as acceptable, right, and civilized as the teaching of the Word of God that has stood the test of time. Or the suggestion that Muslims, following an immoral slaveholder, killer, and desert thief, even compare to Christians is falsehood, foolishness, and folly.

Listen as a church full of **changed** Christians sing, "How Great Thou Art" and then watch Muslims hoot and holler as they throw stones at the devil! But the plan is in place to consider all religions equal, that is, except evangelical and fundamental Christianity! We are the ones the multiculturalists love to hate. They tolerate everyone except us; after all, toleration has its limits!

CATHOLIC STATEMENT

The Roman Catholic Church issued a statement on Islam that is tolerant, gracious, and kind but without any regard for truth. It makes everyone, especially those who constructed the Trojan Horse, feel so warm, fuzzy, and good. The Catholic statement[1] says, "For the Muslim, Allah is none other than the God of Moses and Jesus." Now the authors of that statement and the editor who approved it are either dishonest or uninformed. And it may only be that they are un-informed. Islam teaches that Christ was not Deity; that He did not die on the cross; that He was not part of the Trinity. It is bad enough that Muslims make Christ a mortal man, but that mortality would also make Him a liar or a lunatic. I believe He was neither; He was, is, and always will be Lord.

The Catholics also said, "One can therefore understand the Muslims' protest at the all too frequent custom in European lan-guages of saying 'Allah' instead of 'God' [implying a difference when referring to the god of Islam]." Again, this statement makes the Muslims feel good and accepted by civilized people and it makes the Catholics feel good in being so kind and ecumenical, but to say there is no difference in Allah and the God of the Bible is contrary to the facts of history. In another chapter, I go into more detail on this subject but suffice it to say that Allah was a pagan god known throughout the Middle East hundreds of years before Mohammed was born! Allah was one of 360 pagan gods worshipped in Mecca. It's a matter of history, and all the subterfuge by Muslims and the sentimentalism of Catholics will not change the facts, since facts are very stubborn.

The bleating heart sentimentalists continued: "In fact, Islam was hardly any more fanatical during its history than the sacred bas-tions of Christianity whenever the Christian faith took on, as it were, a political value." Many will be surprised that I agree with that state-ment. I agree because they are not referring to Bible Christianity but to Roman Catholicism. And the Catholic Crusades and the Inquisi-tion are two of the most disgraceful events in history.

Now we are all aware of the deplorable history of the Cru-sades (see chapter 10), but just to keep the record straight, it was the popes, priests, and prelates of the Roman Catholic Church who preached across Europe to promote the Crusades. I'm not mean, or malicious, or mad (well, maybe a little), but I do insist on the truth. You don't find Bible-believing Christians participating in the Cru-sades and loping off the heads of Jews and Turks, nor are Christians steering planes into buildings. As terror is born and bred in Muslim homes and mosques, the Crusades were born and bred in the Roman Church.

Finally, the Roman Catholic Church statement tries to convince us that those who believe "Islam is a hide-bound religion, which keeps its followers in a kind of superannuated Middle Ages" are a bunch of bigots. Wait a minute. Isn't it obvious that Islam is a seventh-century culture right off the desert? They insist that women wear a veil or the burqa (that would be reasonable for desert life); that justice is done by chopping off hands and feet, tearing out tongues, beheading people for minor crimes, and even for converting to another religion. Of course, it is a religion and culture of the Middle Ages, and even the Roman Catholic Church can not change that fact.

INTOLERANT CHRISTIANS

Some liberal "Christians" tell us that Islam is not that much different from Christianity and there is much we can learn from it. One man said that if a monk from the sixth-century Byzantine Empire were to come back today, he would find much more that was familiar in the practices and beliefs of a modern Muslim than he would find in a contemporary American evangelical church. Such a man is obviously uninformed as to Islam, evangelicalism, or both. Television preacher Robert Schuller said that it wouldn't bother him if he came back in a hundred years and found all his descendents followers of Mohammed! Let me remind him that Muslims have always denied the deity of Christ and the Trinity. To suggest that there is any comparison of Islam and Bible Christianity is insensitive, incredible, and insane.

We are seeing Bible-believing Christians demonized in the media to make Muslims appear more acceptable. It is another myth that Bible-believers are an aberration of Christianity. The fact is we are the mainstream; however, there is a continuing trend to demonize conservative Christians. In a recent article in the *New York Times*, the Islamic terrorists are identified as the "radical right." I think maybe I've been called that a few times. Then *Newsweek* reported that the Democrats are going after President Bush by going after conservative Christians.[2] The thinking is that we are at war with terrorists internationally, so at this time we should be more tolerant of all people. And everyone knows Christians are intolerant, don't they? The Democrats are trying to push Bush into a corner where he offends his most loyal and enthusiastic supporters by projecting them as unreasonable, unthinking, and unkind Bible-thumpers. Personally, I seldom thump my Bible. Well, maybe four or five times this month.

NO CHRISTIAN TERRORISTS

The term "fundamentalism" is almost always used in a pejorative and negative way. It is incredible that many educated people don't know what it means: it simply means to get back to the fundamentals! Consider a basketball team that has lost every game during the season and the coach decides that the team must "get back to fundamentals," so he starts a session with his team around him by saying, "This is a basketball. This is a dribble. This is how you pass." This is back to basics.

That is what a Fundamentalist is without going into the historical background of the origination of the word which is not necessary here. There are fundamental Jews, fundamental Muslims, and fundamental Christians. But keep in mind that since all Muslims say they believe in the Koran and the Hadith, they are all supposed to be fundamentalists! Not true with Christians. There is a definite separation of "Christians." There are non-believing liberals who do not accept the Bible as the very Word of God and those of us who do. If unbelieving liberals had any character, they would admit they are not Christians, especially their clergymen who took vows to teach and defend the Word of God.

Christians are often presented as being uneducated, unsophisticated, and unreasonable, but our critics don't understand that we sincerely believe that we have an obligation to obey the Bible; consequently, we may appear inflexible, intolerant, and insensitive to others. One thing is sure: we don't steer planes into buildings. And the "nuts" who beat their kids to death and say "God told me to do it," are not Fundamentalist Christians. Should we be tolerant of those people? After all, who are we to make a judgment and discriminate?

Furthermore, no informed person calls the people at Waco "Fundamentalist" Christians. They were sincere cultists, with no relationship to historic Christianity, who, by the way, did **not** deserve to be killed by our government!

Some have used a few extremists in the abortion movement to tar everyone who takes a pro-life position. First, some of those abortion terrorists have never been involved with the pro-life movement. And none to my knowledge has professed faith in Jesus Christ. They are simply "fruitcakes" who care about unborn babies being ripped from the womb. What our enemy has done is to consider a very few fringe individuals and based on those, indicted the whole class of pro-lifers and Fundamentalists. No, it isn't fair or honest, but no one has ever accused the radical leftist crowd of being fair and honest, have they?

THE REAL ENEMY

Thomas Friedman suggested in a *New York Times*[3] column that the real enemy is not terrorism, but religious totalitarianism—"a view of the world that my faith must reign supreme, and can be affirmed and held passionately only if all others are negated." Well, Christians do believe that our faith is Universal and we do believe that there are no other ways to heaven other than by an experience with Christ; however, we do not believe we have the right to force anyone to accept that truth. In fact, we maintain that such a thing is impossible, that no person has ever been forced to accept Christ as Savior! "Forced conversion" to Christ is an oxymoron.

In November of 2001, television preacher Robert Schuller spoke at a love-in at a Chicago mosque with Black Muslim Louis Farrakhan. Schuller made one of his dumbest statements that day when he said, "The purpose of religion is not to say, 'I have all the answers, and my job is to convert you.' That road leads to the Twin Towers. That attitude is an invitation to extremists." Schuller should be honest and admit that he does not believe the Bible is the Word of God. While I don't have all the answers, it is my job to seek your conversion. And to equate us with terrorists (while he is hugging a Black Muslim leader!) is dishonest, disingenuous, and despicable. It's that kind of statement that causes informed people to say that he is the biggest phony in America.

You see, Christians do teach a rather narrow message. We do preach an exclusive way to heaven but we don't force anyone to agree with us. That is one of the distinct places where we are in disagreement with Islam. Every Muslim on earth has an obligation to see that the whole world accepts Islam anyway possible. Christians maintain that trusting Christ is simply an act of faith and love with no coercion of any kind. There has been much forced conformity but no forced conversions in any Christian church.

PHONY PLURALISM

Freidman would force his view, the religion of secular humanism, upon principled Christians, and his religion is very tolerant of all religions **except** Bible Christianity! Wonder why everything (and I mean everything) is acceptable to the broadminded pluralists except Christianity? It is that phony pluralism that made the U.S. a target for the Muslim attack on September 11.

If we had been realists and not obsessed with broadmindedness, we would have seen the attack coming. Informed people have known that Islam preaches world dominion by speech and sword. They attacked us in 1993 with the first terrorist attack on U.S. soil at the World Trade Center. Even that attack by Muslims did not produce ringing bells, flashing lights, and whining sirens. Why, because our leaders were deaf, dumb, and blind, or in other words, pluralists, multiculturalists, and humanists. Informed, thinking, and concerned people would be aware of any imminent danger from Muslim terrorists who are capable of anything. Those who are unconcerned and unaware are like a man walking waist-deep through a snake and alligator infested Everglades swamp. **They are going to get bit.**

What the multiculturalists want is for Christians to look again at the Scriptures and reinterpret them in the light of modern thought. They tell us that such an approach is only reasonable, and after all, what's wrong with reason? Nothing except, in that event, it would not be reason but treason. Such a person is not a Bible or historic Christian! Hey, we are tolerant; if you want to believe that, go to it, but please tell me why I am intolerant simply because I don't agree with this warped interpretation of Scripture? Must I accept obvious error to prove my tolerance?

NO ABSOLUTES

I am called a totalitarian. Liberals say that I should jump into the twenty-first century pool of pluralism that Friedman says is "an ideology that embraces religious diversity and the idea that my faith can be nurtured without claiming exclusive truth." Maybe we should rewrite the Bible, but I believe they have already done that many times! If the Bible claims exclusive truth, then it claims exclusive truth! However, we are told "that belief" is oppressive to others, but if my affirmation of eternal realities is oppressive to others, then

41

they have major mental, emotional, and religious problems. Why would any sane person expect me to try to change what a sovereign God has settled?

We are told that my thinking is dangerous, but dangerous to whom? Why? How? I say, "Live and let live." If you want to believe in Islam, then go to it. You have every right to accept a seventh-century, desert culture whose members run around the Mecca mosque, then throw rocks at the devil, degrade women, chop off hands of criminals, and execute any who become convinced that Islam is a false cult. Go to it, but understand that there is no eternal salvation in such absurd belief.

Friedman quotes a religious leader as suggesting that the future of the world may depend on whether different religions can understand "that God speaks Arabic on Fridays, Hebrew on Saturdays and Latin on Sundays, and that he welcomes different human beings approaching him through their own history, out of their own language and cultural heritage." It would be interesting to know how that "religious leader" knows God's language. (I know people who think God speaks Southern!)

Friedman's statement sounds broadminded, but he is saying that there are no absolutes. You see, if there is no eternal God who has established absolute authority, then it doesn't matter what you believe. And when a person doesn't believe in the true and living God, he will believe almost anything. If it is true that a sovereign God (as taught in the Bible) really exists, then every person will be held accountable as to what he or she does with His message. It would not be loving and kind if I led people into an error that damns them for eternity. So I am a lover not a hater.

Remember that it is God's Heaven, and He has the right to set the requirement for admission, and that requirement is repentance and faith in the atoning work of Christ. It doesn't really matter what theologians, philosophers, and others think about that requirement. It is settled in Heaven! They don't have to accept it, but if not, they won't gain entrance to Heaven. Rather narrow, isn't it? That's what God called it!

Look folks, let's cut to the chase. Is Jesus Christ who He said He was? Is He God? If so, then there are no concessions, no compromises, and no collaboration with teachers of error. It is astounding that educated people cannot understand that simple fact. Do they want us to say, "Jesus Christ is not God"? Well, we cannot say that because He **is** God. Do they want us to say, "Well, Christ is God, but we will overlook that fact and sit down with others who say He was a liar or lunatic"? Do patrons of pluralism think we are total idiots? He is not a liar or lunatic but Lord of all!

EXCLUSIVE TRUTH

II John, verses 9-11 give Christians some parameters and principles to follow in our every day living: "Whosoever transgresseth, and abideth not in the doctrine of Christ, hath not God. He that abideth in the doctrine of Christ, he hath both the Father and the Son. If there come any unto you, and bring not this doctrine, receive him not into your house, neither bid him God speed: For he that biddeth him God speed is partaker of his evil deeds." As a Christian I may choose to disobey that clear passage, but if I profess to love and follow Christ, I should obey it even if I am accused of being unloving, unkind, unbending. So be it. Just because we don't recognize other religions as true does not mean we would hinder their preaching, teaching, growing, and doing their thing. That doesn't mean that we must revise our theology, knowing we are accepting error just to be tolerant of others to make them feel better.

David Limbaugh wrote, "The left is always complaining about hate speech because such speech is likely to lead to violence. If incitement to violence is the test for hate speech, is it not hate speech to contend falsely that Christianity or other religions, because they claim to have exclusive truths, advocate the extermination of other faiths? Is it not hate speech for the left to engage in such sloppy comparisons as equating Bible-believing Christians with Muslim terrorists?"[4] Great question, David! Christians are not fools or fanatics but followers of Christ who must have the preeminence in all things. Thinking, informed, and honest people will not fall for those myths. They know the reality: that conservative Christians, while not perfect, are the backbone of this nation and have been since the *Mayflower* bobbed on the waves in the bay at Plymouth.

IS CHRISTIANITY UNIVERSAL?

Another myth propagated by Islam is that Islam, not Christianity, is universal. For the treatment of this issue I am indebted to Jens Christensen, author of *Mission to Islam and Beyond: A Practi-*

cal Theology of Missions, chapter 15, "Is Christianity Universal?"[5] Both Christianity and Islam claim to be universal but that is impossible. If one is absolute truth, then the other cannot also be true. If the Bible is true, then its message is for all men, in all times, in all locations–no exceptions. And if that is true of Christianity, then it cannot be true of Islam.

Almost all Christians will wonder what the point is, after all, everyone knows that the Gospel is universal, or do they? Most of you have never questioned it. A Muslim will tell you that Christ did not consider His message universal because He said in Matthew 15:24 that He was "not sent but unto the lost sheep of the house of Israel." There are other verses Muslims will use in this regard. They will say that in Matthew 1:21, the angel is represented as saying to Joseph concerning Jesus: "He shall save His people (the Jews) from their sins," and in Matthew 10, Jesus sends the twelve out to preach His Word, yet He told them not to go to the Gentiles, only to the lost sheep of the house of Israel. However, they do not remember that Christ, following His Ascension, gave His command for His disciples in Acts 1:8, "ye shall be witnesses unto me both in Jerusalem, and in all Judaea, and in Samaria, and unto the uttermost part of the earth." Furthermore, Jesus commanded them in Mark 16:15: "Go ye into all the world, and preach the gospel to every creature." That was "every" creature. Now, we understand what He was expecting them to do, but Muslims say that He was just saying that there are Jews all over the earth, so go tell **only** them the good news. However, the Mark passage refutes that thought.

PETER'S VISION

In Acts 10, Peter went to the home of Cornelius and received a vision that made it very clear that the gospel was to be preached to everyone, not only the house of Israel. The chapter ends with Gentiles having the Holy Spirit poured out upon them. Obviously, Christ had not targeted non-Jews or the incident in Acts 10 would not have happened. In Acts 11, Peter went to Jerusalem and the Christian Hebrews approached him about his association with Gentiles, and he explained his vision and command that all men were to hear and receive the Universal Gospel message.

Christensen suggests that we dispense with moral arguments and stay with our Scriptural command. We must not permit Muslims

44

to get us off the main argument and onto "rabbit trails." Muslims will not be too impressed with Christ other than as another Apostle. They will not accept the fact that He was and is the unique Son of God who died for our sins and was resurrected.

Muslims will point out that the Old Testament prophets were saved by faith, so it was not faith in Christ but faith in God that is universal, saving faith. Of course we maintain that the Old Testament sacrifices spoke prophetically of Christ's death, plus many prophecies spoke of Him, so the Old Testament prophets and others had to exercise faith in the future death of Christ as a basis for personal salvation. But that argument will not fly for most Muslims, and it is easy to get bogged down in all the sacrifices. Simply put: apart from Christ we know nothing and have nothing.

We admit that Christians were isolationists up to the time of Acts 10. It's a fact. We acknowledge the fact that Christ never told the disciples everything they wanted to know, because certain things were to be revealed at a later time. As John 16:12 says, "but ye cannot bear them now." The Spirit would guide them in all truth. After Peter's experience in Acts 10, the Spirit convinced them that the Gospel was truly universal.

ISLAM NOT THE GOOD NEWS

Many liberals and Muslims charge that Paul was the one who took the church in a different direction. He never saw the Lord in the flesh; he was a Johnny-come-lately. He was the one who went to the Gentiles and sought to make the Gospel universal. Not so. Go back to Christ and then to Peter. Remember that the early church accepted this new approach (going to the Gentiles) before Paul came on the scene. After Paul was saved and called, the church leaders in Jerusalem accepted him and his message; they gave him the right hand of fellowship along with their blessings as Paul went out to preach the Universal Gospel to the Gentiles, as the other followers were doing to the Jews.

Unbelievers make much of Paul's teaching a doctrine not mentioned by Christ. I've had that thrown at me many times on talk shows dealing with perversion and the death penalty. I always remind my critics that if the Bible is the very Word of God, it doesn't matter whether Christ spoke about an issue or not. And just because a subject is not recorded in the Gospels does not mean Christ did not

45

deal with the subject. However, what we have in the Gospels is exactly what God wanted us to know on that subject at that time.

Muslims may ask, "But if the Gospel was to be universal, why did Christ confine His ministry to the Jews?" Genesis 12 tells us that all nations of the earth would be blessed through Abraham, and He would make Abraham the father of many peoples. God's plan of the ages was for Christ to be born, to die, and to rise from the dead, for the church to be established and for believers to preach the Universal Gospel to the world. The foundation of His plan goes back into the aeons of eternity, then to the promise in Genesis 3:15 concerning the seed of the woman, then to Abraham, to his seed, and down to the manger in Bethlehem.

So for thousands of years, the Jews were the channel through which the blessings to the world came. Then God permitted events in the world, i.e., the dispersion of the Jews after the fall of Jerusalem, the massive road building of the Roman Empire permitting free access by Gospel preachers to other parts of the world, etc., to facilitate this Universal Gospel to be presented to the world.

Islam is not that message since it is not a gospel of salvation but one of works. Its message came from the seventh-century Arabian Desert and is far from universal. And it would not have become the second largest religion in the world if it had not been for the sword!

NO SEPARATION OF MOSQUE AND STATE

What most Americans don't understand is that with the religion of Islam comes the culture of the desert and Islamic law known as "*sharia*." When Islam takes over, it imposes not only the religion of Islam but also all the laws, customs, and mores that have developed since the seventh century. One custom is the desert code of loyalty. An Arabian proverb says, "My brother and I against our cousin, but my cousin and I against a stranger." There is much loyalty to people–very select people, but little loyalty to principle.

There is also religious exclusivity. No Islamic nation permits religious freedom. The Saudi Arabia royal dictatorship prohibits all non-Muslim religious activity. There are fewer than five Roman Catholic priests in the country, but they must work *incognito*. There are no churches in the land! Saudi citizens are paid $3,000 for reporting a home Bible study to the authorities, and Americans who convert to Islam are paid about $22,000.00. Saudis who convert from Islam are killed.[6]

What has Islamic law and religion produced in many Middle East countries besides a dominate theocracy? The President of Pakistan, Pervez Musharraf, made a very revealing statement in February of 2002 about this: "The Muslim umma (community) is one-fourth of humanity, but we are the poorest, the most illiterate, the most backward, the most unhealthy and indeed the most deprived and weakest of the human race."[7] I would have added the word, "depraved" as well. So, when a nation installs Islam as their religion, they get the "whole package." They don't separate mosque and state.

GOD JUDGES NATIONS

Yes, there are many myths but one of the easiest to explode is that God does not judge the nations that reject this Universal Gospel and the Bible. One thing is sure: God has never said, "oops!" "come to think of it," or "on second thought." None of the terrorist events surprised God because He is an all knowing, all powerful, and yes, all loving God. He is sovereign and does not answer to any entity. The Apostle Paul wrote in I Timothy 6:15-16: "Which in his times he shall shew, who is the blessed and only Potentate, the King of kings, and Lord of Lords." Now since God is sovereign, He not only has the authority but the right to judge nations. Is He judging America at this time with terrorist attacks?

One of our great early leaders, George Mason, aptly wrote: "As nations cannot be rewarded or punished in the next world, they must be in this....Providence punishes national sins by national calamities." Thomas Jefferson suggested the same possibility when he wrote, "Indeed I tremble for my country when I reflect that God is just, that his justice cannot sleep forever."

All Christians are aware that God brought judgment upon the whole world with the Flood of Noah. Genesis 6:17 reveals this fact: "And, behold, I, even I, do bring a flood of waters upon the earth, to destroy all flesh, wherein is the breath of life, from under heaven; and every thing that is in the earth shall die." That was the ultimate judgment upon all people.

Uninformed people cannot visualize God who would bring judgment resulting in the deaths of people, especially innocent children; however, those people have not considered or don't understand a holy God who, by His very nature, must punish sin.

Muslim leaders, U.S. politicians, media personalities, ecumenical preachers, and others are disseminating these and other myths as they seek to "build a bridge between Islam and Christianity," but their bridge is one way, and it leads to Islam. The following allegory, written by Jalal-ud Din Rumi, the beloved Muslim thirteenth-century Sufi, illustrates the pernicious propaganda that is being peddled by preachers, politicians, and pundits in the free world. Jalal-ud lived in a city whose population was almost equally divided among Christians, Muslims, and Jews. When asked about those three incompatible religions he told his now-famous story about a city where every person was blind:

> One day the news came that an elephant was passing outside the city, so the townsfolk decided to send a delegation to report back as to what an elephant was. Three men left and stumbled forwards until they found the beast. They felt the animal and headed back to report. The first man said: "An elephant is like a vast snake!" The second man was indignant at hearing this: "What nonsense!" he said. "I felt the elephant and what it most resembles is a huge pillar." The third man shook his head and said: "Both these men are liars! I felt the elephant and it resembles a broad, flat fan." All three men stuck by their stories and for the rest of their lives refused to speak to each other. Each professed that they and only they knew the truth. Of course all three blind men had a measure of insight. The first felt the trunk of the elephant, the second the leg, the third the ear, but not one had begun to grasp the totality or the greatness of the beast. If only they had listened to one another, they might have grasped the true nature of the beast. But they were too proud and preferred to keep to their own half-truths. "So it is with us," said Jalal-ud Din. "We see the Almighty one way, the Jews have a slightly different conception and the Christians a third. To us, all our different visions are irreconcilable. But what we forget is that before God we are like blind men stumbling around in total darkness...."

But Christians are not blind. God does not leave us "like blind men stumbling," but opens our eyes of understanding to see Him. (See Luke 24:31.) The above writer was a better storyteller

48

than theologian. I am interested in truth not political correctness, unity, diversity, pluralism, multiculturalism, ecumenicity, or making Muslims feel warm and fuzzy. Love without truth can be dangerous.

Christians must correct the myths with the truth of Scripture as the following chapter attempts to do. It's good to know that the facts, while always uncompromising, are on our side.

1. Catholic Statement, Vatican Office for Non-Christian Affairs, "Orientation Between Christians and Muslims."

2. Quoted in *WorldNetDaily*, 1-8-02.

3. *New York Times*, 1-4-02.

4. *WorldNetDaily*, 1-4-02.

5. Jens Christensen, *Mission to Islam and Beyond: A Practical Theology of Mission*, Ch. 15, from internet.

6. Tom Bethell, *The American Spectator*, "Saving Faith at State," April, 1997.

7. *Associated Press*, quoted in *The Sword and Staff*, March, 2002.

Chapter Three

The Myths, II

Mythmakers are Mythtaken!

Since the terrorist attacks on America, especially on September 11, there have risen some myths about God and His dealing with men. Some tell us that if God really exists, He would not permit such tragedies to occur. Others tell us that God did it. Then still another myth is that God does not use such events to bring a nation to repentance. The mythmakers are mythtaken.

The Bible and history are replete with examples of the judgment of God upon the various nations, and if so, can America expect to escape? It is a **fact**, not a myth, that other nations have not escaped His judgment as a cursory examination of early civilizations will show.

There were two impressive (for that day) centers of civilization in mankind's early history: Ur and Babylon. Civilization moved from Ur, (located 200 miles north of the Persian Gulf) and Babylon (located between the Tigris and Euphrates Rivers) to Judea and to Nineveh, respectively, and eventually to Egypt, Greece, and Rome.

Thousands of miles of the Tigris and Euphrates Rivers permitted farmers along their banks to produce prodigious amounts of produce and provided the avenues of commerce for most of the Fertile Crescent. The area became the garden and granary of western Asia.

During the time of Abraham, the Sumerian city of Ur was a center for trade from the Persian Gulf as ships sailed up the Euphrates bringing gold, copper ore, ivory, hardwoods, and other items from Egypt, India, and Ethiopia. Excavations of Ur have proved that it was settled at least 3,000 years B.C. and had developed "a high culture."[1] Intricate and impressive carvings, pottery, and gold head-dresses have been uncovered in the Royal Cemetery. Graves were discovered that contained wealthy occupants, each holding a heavy gold cup to his or her mouth. In time, Ur was eclipsed by other city-states as power shifted from place to place.

EARLY BABYLON

Standing on the sandy shores of the Euphrates amid the wastes of ancient Babylon (known as Babel in Genesis 10:10, and ruled by Nimrod), one would never imagine that there stood the epitome of civilization 700 years before Christ! The various settlements and cities were unified and became Babylonia with headquarters in Babylon.

Hammurabi united lower Mesopotamia with its capital in Babylon, and he changed it from an insignificant river-town to the capital of an empire. He ruled from 1795 to 1750 B.C. and introduced his famous code, said to be given by the Sun god himself.

Babylon reached its zenith under the 43 year reign of Nebuchadnezzar. Soon Babylon controlled all the trade in western Asia, and with the additional funds Nebuchadnezzar built a magnificent city. Daniel quoted him as saying, "Is not this great Babylon that I have built?"[2] Herodotus (born about 484 B.C.) visited Babylon about 150 years after Nebuchadnezzar died, describing it as standing in a spacious plain and surrounded by a wall 56 miles in length that enclosed an area of 200 square miles. He said that a four-horse chariot could be driven along the top of the walls. The Euphrates, lined with stately palms, ran through the center of town and was spanned by a bridge that permitted its citizens to live on either side of the river. The city was built of brick faced with yellow, blue, and white enameled tiles, most of which were emblazoned with, "I am Nebuchadrezzar, King of Babylon."[3]

The most impressive sight when approaching the city was a 650-foot ziggurat that was "probably the Tower of Babel."[4] Six hundred yards north of Babel was one of Nebuchadnezzar's palaces and the Hanging Gardens that he had built for one of his wives who was homesick for the mountains. The Greeks considered the Hanging Gardens one of the Seven Wonders of the World. There had never been a city to equal Babylon in grandeur and few to this day!

An official census taken about 900 B.C. revealed that the

Babylonians worshiped about 65,000 gods! Ishtar was one of those gods. She was sometimes presented as a bisexual deity and sometimes as a nude, offering herself as a willing sexual object to her subjects who called her "The Virgin," "The Virgin Mother," and "The Holy Virgin." "Virgin" only meant that she had not been soiled by marriage! None of the hundreds of gods could give any assurances of life after death! The Babylonian citizen could not trust his gods beyond the grave! And those gods did not produce pure, decent, or magnanimous living. Such worship produced correct ritual rather than a good life.[5]

WICKEDNESS OF BABYLON

The wickedness was so bad that even Alexander the Great, who was an adulterous and bisexual drunk (who died drunk in the palace of Nebuchadrezzar) was shocked by the wickedness of the city![6] Herodotus revealed that every native woman in Babylon was required, once in her life, to go to the Temple of Venus and have sexual intercourse with a stranger! Wealthy women (attended by many maids and eunuchs) would ride up to the Temple in luxury carriages, enter the Temple, and wait for a stranger to throw a piece of silver (of any value) into her lap. She could not refuse anyone for any reason. The two would then go off together in or outside the Temple for their tryst. At the conclusion of the liaison, she would enter her carriage and return home, having obeyed the law and satisfied Venus.[7] She had satisfied the law and could not be required to participate any further in the one-time prostitution. Such was the status of women in Babylon.

Herodotus also revealed that when Babylon was besieged it was common for the men to strangle their wives to keep them from eating the stored provisions.[8] After all, a man can't fight if he is hungry! Such wickedness was followed by even more in the form of effeminate degeneracy. Young men dyed and curled their hair, wore perfume and rouge, wore necklaces, bangles, earrings and pendants.[9] (We're on our way!) After Babylon was conquered by the Persians, it got even worse when women of every class thought it only courtesy to reveal their bodies to as many men as possible. Herodotus even said "every man of the people, in his poverty prostituted his daughters for money."[10]

Durant's summation is appropriate to the U.S. as we face the greatest challenge of our history. He wrote: "Morals grew lax when the temples grew rich; and the citizens of Babylon, wedded to delight, bore with equanimity the subjection of their city by the Kassites, the Assyrians, the Persians, and the Greeks."[11]

WORSE THAN WORTHLESS

Is that the danger Americans face? Have we grown lax in our wealth, good times, easy living, depending on our missiles, bombs, and planes to protect us? Will we calmly, dispassionately permit our society, our culture to be taken over by a foreign element that uses undisguised threats to accomplish their desires? Others appeal to our sense of fairness and assure us that Muslims are not interested in capturing our nation. Should we believe them? At least, should we not inquire deeply into what specific Muslims believe to assure ourselves that they are not part of the Trojan Horse conspiracy? Are we so fearful of being considered bigots and haters that we reject our culture, our civilization, and our convictions? If so, maybe we deserve to lose and become absorbed in the pagan Islamic culture.

The greatness of Babylon had been deteriorating for many years as they indulged themselves in all desires, lost interest in maintaining their strength to repel aggressors, and fanned themselves under the stately palms. They tried one god after another, then an assortment of gods, but none could provide peace, piety, or power over degrading and debilitating wickedness. The pagan priests had them in a lock box from which they could not escape. Only the priests could provide revelation and that was worse than worthless. Finally, the soul, whether good or evil, at death would drop into Hades where it would suffer in outer darkness forever. Is it any surprise that Babylonians gave themselves to revelry, rioting, and ravenous behavior?

BABYLON CRUMBLED

Babylon began to crumble. Nebuchadnezzar was now dead and Nabonidus ruled, or actually, he played at it. Nabonidus was more interested in excavating the desert than in executing directives. While Nabonidus was digging in the sand, his son Belshazzar ruled as co-regent, but Belshazzar had not learned, as had Nebuchadnezzar, that God can put down the mighty. Because of Nebuchadnezzar's pride, God took away his senses and he lived with the beasts of the field until God returned his understanding. Then he said: "Now I Nebuchadnezzar praise and extol and honour the King of heaven, all whose works are truth, and his ways judgment: and those that walk in pride he is able to abase."[12] Nebuchadnezzar learned that God will bring judgment upon people to bring them to Himself.

Belshazzar gave a lavish party for a thousand of his lords and ladies and it was a wild night of desecration, debauchery, and death. Belshazzar purposefully sought to offend God by drinking wine from the sacred vessels that had been taken from the Temple when Jerusalem was sacked. During the revelry, the king suddenly dropped his golden goblet of wine and pointed to the fingers of a man's hand writing on the wall. The king lost control of his body as his mind troubled him, his face was contorted and his knees smote one against the other. That broke up the party.

The court clergy were called but didn't have an interpretation for the supernatural phenomenon, then the queen reminded Belshazzar about Daniel. So when all else failed, they called the preacher! Daniel came before the king, told him to keep his gifts of gold, then listed the royal transgressions. (Daniel was not interested in climbing the corporate ladder.) Daniel said that the meaning of the writing was: "MENE; God hath numbered thy kingdom, and finished it. TEKEL; Thou art weighed in the balances, and art found wanting. PERES; Thy kingdom is divided, and given to the Medes and Persians."[13] Translation: King, you are dead meat. That judgment was fulfilled that very night.

The Persians were at the gates of the city, but it was still a mighty city, so the wily Medes and Persians diverted the river Euphrates (that flowed through the city), and the army marched up the riverbed under the massive walls to take the city: "In that night was Belshazzar the king...slain." Thus ended the world empire of Babylon. Historians write of the military conquests, but they are really writing about the judgment of God upon a civilization. Often one wicked nation is allowed to bring down another wicked nation–all in God's plan.

DANIEL AND HIS FRIENDS

Daniel and his three friends were brought into this wicked Babylonian atmosphere when Nebuchadnezzar was at his height of power. They spent the rest of their lives there, five hundred miles from Jerusalem, away from home, away from the man of God, and they stayed true and pure, positive and productive for a lifetime! While Daniel and his friends were in prominent places during the reign of Nebuchadnezzar, the king wanted them to convert to his religion. That is what the third chapter of Daniel is all about. It is one of the most famous Old Testament stories. Nebuchadnezzar set up a massive idol on the plain and required that all political leaders of his empire come for the dedication of the image of gold. As every Sunday school pupil knows, Shadrach, Meshach, and Abednego (their Babylonian names) refused the king's command and were thrown into the fiery furnace, but God brought them out of the fire without the odor of smoke on their clothes. However, this incident is far more than three young men who stood on their principles and were willing to die for them.

Nebuchadnezzar's image was not as simple as preachers have made it for over 2000 years. He was trying to enforce religious conformity throughout the empire and used threats to accomplish it. Too often we look at this incident through modern eyes and miss its subtleties. People of that day did not consider the worship of the golden image religious oppression. By worshipping the image, the worshippers were not forbidden to worship any other god. They were not required to renounce their favorite god. They simply had to add another god to their pantheon. No big deal.

In fact, heathens thought it only proper to show reverence to any and all gods. If the king wanted another god, so be it. They would pay homage to his god. After all, the king felt rather strongly about it, and bowing before the king's image would save their lives. It would also be a good career move to placate the king. After all, what's one more god? Notice that all the people from the other nations obeyed the king's command. They did that because they did not serve the one, true, sovereign God. The three young Hebrews thought that it is important to stand for what you believe, and this "mature" Gentile believes the same!

Standing on principle exacts a price as the Hebrews discovered. The reigning despots of that day didn't think it was outrageous that all citizens be required to worship the official god of the nation where they lived. Citizens could then add as many gods as they wanted. Most despots have understood that religion could act as glue that would hold society together. Daniel and his three friends were saying: "The state-approved gods are false gods and must be rejected. Worship must be directed to the only true God under heaven." That exclusivity was not permitted, and trouble resulted. Such persons were "atheists" attacking the state. The three Hebrews were not only refusing to worship a false god, but they were also refusing to recognize the authority of the king! Bad news.

CONFRONTATION

This enforced religious conformity is where the early Christians had their trouble. They were not required to forsake the worship of Christ. All they were required to do was to burn a little incense to Caesar. Of course, in doing so, they were affirming that Caesar was lord, and no Christian could, in good conscience, admit that. Christians believed that there was but one true God who desired, deserved, and demanded exclusive worship. That produced a major confrontation resulting in thousands of believers being thrown to the lions, burned at the stake, broken on the rack, drawn and quartered, drowned, lynched, crucified, and killed in other ingenious ways.

Christians in the Roman Empire basically claimed that the pagan gods were worthless, and everyone should recognize Christ as King of kings and Lord of lords. That amounted to heresy in Caesar's court, and it amounts to heresy today. We don't have problems when we say that Jesus Christ is Savior, but when we say that He is the **only** hope for this world, that He is the **only** way to Heaven, then we have trouble. We are saying that other religions are not valid, that their doctrines are untrue, and we become politically incorrect. We become *persona non grata* in most areas of society.

Basically Nebuchadnezzar was saying: (1) all the gods worshipped by others were to be recognized; (2) other gods could be introduced by authority of the State; (3) the gods which the government approved were to be honored by everyone whatever their religious persuasion; (4) if any person denied the new god instituted by the State and refused homage, that person would be recognized as an enemy of the State.[14] This is where we are in the Age of Terror. Men have lost confidence in the Bible as the authoritative Word of a sovereign God and are now guided by how they "feel" about things. Truth is not required or respected. Peoples' feelings are more important than truth. We are told that reality is that America is now a pluralistic society (and it is), and we must all live together peacefully (and we must). Furthermore, we are told that Christianity has "had its place in the sun" but that is now past, and that a sovereign God must step aside, or at best, share the spotlight with other gods.

MYTH OR REALITY

The myth is that God (if there is a God) does not involve Himself in the affairs of men. Most people want to believe that God is a benevolent grandfather (someplace in the heavens) who is forever indulgent with his erring grandchildren, and that He would never bring judgment upon them or their nations. Therefore, modern men have convinced themselves that this myth is reality.

As with Nebuchadnezzar's image, all gods worshipped by others must be recognized by all, and government will endorse all gods (except the God of the Bible!). Anyone who refuses to acknowledge the gods will be considered a religious terrorist who wants to force his intolerant views on everyone. Such a person will be considered an enemy of the state. Was Babylon an early pattern for Mecca and the 360 gods worshipped by the desert Arabs?

The Hebrews had been in Egypt for over 400 years, and the cup of God's wrath was slowly filling. When Moses was 80 years old, God called him to lead the Hebrews out of the land of bondage to the land of blessing. In a confrontation with Pharaoh, God brought 10 judgments upon the nation resulting in Pharaoh and his army being drowned in the Red Sea. Obviously, God does bring judgment upon nations. God brought judgment upon the cities of Sodom and Gomorrah for their vile sin of sodomy. God did not hate them, but He surely hated their sin. Their unrepentant hearts resulted in God's judgment that totally destroyed the cities.[15]

There are many examples of God sending judgment upon Israel because of national rebellion. Numbers 21 is a good example where God infested their camp with poisonous snakes and many of the people died. Those bitten could be healed if they cast their eyes upon a brazen serpent on a pole in the midst of the camp. If they looked, they lived. If not, they died. Jesus mentioned that example in John 3 when He likened Himself to that serpent of brass. In John 12:32, Christ promised: "And I, if I be lifted up from the earth, will draw all men unto me." Just as during that time of wilderness judgment, if men look to Christ, they live. If they don't, they die. It is a personal choice.

Americans can "buy into" the myth that God does not bring judgment upon nations (or individuals) if they choose, but they must understand that such a belief has consequences. Ask Belshazzar!

1. *The Wycliffe Historical Geography of Biblical Lands*, Charles F. Pfeiffer and Howard F. Vos, Moody Press, 1970, p. 14.

2. Daniel 4:30.

3. This was a shock to Bible critics who claimed for hundreds of years that Nebuchadnezzar was fictitious!

4. Will Durant, *The Story of Civilization,* Simon and Schuster, New York, 1935, Book 1, p. 224.

5. Ibid., p. 240.

6. Ibid., p. 244.

7. Ibid., p. 245.

8. Ibid., p. 248.

9. Ibid., p. 248.

10. Ibid., p. 248.

11. Ibid., p. 248.

12. Daniel 4:37.

13. Daniel 5:26-28.

14. Albert Barnes, *Barnes Notes on the Old Testament,* Baker Book House, Grand Rapids, First pub. 1831, p. 212.

15. *The Stringer Report,* Phil Stringer, June, 1997.

Chapter Four

The Monsters

Scheming While We Sleep!

Islam is a religion in which Allah requires you to send your son to die for him, but Christianity is a faith in which God sent His Son to die for you. I have paraphrased Attorney General John Ashcroft whose courageous and accurate statement hit the bull's eye and caused howling and gnashing of teeth from the Redwoods of California to the vacate lot in Manhattan. Some of the "moderate" Muslims went after him with a hatchet seeking his scalp as they have done since his suggestion that all foreigners coming to America from the Middle East be fingerprinted and photographed. (That is now being done as of November, 2002.) What's wrong with that? Some will tell us that many Muslims are moderate so it would be intimidating and unfair to them. Too bad, how do all Americans feel knowing that Muslim men massacred about 3,000 innocent people, including a few Muslims?

A good definition of a Muslim wearing a "moderate" facade is a man who doesn't have the ability to act ruthlessly to seize control **today**. I have spoken to Muslims who are critical of any terrorist acts for any reason; however, the mosques are full of men who do believe in using terror as a weapon. Many Muslim leaders publicly abhor terror while they privately applaud it. So a moderate Muslim true to the Koran is an oxymoron. It's like being a moderate child molester or moderate Nazi. If a Muslim believes what traditional Muslims believe, he is a Fundamentalist, not a moderate; and those Muslims who are really moderate will be the first to die when the true Muslims take control.

Most non-Muslims do not understand the seventh-century, desert culture of Islam. Muslims appear to be one thing to the U.S.

public and something else to the rest of the world. Their allegiance, in addition to Islam, is to family and tribe; immigrating to America, wearing blue jeans, eating pizza, and mouthing "cool" statements will not change them. Remember the old Arab proverb that is inculcated in every Arab that says, "My brother and I against our cousin, but my cousin and I against a stranger." You are a stranger, and you should remember that!

MONSTERS BUT NOT COWARDS

The Muslims who steered the planes into the Twin Towers and the Pentagon have often been called "cowards," but cowards don't study, work, and train for years to carry out an act that results in their deaths. These terrorists are highly motivated followers of their religion. It is not wise to mischaracterize an enemy nor is it necessary. If we make him less than he is, then we can not effectively deal with his desire to do us harm. Giving credit for a minor attribute does not condone his major activity. Why put ourselves at a disadvantage in this battle for our very lives? In fact, we need to look at their motives and grievances; after all there could be **some** truth to them. However, sincere motives and grievances never justify killing innocent people, but knowing does help us understand the reasoning of the perpetrators.

I have sought for a descriptive word for the terrorists and "monster" seems very appropriate. There were many examples of such monstrous acts and attitudes following the September 11 attack. Notice the following vicious statements and headlines by leading Muslims:

"Ex-president of Iran backs nuking Israel"

"Islamic terrorists threaten Taj Mahal"

"Christians terrorized in Muslim Indonesia–Islamic militants praising bin Laden; promise believers 'bloody' December"

"The Jews are taking over the world."

"Terrorists shoot 18 during church service."

"U.S. Go to Hell!"

"Go To Hell America" and "Destroy America." "Death to America."

"Death to America, Death to Israel, Taliban, we salute you."

"Bin Laden we are with you."

"America is the enemy of God."

"America is a great Satan."

"U.S. go to hell, Afghans will prevail."

"Down, down USA!"

"Long live bin Laden."

"Tony Blair burn in hell."

WHERE ARE THE MODERATES?

Salman Rushdie, a native of India but now a citizen of England, wrote a book considered critical of Islam. He, a former Muslim, bravely titled the book, *The Satanic Verses,* a subject I deal with in another chapter. The top Muslim in Iran put out a contract on his life! Ayatollah Khomeini of Iran said, "Even if Salman Rushdie repents and becomes the most pious man of all time, it is incumbent upon every Muslim to employ everything he has, his life and his wealth, to send him to hell." That was one of the leading "holy" men of Islam speaking!

My question: Where were all the "moderate" American Muslims at that time? Not **one** came to Rushdie's defense! Not one deplored the book burnings, riots, and killings that followed the publication of the book. It seems that many Muslims don't walk the talk! To their credit, 127 Muslim international intellectuals (no Americans) came to Rushdie's defense in a signed protest statement.

One thing is sure: Muslims feel deeply about what they believe! The two men who translated Rushdie's book into Japanese and Italian were both killed by Muslims! But then, that's not unusual for dedicated Muslims. As I write, militant Muslims are training young Muslims to be dedicated terrorists to further their cause. All Muslims confess that world domination is their cause. Many have disavowed terror, while many others have not. Those are the ones hidden deep in the bowels of the Trojan Horse that concern me.

FRENCH TERRORISTS

Terrorists have been reared for many years in the slums of

Beirut, the hovels of the West Bank, Pakistan, Saudi Arabia, etc. They are being trained in London and Paris! Chuck Colson, who works with U.S. prisoners, charges that al Qaeda training manuals specifically target black prisoners in the U.S. for Islamic conversion. Richard Reid, who tried to blow up an international flight with a shoe bomb, was converted to Islam while in a British prison. (*The American Sentinel*, September 2002.) Furthermore, we know that Abdullah al-Muhajir, alias Jose Padilla, the "dirty bomber," was converted to Islam in an American prison. In fact, more than 10 percent of the 2 million-plus U.S. prison population is Muslim! But it's worse in France.

The Sante Prison, located on the Left Bank in Paris, is where many Muslim terrorists have been incarcerated for ten or more years. Inflammatory literature has been circulated throughout the prison, highlighting real and imaginary complaints of Muslims against Israel and the West. The prison is a recruiting station for Islamic terrorists.

Over half of France's 45,000 prison inmates are Muslim according to Frank Viviano of Hearst Newspapers. Viviano reports that extremists have built what amounts to an extensive and highly organized "terrorist university" behind bars, according to his sources in the prison guards' union. Smuggled tapes, books, and pamphlets preach the fiercely anti-Western and anti-Semitic gospel of al-Qaeda. Some inmates claim to have been offered instruction in the manufacture of homemade mines, bombs, detonators, and fuses. Prison officials, aware of the magnitude of the problem, have transferred the extremists to other prisons; however, that has only exacerbated the problem: The leaders are able to recruit new members with each move! The Muslim prisoners are going after the other prisoners with a missionary zeal. (Would that the average Christian had their zeal.) But there is a major problem in an effort to dampen the Islamic terrorists' zeal: prison authorities are restricted by a law that guarantees each "detainee must be able to satisfy the demands of his religious, moral or spiritual life."[1] The inmates have taken over the asylum!

TERRORISTS IN LONDON

The city of London is being overrun with Muslims, and experts expect England to become the first European nation that falls into the Muslim community of nations! Think of that, in the land of John and Charles Wesley, Charles Spurgeon, etc. The English waited too long to do anything about their Trojan Horse, and now they are **fearful** of doing anything about it.

Dr. Gary North quoted a London *Times* column about what is happening in the town of Luton:[2]

> There is a terrible, visceral rage among Luton's young Muslim brotherhood, a fury so powerful that already dozens of men, all British born and highly educated, have disappeared to fight for the Taleban. It has left parents terrified, the town's mosques full of loathing and yesterday, as *The Times* discovered first-hand, seen journalists and photographers physically attacked....Within a minute of arriving outside the mosque, this *Times* reporter and cameraman were set upon by a Muslim man, who had rushed, enraged, from a halal butcher shop.
>
> "You insult Islam, you corrupt Islam!" he screamed, smashing the camera to the ground and grabbing another photographer by the throat. "You don't understand how angry we Muslims are!" Five other Muslim men joined him, surrounding us, as he demanded the other camera. Their sense of fury was frightening. . . .
>
> "They want to die there," Mr. Abdullah said. "These are well-educated people. They have families. I knew Afzal. He loved his wife. But you must understand: all Muslims in Britain view supporting the *jihad* (holy war) as a religious duty. All of us are ready to sacrifice our lives for our beliefs. I am jealous of Afzal. He has reached paradise."
>
> He continued: "There are people leaving all the time. Not just in Luton, but all over Britain. We, as Muslims, don't perceive ourselves as British Muslims. We are Muslims who live in Britain. All we want to do is go to Afghanistan to defend the honour and sanctity of Islam."

These people drip with violence and hatred and are examples of the old saying that rage burns hottest in the weakest minds. These people are pursuing death. That isn't normal. We are born to seek life not death. It comes sooner or later. And if you are a Muslim, it often comes sooner than later. However, we are not at war with all Muslims but with monsters that practice Islam. And we had better differentiate between them.

GIFTS TO TERRORISTS ARE TAX DEDUCTIBLE

If we were at war with Muslims in general, why did we drop millions of dollars of food to them during the war in Afghanistan? And why permit Muslims to come to the U.S. to freely practice their religion (when Muslim nations don't permit religious freedom)? Obviously our war is with terrorists, and thus far, they have all been Muslims. More frightening, Muslim terrorists are being recruited right here in America often with tax exempt dollars! On February 24, 1998, Steven Emerson appeared before the U.S. Senate Judiciary Subcommittee with an incredible story of Muslim terrorist organizations that are operating in America. Emerson, a professional journalist, produced a 1994 prize-winning PBS documentary on militant Muslim organizations in the U.S.[3] that use our laws to attack our culture!

Emerson testified as to what he called "networks of Islamic extremists" inside the U.S. He concluded that "for these militants *jihad* is a holy war, an armed struggle to defeat nonbelievers, or infidels, and their ultimate goal is to establish an Islamic [worldwide] empire." Emerson was very clear that Islam is the impetus behind terrorism.

After his PBS special, he received an alarming phone call that summoned him to a meeting of Washington D.C. law officials where he was informed that a group of foreign Islamic fundamentalists had been assigned to assassinate him. He was told that he could not be protected unless he entered a Witness Security Program with a new identity. It is incredible that not one American Muslim cleric came to his defense and protested the threats on his life! Where are the moderates? "I became the target of radical fundamentalist groups throughout the United States (and internationally) who fiercely denied the existence of 'Islamic extremism' and accused me in engaging in an 'attack against Islam.' For this transgression, my life has been permanently changed," said Emerson. (Emerson is now in hiding because of those "peaceful" Muslims.)

Emerson told the Senate committee that after the bombing of the World Trade Center Building in 1993, various Muslim groups created a network of nonprofit organizations under 501 c (3) tax-free legislation. He said that under the cover of humanitarian causes, these organizations fanned the flames among American Muslims, sometimes inciting them to violence in huge conferences and rallies unnoticed by the American government.

IDEOLOGICAL HATRED OF U.S.

Emerson further revealed that the Muslims raised money for "suicide martyrs" in Palestine and elsewhere, operated a military training camp in Arizona, and provided the money for a stream of terrorists to enter and leave the U.S. at will. In short, militant Islamic groups in America "experienced freedoms and maneuverability they never experienced in their native lands" while they used these freedoms to express their "ideological hatred for the United States." Well, the Senators surely got an "ear full," but did little about it.

Emerson quoted Iran's Ayatollah Khomeini, saying, "The purest joy in Islam is to kill and be killed for Allah." Monsters like Khomeini are, without a doubt, within America's Trojan Horse, working, planning, and scheming while we sleep.

Mohammed and his followers slaughtered thousands in spreading Islam. Mohammed ordered Muslims, "Who relinquishes his faith, kill him." And "I have been ordered by Allah to fight with people till they testify there is no god but Allah and Mohammed is his messenger." Since Mohammed preached terror and violence, is it unusual that Muslims are responsible for most terrorism in the world today? All Muslims are not terrorists but **all** the September 11 killers were Muslims! Could there be some connection between terror and terrorist teaching? If not, then the educational foundation of the free world is based on a fallacy. Of course, there is a connection between what is taught and what is wrought.

Emerson quoted Fayiz Azzam in Brooklyn in 1989: "Blood must flow, there must be widows, orphans, [and] hands and limbs must be severed and limbs and blood must be spread everywhere in order that Allah's religion stand on its feet!" Religion of peace?

In Kansas, in 1988, another leader recruiting Islamic holy warriors against the United States exults, "O, brothers! After Afghanistan [where Muslim 'freedom fighters,' aided by the CIA, drove out the Soviets and installed the brutal Taliban regime] nothing in the world is impossible for us any more! There are no superpowers or minipowers. What matters is **will power** that springs from our religious belief!"

Many Muslim leaders reject the use of violence to advance Islam; however, every Muslim scholar knows that the Koran teaches that every single Muslim has an obligation to support conversion efforts until Islam has taken over the world. I write that with reluctance because it will turn some people off; however, reluctance will keep many people from hearing the truth: still there is a Trojan Horse inside America and it is full of trained extremists who will do **anything** to advance their cause!

TRAINING CHILDREN TO HATE

What kind of monsters dedicate themselves to killing helpless, innocent civilians, even children? They are people who have been trained all their lives to do just that. A *WorldNetDaily* column reported that Palestinian children are taught to kill Jews through "Sesame Street"-type television shows![4] The column reported that "Palestinian children are taught to hate Jews, to glorify *jihad* (holy war), violence, death and **child martyrdom** almost from birth, as an essential part of their culture and destiny." In 1998, Israelis documented this proving the "Children's Club," along with puppets, songs, and other characters, promoted hate toward Jews. Kids were told of the perpetual *jihad* that would continue until the Israeli flag comes down from "Palestinian land" and the Palestinian flag is hoisted.

I have seen that video and it is shocking and nauseating as small children sing lustily about becoming suicide warriors! Groups of children are gathered shouting "*Jihad* against Israel." Others want to take a machine gun against the hated Israelis. A very little girl chants, "When I wander into Jerusalem, I will become a suicide bomber." Another boy is shown in class proclaiming, "We will settle our claims with stones and bullets." Now, is there any question why children throw stones at tanks when such monstrous men teach them?

CHASING DEATH

It is impossible to understand how parents can promote death to their children. They are teaching small children that death, rather than life, is to be pursued! They don't only risk death; they chase it! That is monstrous! They are told that the government will compensate their families if they give their lives for "the cause."

Gerald M. Steinberg, writing in the *Jerusalem Post*, provided details of statements made by Palestinians to reporters after their children had been killed in fighting. "Interviewed by journalists after [recent] tragedies, some of the parents of these young victims refer to their children as *shaheeds* (martyrs), whose lives were given willingly and proudly to the Palestinian cause in fighting the hated Zionist enemy," Steinberg said. There was a Palestinian man teaching children how to fire M-16 automatic assault rifles, and "In an unbelievably shocking scene, one mother boasted that she bore her son precisely for this purpose, and the father proudly claimed credit for providing the training."[5]

The *Whistleblower* magazine published an article titled, "The secret world of suicide bombers" that profiled the Hotari family as they prepared for a party to celebrate the killing of 21 Israelis earlier in the month by their son, a suicide bomber! The article reported: "Neighbors hang pictures on their trees of Saeed Hotari holding seven sticks of dynamite." Kelley, a reporter for *USA Today* wrote, "They spray-paint graffiti reading '21 and counting' on their stone walls. And they arrange flowers in the shapes of a heart and a bomb to display on their front doors."

The boy's father, 54-year-old Hassan Hotari, reports Kelley, says he is "very happy and proud of what my son did and, frankly, am a bit jealous." His son was responsible for the June 1, 2001, terrorist bombing outside a disco in Tel Aviv. Mr. Hotari gushed, "I wish I had done it. My son has fulfilled the Prophet's (Mohammed's) wishes. He has become a hero! Tell me, what more could a father ask?" Now **there** is a legitimate case of child abuse where a father reared a monster.

"The secret world of suicide bombers" reports that in Hamas-run kindergartens, signs on the walls read: "The children of the kindergarten are the *shaheeds* (holy martyrs) of tomorrow." And there is promotion of terror at the university level as well. The classroom signs at Al-Najah University in the West Bank and at Gaza's Islamic University say, "Israel has nuclear bombs, we have human bombs."

HUMAN BOMBS

Hamas runs an Islamic school in Gaza City where 11-year-old Palestinian student Ahmed boasts, "I will make my body a bomb that will blast the flesh of Zionists, the sons of pigs and monkeys." Ahmed says, "I will tear their bodies into little pieces and cause them more pain than they will ever know." Ahmed's teacher shouts, "May the virgins give you pleasure," referring to one of the rewards waiting martyrs in Paradise. The principal smiles and nods his head in approval.[6] An empty head!

Of course, all this is going according to plan. Osama bin Laden told all Muslims in 1998 during one of his diatribes: "To kill Americans and their allies, civilians, and military is an individual duty for every Muslim who can do it in any country in which it is possible to do it." It is noteworthy that all the homicidal bombers have been relatively young people. Where are the old dudes who push them into the grave? Some of the terrorist leaders praise the young killers, and they have talked of being a "martyr," but none have volunteered yet! Come on guys, step up to the line. Put your mark on the volunteer list to commit suicide.

I asked earlier what kind of people would train children to become assassins of innocent, helpless people, but there have always been dedicated people willing to give their lives for a cause. We saw that with the Japanese pilots during World War II who flew their explosive-loaded planes into allied ships. But it goes back into the distant past when young Shiite Muslims trained to be assassins under the influence of hashish. In fact, that is where the word "assassin" comes from.

OLD MAN OF THE MOUNTAIN

Muslim history reveals that in 1094 Hasan-i Sabbah, a native of Khurasan and supporter of the caliphate in Cairo until the caliph's death, refused to recognize the new caliph. Hasan and the Persian Muslims transferred their allegiance to the deceased caliph's deposed elder brother, Nizar. However, Nizar and his son were murdered in an Egyptian prison, but an infant grandson was smuggled out to Persia and reared by Hasan to start a new line of Nizari imams.[7] Hasan and his followers adopted assassination as a "sacred religious duty," and assassins were promised Paradise if they died carrying out instructions. This group was known as the "Assassins."

Hasan became the first "Old Man of the Mountain," and all future leaders assumed the same title. He seized the castle of Alamut in an impregnable valley near Kazin in Iran. It had sheer sides about

600 feet high and accessed, by steps, one man at a time. When an assassin's mother heard that her son had been killed in carrying out his "religious" duties, she rejoiced and dressed in gay clothing, but if he returned alive, she wore mourning attire. The training of monsters goes back more than a thousand years.

When a visiting emissary visited the castle of assassins, Hasan wished to display his power and ordered one young man to slit his own throat which he did to the horror of the emissary. Then a youngster was ordered to throw himself from the precipice, which he did without a moment's hesitation! And with a smile on his face! That was the kind of terrorists who steered the planes on September 11 and who are waiting in America's Trojan Horse!

MARCO POLO AND TERRORIST TRAINING

How could human leaders instill bright, dedicated young men with a murderous instinct to train to be assassins and to give their lives for such a cause? Marco Polo (1254-1324 A.D.) had very enlightened information on the "Old Man of the Mountain" and his killing cadre in his best selling book:

> In a beautiful valley, he [the Old Man of the Mountain] formed a luxurious garden, stored with every delicious fruit and fragrant shrub. Palaces were erected in different parts of the grounds, ornamented with gold, paintings and furniture of rich silks. The inhabitants of these palaces were elegant and beautiful damsels, accomplished in the arts, especially those of dalliance and amorous allurement.

> The object which the chief had in forming a garden of this fascinating kind was this: that Mohammed having promised to those who should obey his will the enjoyments of Paradise, where every species of sensual gratification should be found, in the society of beautiful nymphs, he was desirous of it being understood by his followers that he was also a prophet and the compeer [peer, an equal] of Mohammed, and had the power of admitting to Paradise such as he should choose to favor.

> At his court, this chief entertained a number of youths, from the age of 12 to 20 years, selected from the inhabitants of the surrounding mountains, who showed a disposition for martial exercises and daring courage and at certain times he

71

caused opium to be administered to 10 or a dozen of the youths; and when half dead with sleep he had them conveyed to the palaces in the garden. Upon awakening, their senses were struck with all the delightful objects that have been described and each believed himself assuredly in Paradise.

When four or five days had thus been passed, they were thrown once more into a state of somnolency, and carried out of the garden. The chief thereupon addressing them, said: "We have the assurances of our prophet that he who defends his lord shall inherit Paradise, and if you show yourselves devoted to the obedience of my orders, that happy lot awaits you."

The consequence of this system was, that when any of the neighboring princes, or others, gave umbrage to this chief, they were put to death by these his disciplined assassins; none of whom felt terror at the risk of losing their own lives.[8]

Some have said that Marco Polo's account is fanciful if not fabricated, although there is no doubt that the group existed and the mountain fortress just northwest of modern Tehran was a reality. In recent years scholars such as Charles Van Doren have confirmed the "solid core of historical and geographical information in the volume." (*History of Knowledge*, p. 170.)

CULTURE OF TERROR

Does the above training of Muslim assassins reveal Islam to be superior or even equal to Christianity? Can you even imagine Christians training to be killers? How can Islam be "superior" to Christianity when it is a violent and vindictive religion unlike Christ's teachings of love, peace, and forgiveness? **Professing** Christians have done horrible things, but never can the blame fall at the feet of the Savior who said in Matthew 5:44: "Love your enemies,... do good to them that hate you...."

Those men who steered the planes into the Pentagon and the World Trade Center were doing what Muslims have been trained to do for centuries. And while many Muslims reject the actions of the fanatics, they don't reject the Koran, the Hadiths and Islamic doctrines that promote terror. Furthermore, many "moderate" Muslims

72

decry the terrorist attacks but secretly raise money to train future terrorists and according to the Bush Doctrine that makes them terrorists! When those "moderates" in the U.S. and England start acting consistently, I'll believe them when they show disgust for terrorists.

Dr. Jerry Falwell called Mohammed a "terrorist" on CBS and the Muslims and the media went after his scalp. Ibrahim Hooper, communications director for the radical Council on American-Islamic Relations, said: "What concerns us the most is the complete failure of mainstream religious and political leaders to repudiate this kind of anti-Muslim hate speech." He added, "On the issue of bigotry, silence equals consent." No one asked, "Is the statement true?" Was Mohammed a terrorist? Of course he was. He instilled terror all over the Arabian Peninsula; however, truth is not as important as political correctness. In any war, truth is the first casualty–and be assured we are in a war. We are observing Muslim leaders rewriting history before our eyes. They are trying to sanitize their bloody religion.

I remind Mr. Hooper that silence on the issue of terror is treason! I challenge Mr. Hooper to:

♦ demand religious freedom in Saudi Arabia and all Muslim nations.

♦ demand that Sudan stop its slavery and imprison all slavers–buyers and sellers.

♦ declare that the 19 terrorists on September 11 were murderous monsters who dropped into the lowest hell not into the arms of dark-eyed virgins in Paradise.

♦ declare that no one should give a dollar to any Islamic organization that supports any kind of terror.

♦ declare that Arafat is a thief, a liar, an opportunist, and terrorist who should be repudiated by all Muslims everywhere. In other words, he's not just another pretty face!

♦ declare that bin Laden is a fool, a fanatic, and a fraud.

♦ demand that airlines start profiling all passengers from the Middle East.

♦ declare that there is no such thing as a "good" terrorist. They are all bad.

73

Until Hooper is willing to do the above I consider him a sanctimonious hypocrite and one who aids and abets terrorism. According to Bush, that makes Hooper a terrorist! So I challenge him to do the above then announce it on national television. I will be totally convinced of his sincerity and loyalty to America when he stands before the television cameras with an American flag in his right hand and a copy of the U.S. Constitution in his left hand held close to his heart as he sings all the verses of "It's a Grand Old Flag" and, while the cameras fade out, he whistles "Yankee Doodle Dandy (or maybe, Dixie!) Then he'll make me a believer in his sincerity.

American Muslims must take an unequivocal stand against monstrous acts done by their own, and we must not give them any wiggle room! The men who attacked the U.S. on September 11 were monsters and those who sent them and financed them, gave them shelter and encouraged them are all monstrously evil men who must pay the price for their terror.

American and British politicians must realize that there is no total victory over "evil" and "terror" as long as evil men walk among us. We would be wiser and safer if we heed the admonition of Edmund Burke: "There is no safety for honest men except by believing all possible evil of evil men."[9] He was observing the total depravity of man. We are sentimental fools and slaves to multiculturalism if we don't recognize the culture of terror promoted in the Islamic movement. The fuse is lit and burning!

1. Hearst newspapers, 11-2-01.

2. *London Times,* 10-30-01.

3. Steven Emerson, *Jihad in America,* PBS Special, 1994.

4. *WorldNetDaily,* 12-3-00.

5. *Jerusalem Post,* 10-27-01.

6. *Whistleblower* magazine, Nov. 2001.

7. *Encyclopedia Britannica,* vol. 2, 1960, p. 553.

8. *The Travels of Marco Polo* and various web sites.

9. Edmund Burke, from his second speech on conciliation with America, March 22, 1775.

Chapter Five

The Movement, I

Loot, Land, and Ladies

Since Islam is one of the largest movements in the world and the fastest growing, we must look closely at what it is, **not** what some people claim it is. On April 25, 2002, I interviewed three Muslim leaders in Indianapolis, one of their main centers in the U.S. In that interview I asked: "Are you willing to characterize the suicidal bombers as homicidal bombers?" I thought I might get such an admission; however, I got much more than I expected. One of their most respected leaders calmly asserted that they "were freedom fighters." He confirmed this statement a few weeks later by telephone. "They are freedom fighters." That is proof that some "moderate" Muslims are supportive of terrorism. It further substantiates the fact that U.S. leaders are uninformed or are dancing around the issue when they say, "extremists have hijacked a peaceful religion."

U. S. OFFICIALS WRONG

President Bush told Muslims at a Washington area mosque: "The face of terror is not the true face of Islam," and he told a Joint Session of Congress: "Its teachings are good and peaceful, and those who commit evil in the name of Allah blaspheme the name of Allah." Is that true or not? If it is **not** true, then Christians are obligated to reprove, rebuke, and rectify the error, even error coming from the President! After all, he is only the President of the United States, not a member of the Trinity! (Don't tell that to fanatic Republicans who think the GOP is the fount from which all blessings flow.)

At a White House press briefing, spokesman Ari Fleischer said, "This attack had nothing to do with Islam. This attack was a

75

perversion of Islam...." Bush and Fleischer were not served well by their fact checkers and speechwriters.

Attorney General John Ashcroft, referring to a four-page document belonging to one of the terrorists, said the "references were a stark reminder of how these hijackers grossly perverted the Islamic faith to justify their terroristic acts...." Ashcroft was wrong. The terrorists were simply carrying out many injunctions found in the Koran, the holy book of **all** Muslims.

U.S. Government leaders are fearful of giving the impression that we are fighting a "religious" war. They cannot admit the terrorists are true Muslims because if they did, the U.S. would be perceived as anti-Muslim, and the U.S. would then be declaring a war against a religion! Of course, politics must be considered, but it is not helpful to dance around the truth: the U.S. did not start this war. It was declared by a bunch of Muslim terrorists. Our government will not admit that we are involved in a clash of cultures and a religious war that could last a hundred years! It is not a war of our making. When the next terrorist attack happens you will notice that Bush and Company's unwisely and hastily adopted sympathy and pandering to all things Muslim will be discarded as quickly as long underwear in a Texas heat wave.

CHRISTIANS ARE NOT TERRORISTS

Authorities get very uneasy around committed Christians who declare that there is one genuine, authentic, reliable religion that is totally different from all other religions. That is breaking the first rule of multiculturalism and authorities don't really want us to admit the possibility of one religion being superior. And it is a fact that our government is much more fearful of Muslims than they are of Christians. For once, they have made a correct assessment. Christians aren't flying planes into buildings! Many are just sipping a cold drink as they watch "Gilligan's Island" for the 34th time!

The message that the world is getting from our politicians, preachers, and pundits is that there are many religions and each one is as good as any other. All are equal. Of course, that is heresy and nonsense. All religions fall into one of two categories: the religion of Abel or the religion of Cain. Abel offered a God-required sacrifice while his brother offered the crops he had produced. Abel's offering was accepted and Cain's was rejected. On one side you have salvation becoming reality through repentance and faith, only through the meritorious work of Christ in dying for man's sins. Personal salvation comes through regeneration, not reformation or rehabilitation or religion. On the other side you have all the other religions of the world: religions of works.

In America (an America that was founded upon the fact of Christ's finished work!), it is almost a hate crime to assert that one religion is true and all others are false. I would further remind you that following the terrorist attacks, almost no one has mentioned Jesus Christ, but always some unknown god out there somewhere. We are seeing government, at all levels, trying to placate the non-thinking public by calling upon an unknown, ambiguous god to support their policies. Everyone is saying, "God bless America," but we must ask, "Whose God?" The God of the Bible, I trust. One thing is sure: we can not expect the blessings of God if we are fearful and reticent to proclaim that Jesus Christ is the only hope for this nation and world!

Christians must not give anyone a reason to mistreat others. We are obligated to truth, not error. And Americans can discuss, debate, and disagree on any issue without fear. While there are many Muslims who are embarrassed and horrified at the terrorism that took place on September 11, we must not permit them to distort facts, the facts about the Koran, to make themselves more comfortable. In this chapter I will provide documented facts as to the real face of Islam and the real Mohammed.

THE REAL MOHAMMED

We need to examine some facts about Mohammed, the founder of Islam. Mohammed, with its various spellings, is the most common name in the world![1] He was born in Mecca (Saudi Arabia) in 570 of the Quraysh tribe to Abdullah (Abd-Allah) and Aminah. He was distantly related to the royal family; however, his parents were poor. After the death of his parents, Mohammed was passed among different wealthy relatives and was finally reared by a poor uncle.

Mohammed had visions even as a youngster and some historians think they were epileptic seizures. Muslims get indignant when this is suggested, but he had the symptoms of epilepsy: he fell to the ground, foaming at the mouth, throwing his head from side-to-side, his eyes rolling back in his head, his heart thumping wildly, and his body jerking and perspiring heavily. Sometimes, he heard bells. I'm not sure what he had, but I sure don't want it, and it sounds like epilepsy to me. During these episodes Mohammed received his visions. McClintock and Strong reveal: "Muhammad, as we gather from the oldest and most trust-worthy narratives, was an epileptic, and as such, was considered to be possessed of evil spirits."[2] Historian Norman Cantor also says Mohammed was given to epileptic fits. Muslims have every right to disagree with such an assessment, but are obligated to explain his seizures.

Mohammed's problem, as suggested above, may have been demon possession. Vol. 4, book 53, no. 400 and vol. 4, book 54, no. 490 of the Hadith (one of Islam's holy books) reveals that he was bewitched, at times seeing things under satanic inspiration. In fact, at one point that's what Mohammed thought his problem was, and he decided to commit suicide when he had another seizure. His family convinced him that he was not possessed because he was such a "good" person; however, we do know that his mother claimed to be visited by spirits, had visions, and was involved in the occult arts. Mohammed could have been epileptic or demon possessed! Or, it could have been both! If I had my choice, I would rather be an epileptic than demon-possessed. I mean no disrespect to sincere Muslims, but I am not going to "waltz around the issue" just to make them more comfortable with their religion. Just as I will stand with Christ and His preaching, His person, and His program of world evangelism, the Muslims must stand with Mohammed's deception, demonism, debauchery, and depravity.

HIS EARLY YEARS

The facts of his life are really not disputed: When he was age 25 he married Khadija, a rich widow 15 years his senior who had hired him to manage her caravan trade. They had two sons who died young and four daughters. At age 40 he received his "calling" as an "apostle" or "prophet." He wanted to appeal to Christians and Jews as his first converts (after his family of course), so he thought "apostle" and "prophet" would "open doors" for him. He was wrong. The Jews and Christians could see that he was a charlatan.

Allah couldn't get his facts straight as to Mohammed's calling! In sura (chapter) 53:2-18 and 81:19-24, Mohammed had a personal appearance from Allah. Then we are told in sura 16:102 and sura 26:192-194 that his call came from Gabriel. Again, in sura 2:97 it was the angel Gabriel who gave him his call and provided him with the perfect Koran right from the throne of Allah. According to Muslims there was no human author of the Koran and it was handed down to mankind from Allah through the angel Gabriel.

Mohammed won a few members of his family to Islam but only received ridicule, resentment, and rejection from the Mecca community. The leaders of Mecca were fearful that this new religion would hurt their business at the Kaaba where the worship by Arab pagans of 360 gods brought many rich caravans and pilgrims to the city. The financial success of the city, especially Mohammed's Quraysh tribe (who controlled Mecca), depended on the caravans that planned their route to go through Mecca so the caravan workers could stop and worship their god at the Kaaba. (And throw a few rocks at the devil. More about that exciting event later.)

The followers of Islam react angrily when we speak of Islam's having pagan origins but Arab scholar Nazar-Ali commented, "Islam retained many aspects of pagan religion."[3] Professor of Arabic Alfred Guillaume admitted, "The customs of heathenism have left an indelible mark on Islam, notably in the rites of the pilgrimage."[4]

RELIGIOUS DESPOT

Mohammed left town in a hurry for Ta-if but was no more successful there than he was at Mecca. In fact, they ridiculed him and pelted him with stones. He returned to Mecca and found that the anger had not abated but had intensified, so in 622 he went to Medina (250 miles north) where he found some success by uniting two Arab clans and neutralizing various Jewish tribes. Rulers in Medina invited Mohammed and his followers to that city because they needed to restore order. Mohammed agreed to move if they accepted him as prophet. His move to Medina is known as the *hijra*.

It is believed that in Medina Mohammed was a sincere (although misguided) seeker of religion, but that was lost quickly with the acquisition of power, position, and popularity. That should not be unexpected since he was, like others of the Arabian Peninsula, deprived of education and culture and driven by his instincts. Add to that his twisted, fragmented ideas of Judaism and Christianity, along with his visions and vivid imagination, and it is not surprising that he changed from a religious devotee to radical despot. It is no surprise that he could not differentiate right from wrong or truth from falsehood. Mohammed could justify every assassination, every beheading, every robbery, every truce breaking, every act of adultery with the help of his personal heavenly emissary, Gabriel.

PREACHING AND PLUNDERING

With every new convert, Mohammed grew more hostile and led three unsuccessful attacks upon Meccan caravans as they were going to or returning from Syria. In his Nakhla Raid he attacked a caravan and a man was killed. His followers split the loot (and Mohammed took his 20%), and the plunder brought him more converts. (Well, if preaching won't do it, plunder will.) Wonder why a prophet who gets direct messages from heaven has to fund his new religion with plunder? Is Allah in Chapter 11 bankruptcy? Is he broke? Doesn't he own even a few cattle on a few hundred hills and maybe a copper mine someplace?

Mohammed led the next raid known as the Battle of Badr where 49 Meccans were killed and about that number taken prisoner and his plunder pile grew. He had hit the jackpot. Religion **was** paying off. At the conclusion of the battle, the bloody head of Mohammed's enemy was hurled at his feet, and Mohammed cried out, "It is more acceptable to me than the choicest camel in all Arabia." To justify his blood thirst, Mohammed said, "I have been ordered by Allah to fight with people till they testify there is no god but Allah and Mohammed is his messenger." So, it wasn't the devil who made him do it, but Allah! Compare that with Christ who said in Matthew 5:44, "Love your enemies, bless them that curse you, do good to them that hate you...."

MOHAMMED THE ASSASSIN

Mohammed was bursting with power, and he exercised it by taking vengeance against his enemies. One was a poetess who had accused him of using her dead father's writings in the Koran. One night, Mohammed's designated assassin crept into her home and found her sleeping, surrounded by her children, one at her breast. He removed the suckling baby and plunged a sword into the poetess. The next morning the assassin went to morning prayers where Mohammed asked if he had slain her. Mohammed was pleased to hear the positive news. The assassin asked, "Is there a cause for apprehension?" Mohammed assured him that all was well and said, "a couple of goats will hardly knock their heads together for it." Later, Mohammed had another poet, a man over 100 years old, killed as he slept. Seems he, too, had written some poems that offended the prophet. I've read some of their poetry and while it wasn't very good, it didn't require the death penalty!

Mohammed was very disappointed when the Jews refused his convoluted message and ridiculed his calling as prophet. He tried to placate the Jews by insisting all Muslims pray toward Jerusalem; preaching there was only one god (Allah); observing the Jewish Sabbath; and even adopting some Jewish dietary laws. Sounds as if he were pandering to the Jews. But the pandering didn't pay. They rejected him so he changed his beliefs! No, don't observe Saturday but use Friday as the day of worship. No, don't pray toward Jerusalem but pray toward Mecca. He now was killing individual Jews who had offended him.

A Jewish poet named Kab, who had also written poems condemning the Muslims' killing at the Battle of Badr, was lured to a waterfall and murdered. Every Jew now feared for his life. The Jews had not responded to Mohammed's office of "prophet," so now the prophet would have his way with them. Kab's death was ordered by Mohammed:

> Narrated Jabir bin 'Abdullah: Allah's Apostle said, "Who is willing to kill Ka'b bin Al-Ashraf who has hurt Allah and His Apostle?" Thereupon Muhammad bin Maslama got up saying, "O Allah's Apostle! Would you like that I kill him?" The Prophet said, "Yes," Muhammad bin Maslama said, "Then allow me to say a (false) thing (i.e., to deceive Kab)." The Prophet said, "You may say it." (Bukhari, vol. 5, book 59, no. 369.)

The morning after Kab's murder, Mohammed said, "Kill any Jew who falls into your power," so Muhayyisa b. Masud killed Ibn Sunayna, a Jew with whom he and his family had had some commercial relations. When Muhayyisa's brother Huwayyisa badgered him about killing the Jew, Mkuhayyisa told him that if Mohammed had told him to kill him (his brother) then he would do so. Then Huwayyisa, not yet a Muslim, said, "Any religion that can bring you to

81

this is indeed wonderful!" Wonderful? How about wicked?

OVER 800 JEWS BEHEADED

As he built his army, Mohammed discovered that Jewish towns were an easy and rich target, so he and his holy robbers started attacking their settlements, especially those who specialized in gold and silver. Mohammed continued to raid Meccan caravans with sporadic success. Back at Mohammed's hometown of Mecca there was concern that he was "getting too big for his britches," so they attacked him. During the battle Mohammed was hit in the mouth with a sword (Gibbon says, a javelin). Historians can not explain why the Meccans did not pursue the battle and devastate their opponents, but they did not. Of course, Mohammed still had influential family members in Mecca who did not recognize his new religion but probably did not wish him dead.

The Meccans began a two-week siege on Medina in 627, known as the Battle of the Trench; some Jews helped in defense of the city, but most were neutral. Mohammed questioned their loyalty, and after the battle, Mohammed had all the Jews in the crosshairs. He said that the judgment of God was "the Jews shall be killed." During the night, ditches sufficient to contain the dead bodies of the men were dug across the market place of the city. In the morning, Mohammed ordered the male captives to be brought forth in companies of five or six at a time. Each company was forced to sit in a row on the edge of the trench (mass grave) and were there beheaded. The bodies were cast in the trench. Some of the women were given to his troops and others sold into slavery. The butchery lasted all day and into the night with the killing of about 800 men. After the killing spree was over, Mohammed relieved his stress by sleeping with Rihana whose husband and all her male relatives had just been beheaded! War is so stressful! And civilization marches on.

Of course, the above massacre (admitted by Muslim and Western historians) was very profitable. After Mohammed squirreled away his normal 20% of the booty, the rest was divided among his followers. And he got **more** followers. After all, there were loot, land, and ladies available for the taking, and they took.

The above massacre is denied by uninformed or dishonest Muslims, but it is a fact of history recorded in the *New Encyclopedia Britannica*: "Some of the evidence against him such as his connivance at assassinations and his approval of the execution of the men of a Jewish clan, are historical matters that cannot be denied."[5]

MOHAMMED TAKES MECCA

With every month, Mohammed grew stronger as more converts showed up at his tent. (Loot, land, and ladies will do that.) Now was the time to take Mecca for good. A treaty was made between the leaders of Mecca and Mohammed whereby he and his followers could make the pilgrimage to the Kaaba; Mohammed could "preach some revivals" but could not engage in any forced conversions. However, true to his lack of character, Mohammed broke the treaty within a year, since he believed it was legitimate to fake a peace when you are weak so that you can smash your enemy when you are eventually strong. Muslims call that *takiya*. Principled people call it "deception." His impressive army forced the leadership of Mecca to capitulate. Mohammed was back home as the "top honcho" religiously and politically with the necessary troops to have his way. And his way was to destroy the idols at the Kaaba and institute one true god–Allah and Mohammed as his prophet.

CHRISTIANS AND JEWS GO TO HELL

But we are told Mohammed was a man of peace! Yes, he brought peace (of the grave) to thousands of people; his followers have brought "peace" to millions. But Mohammed, like Hitler, Stalin, and Mao, made clear his intentions, and his followers have been carrying out his instructions since his death. He said that Muslims are to "Fight against those who believe not in Allah...(Jews and Christians), until they pay *Jizyah* [tribute] with willing submission and feel themselves subdued" (sura 9:29). "Moderate" Muslims want us to believe that Mohammed was supportive of Christians, but that was only in the early days when he thought he could get their allegiance. Later, he considered them unbelievers consigned to hell:

> Verily, whosoever sets up partners (in worship) with Allah, then Allah has forbidden Paradise to him, and the Fire will be his abode....Surely, disbelievers are those who said: "Allah is the third of the three (in a Trinity)"....And, if they cease not from what they say, verily, a painful torment will befall on the disbelievers among them. (Sura 5:72-73.)

When you hear Muslims speak about tolerance and building bridges between Islam and Christianity, remember the following:

Vol. 6, book 60, no. 105: Narrated Abu Said Al-Khudri:

During the lifetime of the Prophet some people said, "O Allah's Apostle! Shall we see our Lord on the Day of Resurrection?" The Prophet said, "Yes; do you have any difficulty in seeing the sun at midday when it is bright and there is no cloud in the sky?" They replied, "No." He said, "Do you have any difficulty in seeing the moon on a full moon night when it is bright and there is no cloud in the sky?" They replied, "No." The Prophet said, "(Similarly) you will have no difficulty in seeing Allah on the Day of Resurrection as you have no difficulty in seeing either of them. On the Day of Resurrection, a call-maker will announce, 'Let every nation follow that which they used to worship.' Then none of those who used to worship anything other than Allah like idols and other deities but will fall in Hell (Fire), till there will remain none but those who used to worship Allah, both those who were obedient (i.e. good) and those who were disobedient (i.e. bad) and the remaining party of the people of the Scripture. Then the Jews will be called upon and it will be said to them, 'Who do you use to worship?' They will say, 'We used to worship Ezra, the son of Allah.' It will be said to them, 'You are liars, for Allah has never taken anyone as a wife or a son. What do you want now?' They will say, 'O our Lord! We are thirsty, so give us something to drink.' They will be directed and addressed thus, 'Will you drink,' whereupon they will be gathered unto hell (fire) which will look like a mirage whose different sides will be destroying each other. Then they will fall into the Fire. Afterwards the Christians will be called upon and it will be said to them, 'Who do you use to worship?' They will say, 'We used to worship Jesus, the son of Allah.' It will be said to them, 'You are liars, for Allah has never taken anyone as a wife or a son,' Then it will be said to them. 'What do you want?' They will say what the former people have said. Then, when there remain (in the gathering) none but those who used to worship Allah (alone, the real Lord of the Worlds) whether they were obedient or disobedient. Then (Allah) the Lord of the worlds will come to them in a shape nearest to the picture they had in their minds about Him. It will be said, 'What are you waiting for?' Every nation have followed what they used to worship.' They will reply, 'We left the people in the world when we were in great need of them and we did not take them as friends. Now we are waiting for our Lord Whom we used to worship.' Allah will say, 'I am your Lord.' They will say twice or thrice, 'We do not worship any besides Allah.'"

Koran-believing and Hadith-believing Muslims believe that only Muslims are going to heaven. Everyone else is going to hell. Don't believe them if they tell you otherwise. Mohammed cursed Christians in his dying breath: Bukhari vol. 1, book 8, no. 427:

Narrated 'Aisha and 'Abdullah bin 'Abbas: When the last moment of the life of Allah's Apostle came he started putting his "Khamisa" on his face and when he felt hot and short of breath he took it off his face and said, "May Allah curse the Jews and Christians for they built the places of worship at the graves of their Prophets."

FRAUD AND DECEPTION

Mohammed commanded: "Fight those of the disbelievers who are close to you, and let them find harshness in you" (sura 9:123). In fact, Muslims are told in sura 8:39 to, "Fight them until there is no more (disbelief and polytheism, i.e. worshipping others besides Allah) and the religion (worship) will all be for Allah Alone [in the whole of the world]." Peaceful religion? I think not. Gibbon, in his *Decline and Fall of the Roman Empire* supports my contention: "The use of fraud and perfidy, of cruelty and injustice, were often subservient to the propagation of the faith; and Mahomet commanded or approved the assassination of the Jews and idolaters who had escaped from the field of battle."[6]

Will Durant in his *History of Civilization* was a little kinder to Mohammed and Islam but quoted Mohammed's successor as saying: "'compel the rest of mankind to become Moslems or pay us tribute. If they refuse these terms, slay them.' The choice given the enemy was not Islam or the sword; it was Islam or tribute **or** the sword."[7] Many non-Muslims converted to Islam to save a buck!

Non-Muslims must not be confused and deceived by statements of Muslim leaders that seem to contradict some of the above quotes. The Koran, while the most influential book written by one

85

man, is not without error nor is it balanced. It is not a cohesive, systematic treatise on what Mohammed believed. It has contradictory statements that Muslims can use to soften their violent image. It was written on scraps of paper, palm leaves, leather, bones, etc., that were collected by others after Mohammed's death. Obviously, it did not come from Heaven!

MOHAMMED: CHILD MOLESTER

Mohammed was betrothed to Aisha, a six-year-old girl (still playing with dolls!), but managed (we are told) to constrain his ardor until she was nine! (See vol. 7, book 62, no. 64.) One politically correct historian was disingenuous when he mentioned the marriage but added, "who lived with her parents until she came of age."[8] Has a nine-year-old come of age, even on the Arabian desert? Even the liberal *Encyclopedia Britannica* reports that she "had scarcely passed the period of infancy."[9]

I believe all civilized people would consider that child molestation, right? I was told by a Muslim cleric that on the Arabian Peninsula it was not uncommon to take a child bride. It was common. O, all right. That means that child molestation was common in Arabia, doesn't it? And can any sane, sensitive, person believe otherwise, whatever his religious belief? The above Muslim leader told me that Mohammed did not "take her as his wife" until she was **eleven** years old; however, no other source reports that to my knowledge. Besides, does that make a difference? What it means is that in Arabia during that time, the male sexual appetite was to be satisfied without confining notions of morality. The rights of women and children were not considered. But even in that desert "culture," Mohammed got flack for his marriage to Aisha; but surprise, surprise, surprise, he had another vision from Gabriel who said that his pedophilia was all right with Allah! Allah endorsed sexual perversion, but Christ said that if we even thought about unlawful sexual activity it was adultery! Yet we are to believe that Islam is superior to Christianity!

Muslims have great difficulty in a civilized culture with Mohammed's marriage to Aisha, and there has been a great amount of dissimulation, but let me nail it down. Their own "holy" book could not be any clearer that the marriage was a fact. In vol. 7, book 62, no. 65:

Narrated 'Aisha: that the Prophet married her when she was six years old and he consummated his marriage when she was nine years old. Hisham said: "I have been informed that 'Aisha remained with the Prophet for nine years (i.e. till his death)."

Again, in vol. 7, book 62, no. 88:

Narrated 'Ursa: The Prophet wrote the (marriage contract) with 'Aisha while she was six years old and consummated his marriage with her while she was nine years old and she remained with him for nine years (i.e. till his death).

Let Aisha speak again in vol. 5, book 58, no. 234:

Narrated Aisha: The Prophet engaged me when I was a girl of six (years). We went to Median and stayed at the home of Bani-al-Harith bin Khazraj. Then I got ill and my hair fell down. Later on my hair grew (again) and my mother, Um Ruman, came to me while I was playing in a swing with some of my girl friends. She called me, and I went to her, not knowing what she wanted to do to me. She caught me by the hand and made me stand at the door of the house. I was breathless then, and when my breathing became Allright, she took some water and rubbed my face and head with it. Then she took me into the house. There in the house I saw some Ansari women who said, "Best wishes and Allah's Blessing and a good luck." Then she entrusted me to them and they prepared me (for the marriage). Unexpectedly Allah's Apostle came to me in the forenoon and my mother handed me over to him, and at that time I was a girl of nine years of age.

The greatest historian of Islam was Tabari (839-923) who was a Jew (!) who had converted to Islam. He was a physician, philosopher, astronomer, and mathematician who wrote a 39 volume history from creation to 915 A.D. He wrote in volume 7, page 7 quoting Aisha: "My marriage (to Muhammad) was consummated when I was nine...." On page 131 of volume 9 he quoted Aisha: "then the men and women got up and left. The Messenger of God [Mohammed] consummated his marriage with me in my house when I was nine years old."

The above information should be sufficient but I will add

two more authorities: The *Encyclopedia of Islam* informs us under "Aisha": "Aisha went to live in an apartment in Muhammad's house, later the mosque of Median. She cannot have been more than ten years old at the time and took her toys to her new home." Then from a Muslim book, *Women in Islam* published by Islamic Publications in Pakistan: "She (Aisha) was the youngest of his wives. It is said that she was nine years of age when he married her." So, there is no doubt except in the minds of fanatics that Mohammed married a six-year-old girl and consummated the marriage when she was nine. That is child molestation!

MOHAMMED'S SEXUAL APPETITE

Gibbon was right when he said that Mohammed "indulged the appetites of a man, and abused the claims of a prophet."[10] It seems that whenever he was caught in an embarrassing situation, the angel Gabriel paid him a visit to extricate him from his problem. Example: when Mohammed wanted Zaynab, his adopted son's wife, he took her (with his son Zaid's approval). It caused a stir since it was considered incestuous because an adopted son had the same standing as a natural born son. But not to fear because Gabriel was near. Mohammed went into one of his famous swoons, fits, visions, or whatever and when he came out of it he said, "Who will go and congratulate Zaynab (his new bride) and say that the Lord has joined her to me in marriage?" Sura 33:36-38 is his justification for taking his son's wife. His young wife Aisha had an interesting retort to Mohammed following the above "vision." She said, "Truly your God seems to have been very quick in fulfilling your prayers." Sarcasm is not called for, Aisha, but how about fresh poison mushrooms for your husband?

Mohammed's sexual life was the talk of the desert since it was claimed he had sexual relations with **each** wife every day–before prayers! He had the stamina of 30 men and needed it since he had more than 20 women including his concubines and slaves in his harem!

Narrated Qatada: Anas bin Malik said, "The Prophet used to visit all his wives in a round, during the day and the night and they were eleven in number." I asked Anas, "Had the Prophet strength for it?" Anas replied, "We used to say that the Prophet was given the strength of thirty (men)" (vol.

1, book 5, no. 268). Aisha said, "I scented Allah's prophet and he went round (had sexual relation with) all his wives" (vol. 1, book 5, no. 270 and 267).

The above ridiculous and immature boast that Mohammed was capable of being with each of his wives every day was only wishful thinking. The Hadith vol. 7, book 71, no. 660, tells us magic was working on Allah's Apostle so that he used to think he had had sexual relations with his wives while he actually had not.

IT GETS WORSE

Mohammed spent each night with a different wife but when it was Hafsa's turn she was visiting her father, so what's a man to do? Mohammed took Mary his Egyptian slave to bed, but Hafsa returned early to find Mary in her bed with her husband. Fireworks in old Arabia! Hafsa agreed not to tell anyone but decided to tell Aisha, and soon all Mohammed's wives were in rebellion. Mohammed promised to stay away from Mary if the harem would calm down; however, he had another fit and Gabriel gave him special revelations to change the rules. Sex with a slave was acceptable. Rank hath its privileges–and in spades for the Prophet!

Sura 66 is the message that Allah gave to Mohammed that solved his marriage mess: "O Prophet! Why do you forbid (for yourself) that which Allah has allowed to you [i.e., Mary], seeking to please your wives?... Allah has already ordained for you the absolution from your oaths....when the Prophet disclosed a matter in confidence to one of his wives then she told it (to another i.e. Aishah) And Allah made it known to him....It may be if he divorced you (all) that his Lord will give him instead of you, wives better than you...." Principled Muslims have gagged on that sura for centuries.

It gets worse, if possible. Mohammed conjured up the temporary contractual marriage (see book 8, no. 3243) whereby a man was permitted to "marry" a woman for 15 minutes for the purpose of sex! This fact is endorsed by one of Islam's top leaders, Al Baydaivi, who wrote, "The purpose of the contractual marriage is the mere pleasure of intercourse with a woman...."[11] Mohammed later forbade the practice.

ILLITERATE BARBARIAN

Mohammed had some strange habits especially for a desert

Arab. He wore a veil, dyed his hair a reddish orange color and painted his eyes each night. While the red dye colored his graying hair, it did not get rid of the lice that lived there. (See Hadith vol. 1, book 4, no. 167; vol. 9, book 87, no. 130.)

Gibbon characterized him correctly as being "an illiterate barbarian" who united "the professions of a merchant and a robber."[12] Mohammed also permitted, in his presence, the torture of a tribal chief to discover his hidden treasure. He accepted slavery as a law of nature, but mitigated it somewhat by saying that families should not be separated at the time of sale! While he did unify numerous Bedouin tribes and made significant improvements in the social welfare of the people (those he didn't kill), he left a legacy of hatred, treachery, and slavery.

JIHAD! JIHAD! JIHAD!

Mohammed seldom taught about the love of God or man's love for God, but he sure spent a huge amount of time talking about judgment, hell, death, and war. Muslims get very uneasy when we speak of their easy acceptance of violence. They tell us that all Muslims are not terrorists as those who steered planes into the World Trade Center and the Pentagon; however, **all the terrorists were Muslims!** When *jihad* is discussed, Muslims get as uncomfortable as a dog in hot ashes, but it is a major part of Islam. A cursory reading of the Koran and the Hadith easily proves Islam's propensity toward violence. Vol. 1, book 2, no. 25 tells us: "Allah's apostle was asked, 'What is the best deed?' He replied, 'To believe in Allah and his Apostle.' The questioner then asked, 'What is the next (in goodness)?' He replied. 'To participate in *Jihad* (religious fighting) in Allah's cause.'" The Hadith, vol. 1, book 2, no. 35; vol. 4, book 53, no. 386 assures any Muslim killed in a *jihad* that he will go straight to Paradise and experience incredible sexual pleasures for eternity.

Every Muslim has a lifetime obligation to fight for the faith, expanding Islam to every nation on earth. "Moderate" Muslims are disingenuous or dishonest when they deny that Islam requires all Muslims to spread their doctrine by sword or word. Some examples:

Sura 2:191 and 193 teaches: "Kill them wherever you find them...." And "fight them until there is no more disbelief and worshipping of others...." Sura 2:216 tells all faithful Muslims, "Holy fighting in Allah's cause is ordained for you...." Muslims are promised rewards if they die for their cause: "And if you are killed or die in the Way of Allah, forgiveness and mercy from Allah are far better than all that they amass (of worldly wealths)" (sura 3:157).

Sura 47:4: "So, when you meet those who disbelieve, smite (their) necks till when you have killed and wounded many of them, then bind a bond firmly (on them, i.e. take them as captives)." Sura 9:5-6 says, "Kill those who join other gods with God wherever you may find them."

Sura 17:16: "When We decide to destroy a town (population), We (first) send a definite order (to obey Allah and be righteous)...Then we destroy it with complete destruction."

"Believers, take neither Jews nor Christians for your friends" (sura 5:51).

"Fight and slay the pagans [unbelievers] wherever ye find them, and seize them, beleaguer them, and lie in wait for them in every stratagem of war" (sura 9:5).

"Prophet make war on the unbelievers and the hypocrites and deal rigorously with them. Hell shall be their home" (sura 9:73).

"Believers, make war on the infidels who dwell around you. Deal firmly with them" (sura 9:124).

"Fight for the cause of God with the devotion due to Him...He has given you the name of Muslims..." (sura 22:78).

And when people resist Islam, sura 5:33 commands, "Their punishment is...execution, or crucifixion, or the cutting off of hands and feet from the opposite sides, or exile from the land."

Islam would always kill pagans who refused to convert but would often permit Christians and Jews to pay the *jizya*, a very heavy tax that seemed to lead to many "conversions." In paying that tax, they were to be humiliated as a normal procedure.

NON-MUSLIMS ARE SECOND-CLASS CITIZENS

American Muslims strive diligently to project a false image and have used excuses such as the following author wrote to deny the obvious:

> Islam does not permit discrimination in the treatment of other human beings on the basis of religion or any other criteria....it emphasizes neighborliness and respect for the ties of relationship with non-Muslims...within this human family, Jews and Christians, who share many beliefs and values with Muslims, constitute what Islam terms Ahl al-Kitab, that is, People of the Scripture, and hence Muslims have a special relationship to them as fellow "Scriptuaries."[13]

One must remember that the above writer is trying to impress the free world (as opposed to the real world behind the black curtain of Islam). If the nation were an Islamic nation ruled by Muslim clerics he would write something else. He would tell you that you are a second-class citizen, that you cannot have a public worship service, that you will be arrested if gospel singing is heard from your home, that in court a Muslim always will be believed before you are, etc. Muslim countries are totalitarian and the people are slaves to Islam. The only concession I make to them is that they really believe what they believe.

Today, in Saudi Arabia U.S. female soldiers must wear the head-to-toe black dress when they are off base! Furthermore they must sit in the back of cars, and must be escorted by a male soldier! Did you know that when President Bush the First was in Saudi Arabia during the Gulf War, he was told by Saudi officials not to say grace during the Thanksgiving Day meal with American troops? We were there to keep them from being invaded by their Muslim pal in Iraq, and they gave our President orders about praying before a meal! Bush had dinner on a ship in international waters. I think he should have prayed anyway, loudly, and in the name of Jesus of Nazareth who died and rose again on the third day. But then, Bush the First always needed a spinal transplant!

ISLAM AND WOMEN

Non-Muslims are turned off when they discover the Islamic attitude toward women. Paradise seems to be filled with dark-eyed virgins that are available to the men who arrive there. Sura 55:52-66 promises Muslim men: "Shall the reward of goodness be anything but good?...Dark-eyed virgins sheltered in their tents....They shall recline on green cushions and fine carpets...Blessed be the name of

92

your Lord...." Thinking female Muslims should want to know what awaits **them** in paradise? Mohammed didn't say.

If that's not clear enough, sura 78:31-33 promises: "But for the God-fearing is a blissful abode, enclosed gardens and vineyards; and damsels with swelling breasts for companions; and a full cup." Translation: plenty of sex and wine. Sura 55:70-74: "In these gardens will be chaste and beautiful virgins....nymphs, cloistered in their tents....which neither man nor demon will have touched before them."

CONVERTS FROM ISLAM

What happens if one wants to leave this religious movement? Mohammed made that very clear. Kill him! Bukhari vol. 9, book 84, no. 64: Narrated 'Ali:

> Whenever I tell you a narration from Allah's Apostle, by Allah, I would rather fall down from the sky than ascribe a false statement to him, but if I tell you something between me and you (not a Hadith) then it was indeed a trick (i.e., I may say things just to cheat my enemy). No doubt I heard Allah's Apostle saying, "During the last days there will appear some young foolish people who will say the best words but their faith will not go beyond their throats (i.e., they will have no faith) and will go out from (leave) their religion as an arrow goes out of the game. So, where-ever you find them, kill them, for who-ever kills them shall have reward on the day of resurrection."

Most thinking people will agree that the above clearly commands all followers of Islam to kill those who leave the religion.

ISLAM DOES NOT MEAN PEACE

Muslims are working full time to convince us that Islam means peace. It does not. It means "submission." Its original meaning was "defiance of death; heroism; to die in battle." We must spend some time looking at Islam, its teachings and practices. Any honest Muslim will confess that Islam is the only true religion. Their mission is to convert the world. Similarly, Christians are commanded to preach the Gospel to the whole world. We could do it more effectively, I might add. Islam seeks to conquer with error while Christians seek to convince with truth. (What did you expect me to say? I'm a born-again Christian!)

Islam is a religion that soaked the Middle East, India, North Africa, and Europe in blood. To deny that is to deny history. Will Durant, who smacks Islam and Mohammed with a soft hand (whereas Gibbon does so with a mailed fist), asserts that the Muslim "conquest of India is probably the bloodiest story in history."[14] Wherever they fought and conquered, there were loot, land, and ladies for the taking. Not a good foundation for a world religion! But it worked!

Folks, the barbarians are not at the gates; they are **inside** the gates while U.S. politicians and religious leaders stand around sucking their thumbs as a strange wooden horse is pulled even deeper inside our national walls.

1.   Asma Gull Hasan, *American Muslims,* Continuum, New York, 2000, p. 9.

2.   John McClintock and James Strong, *Cyclopedia of Biblical, Theological, and Ecclesiastical Literature,* Grand Rapids, Baker Book House, 1981 reprint), 6:406.

3.   Michael Nazar-Ali, *Islam: A Christian Perspective,* Philadelphia: Westminster Press, 1983, p. 21.

4.   Alfred Guillaume, *Islam* London: Penguin Books, 1954, p. 6.

5.   *New Encyclopedia Britannica,* Edition 15, vol. 22, p. 4.

6.   Edward Gibbon, *The Decline and Fall of the Roman Empire,* D. M. Low, ed., 1960, p. 690.

7.   Will Durant, *The Story of Civilization,* Book 4, 1950, p. 188.

8.   Bruno Leone, ex. ed., *The Spread of Islam,* Greenhaven Press, San Diego, CA, 1999, p. 19.

9.   *Encyclopedia Britannica,* vol. 15, 1960, p. 648.

10. Gibbon, op. cit. p. 691.

11. *Voice of the Martyrs,* April, 2002.

12. Gibbon, op. cit. p. 663 and 679.

13. Suzanne Haneef, *What Everyone Should Know About Islam and Muslims,* Kazi Publications, Lahore, 1979, p. 173.

14. Will Durant, *Story of Civilization*, Book 1, p. 459.

Chapter Six

The Movement, II

Muslim Leaders Must Take a Stand!

Civilization has come a long way driven by Christianity, but Muslims would drag us kicking and screaming back to a seventh-century, desert culture where passions ruled over principles. I don't want to go there.

Muslims insist that Allah is the God of the Bible. Not so. Allah was just one of 360 gods that was worshipped by desert pagans at the Kaaba in ancient Mecca. Religious zealots of the day ran seven times counter-clock-wise around the cube-shaped Kaaba (temple), kissed the black stone, then sometimes ran about a mile to a dry river bed and threw stones at the devil! (Before Mohammed the zealots were naked!) That sounds more exciting than a revival meeting but it will never catch on. Too much work for so little pleasure.

Muslims believe that the Kaaba was first constructed in heaven and Adam built it on earth; however, the Flood swept it away. They believe that Abraham was instructed to rebuild it and did so with the help of Ishmael. However, Abraham was never in Arabia, but adding Abraham gives the tale a little credibility. They need some credibility since some scholars say that the Arabs have no connection to Abraham and his descendants! But then, Josephus informs us that the Arabs **are** descendents of Ishmael. Muslims believe that Gabriel gave Abraham a completely white stone that was used in the building but has since turned solid black by the sins of those who touched it.

Running around temples was not uncommon to pagans of the era, but throwing rocks at the devil was not as common. Mohammed institutionalized the rock throwing by teaching that Satan allegedly appeared to Abraham, Hagar, and Ishmael and they each threw seven rocks at him, and at that place (where the incident did **not** happen) Muslim pilgrims throw rocks at the same devil today. The rock throwing could be an attempt to dispose of a dangerous spirit or to throw away personal evil in the stones. Or, they may **really** be throwing rocks at Satan.

ALLAH: PAGAN GOD

Any good resource book will reveal that Allah was the male, pagan moon deity who married the sun and had daughters as a consequence of that celestial union–the stars! And all those heavenly bodies are gods! Temples to the moon god have been uncovered all over the Middle East. Not unusual since it was the most prevalent religion. Some think that Allah was the leading god of the 360 gods in the Kaaba. It is also a fact that the crescent moon, found in numerous archeological digs in the Middle East, was the symbol of the moon god, and it is also the symbol of every Muslim on earth.

The *Encyclopedia of Religion* agrees about Islam's origin: "'Allah' is a pre-Islamic name....corresponding to the Babylonian Bel."[1] Scholar Henry P. Smith of Harvard stated: "Allah was already known by name to the Arabs."[2] Middle East scholar E. M. Wherry stated that "Allah worship and the worship of Ba-al involved the worship of the sun, moon and stars."[3] So Mohammed did not get knowledge of Allah from heaven, but from the pagan Kaaba temple. A good question for Muslims: how could Mohammed have received the Allah revelation from Heaven when his own father was named "Abd-**Allah**"? Allah was a common name for a pagan god long before Mohammed walked the Arabian Desert. Mohammed only cleaned the Kaaba of all **other** gods.

HEART OF ISLAM

Mohammed did not preach a new revelation to his desert buddies. They were all familiar with Allah and the "buffet of gods" at the Kaaba, so it was much easier for them to accept Mohammed's pagan religion than if it had been a new revelation as claimed. Islam was simply a new twist on the old religion familiar to everyone.

He instituted five pillars of Islam for every Muslim:

- ♦ They must confess, "Allah is God and Mohammed is his prophet."

- Muslims must pray five times a day toward Mecca.
- They must give 2 to 10% of their income to the poor.
- They must fast during Ramadhon.
- They must make a pilgrimage to Mecca once in their lifetime.

Cantor and other historians report that "holy war" is the sixth pillar of Islam.[4] Most "moderate" Muslims disagree, but history would support those historians.

EMISSARIES OF ISLAM

Blerime Topalli, a Muslim, wrote a column criticizing Muslim terrorists and called them "enemies of Islam." However, the terrorists were not enemies of Islam but **emissaries** of Islam. They were doing what Islamist extremists demand. About the Koran, Topalli falsely said, "It is a book of faith and a way of life, not a weapon with which to manipulate people." No, that is exactly what it is. He closed by requesting "firmly" that American flags "be raised at each mosque so that the communities that surround us can view our solidarity with them as Americans."[5]

I appreciate, applaud, and approve his condemnation of terrorists, and I think he is sincere; however, Islam will never be respected by an informed, civilized society unless leading Muslims repudiate the oppression and hate as taught in the Koran and the Hadith! But that would dismantle Islam which they will not do. People like Topelli are decent, law-abiding Americans as loyal as I; however, there are numerous Muslims in America who would never be terrorists but would apparently approve of their attacks! And they do plan to change our nation, make no mistake about that. They are part of a dangerous Trojan Horse. Their plan is literally to conquer the world, nation by nation. The first Muslim missionaries who came to America in the 1920s bluntly boasted, "Our plan is to conquer America." And they are doing it, even as I write.

REALITY NOT RHETORIC

We must get below the rhetoric to the reality. What are they really saying? What do they really intend to accomplish? Pass over their public comments and listen to what they say to their own people. We saw this in November of 2001 when Yassar Arafat tried to keep the Israelis from blowing him into Paradise. He talked like a pacifist with doves flying around his head, but a few days later he was breathing out fire and thunder to his extremist followers. Such duplicity is illustrated by Daniel Pipes who wrote an article in November of 2001:

> In June 1991, Siraj Wahaj, a black convert to Islam and the recipient of some of the American Muslim community's highest honors, had the privilege of becoming the first Muslim to deliver the daily prayer in the U.S. House of Representatives. On that occasion he recited from the Qur'an and appealed to the Almighty to guide American leaders "and grant them righteousness and wisdom."
>
> A little over a year later, addressing an audience of New Jersey Muslims, the same Wahaj articulated a rather different vision from his mild and moderate invocation in the House. If only Muslims were more clever politically, he told his New Jersey listeners, they could take over the United States and replace its constitutional government with a caliphate. "If we were united and strong, we'd elect our own emir [leader] and give allegiance to him....[T]ake my word, if 6-8 million Muslims unite in America, the country will come to us." In 1995, Wahaj served as a character witness for Omar Abdel Rahman in the trial that found that blind sheikh guilty of conspiracy to overthrow the government of the United States. More alarming still, the U.S. attorney for New York listed Wahaj as one of the "unindicted persons who may be alleged as co-conspirators" in the sheikh's case.
>
> The disparity between Wahaj's good citizenship in the House and his militant forecast of a Muslim takeover—not to mention his association with violent felons—is only one example of a larger pattern common to the American Muslim scene.[6]

MUSLIM FANATICS

Pipes reports that Ahmad Nawfal, a leader of the Jordanian Muslim Brethren and frequent speaker to U.S. Muslims, said the United States has "no thought, no values, and no ideals." If militant Muslims "stand up, with the ideology that we possess, it will be very easy for us to preside over this world."[7] If you think these people are not serious, you are living in a state of denial, and denial is dangerous and deadly.

Another Islamic fanatic is Shamim A. Siddiqi who wrote a 1989 book about the need to convert Americans to Islam. He said that all Muslims in America must be involved in this great missionary effort to win America to Mohammed using "all of their energies, talents, and resources." He said that every Muslim will face consequences on the Day of Judgment about how energetic they were in their missionary efforts. He wrote: "Every Muslim living in the West will stand in the witness box in the mightiest court of Allah . . . in *Akhirah* [the last day] and give evidence that he fulfilled his responsibility . . . that he left no stone unturned to bring the message of the Qur'an to every nook and corner of the country."[8]

Islamic dominance in America will completely change it. Is that what you want? Muslims want students in public schools to be permitted to recite "In the name of God, the Merciful, the Compassionate" each day. They want to broadcast the calls to prayer five times each day. They demand that affirmative action for Muslims be established (as we try to dismantle all affirmative actions for others). They want laws that would restrict any criticism of Islam and Mohammed! They would institute the chopping off of hands and feet for minor crimes, beheading for adultery (Saudi Arabia beheaded 81 people during 2001!), no radio, no television or record sales, no pork sales, etc.

MULLAH IN THE CATBIRD SEAT

America would not be America with a Muslim mullah in the catbird seat. Since the Muslim attacks on America, California public school districts are teaching a required, three-week course on Islam! Children memorize verses from the Koran, adopt a Muslim name, wear Muslim robes, study the tenets of Islam, learn about their main leaders, and form their own *jihad*! Children are taught to pray "in the name of Allah, the Compassionate, the Merciful" and are instructed to chant, "Praise to Allah, Lord of Creation."[9] The textbook used always presents Christianity in a negative light highlighting the Salem witch trials, the Inquisition, etc., in bold type while Islam is broadly presented in a very positive light with no mention of the oceans of blood shed to spread its culture/religion! (And some people still defend public education!)

Well, of course the ACLU and other Protectors of the Oppressed such as Americans United for the Separation of Church and State (who recently held their national meeting in a phone booth) and People for the American Way all had a collective fit. No, not a word. Not a fax. Not a news conference. Can you imagine if those schools were teaching **Bible** verses, and the tenets of Christianity, teaching kids to pray in the name of Jesus Christ? This further proves that liberals are the biggest hypocrites in the world.

FEMALE CIRCUMCISION

Muslims in control would legislate the way we dress, eat, rear our children, shop, what we purchase, how and where we worship, and how we treat our daughters and wives. Muslims are not female friendly! Muslims show their hatred of women by their angry, aggressive, and abusive policy of female circumcision. First, it must be understood that the Koran never commands circumcision of males, much less females. Secondly, most people have never heard of female circumcision. *FrontPageMagazine.com* had a chilling article titled "Islam's Hatred of the Clitoris" that dealt with female circumcision. It said that it is "about obliterating the clitoris, or the entire outer vagina. It is the barbarity that exists where misogyny festers most: in the Muslim and African world." The article reveals that 97% of women in Egypt have been circumcised, meaning their clitorises have been amputated. And in places like Sudan, **all** of a woman's external genital organs are removed!

How is the mutilation accomplished? Women hold down a child as young as one month but usually about seven or eight years, and the "surgery" is always done without anesthetics! And is often done with broken glass! As I think about the possibility of my daughters and granddaughters going through such barbaric mutilation, I would like to get my hands on those "surgeons"! What kind of culture or religion would permit something like that to flourish? Note that this practice is common. In fact, if a female has not had this "surgery," she is considered unclean and only the surgery can make her clean!

Many times the victim dies after going through the torture; others suffer from chronic infections for a lifetime. But possibly worse than the suffering is that the surgery makes them less than God intended them to be. God gave females the clitoris to permit them to have sexual pleasure within the confines of marriage. It is

100

not an exaggeration to say that about 75% of women do not achieve orgasm without clitoral stimulation. The clitoris has nothing to do with child bearing, only sexual pleasure. However, warped Muslims apparently believe women should have no sexual pleasure, so they try to undo what God did. (On the other hand, eternal reward for Muslim men is unlimited sexual pleasure.) Many of those unfortunate women are traumatized for a lifetime with sexual, emotional, and mental repercussions.

In Somalia and some other parts of the Arab and African world, the entire vaginal area is sewed up around a hollow reed to permit urination and menstrual flow to take place. On the wedding night the husband beats his wife with a whip, then after this bit of foreplay, he cuts the vagina open with a razor to permit penetration. For the following week, they have frequent intercourse to prevent the vagina from closing again. Following the "honeymoon," the husband takes his bloody razor or knife to all the local hangouts to show his buddies the proof of his wife's virginity.[10]

DARK SIDE OF DIVERSITY

Female sexual mutilation is the dark side of diversity and a curtain of silence has been pulled to cover it. I have had Muslims even deny that it is a common practice in the Islamic world. They say that it is only a local African custom, and "maybe a few Muslims" practice it.

Can any person, Muslim or non-Muslim, defend such a barbaric practice? A British daily reported: "Local authorities and social workers have turned a 'blind eye' to the genital mutilation of young girls among African and other Third World communities in Britain for fear of being labeled racist."[11] Female circumcision has been illegal in Britain since 1985! Medical and social service staffs are "nervous" about reporting female circumcision, no, call it what it is, female mutilation. Why? Because it may be racist! One health official, quoted in the previous article, said, "There continues to be confusion as to what is legitimate in culture, which should be respected, and what is human rights abuse." Incredible, but understandable! When a nation is set adrift without a compass, it is no wonder people make such stupid statements. England was not only adrift years ago, but their ship also went down. They forbid the spanking of children but wink at female mutilation!

DESPOTIC RELIGION

When the Taliban controlled Afghanistan, they prohibited all music, photographs, clean-shaved men, and women in high heels. Men could go to soccer games but they could not enjoy them too much! If people yelled too loudly, a member of the Vice and Virtue Squad whipped them where they sat! (As shown on an *MSNBC* special.) And you may remember that halftime **was** very special. They executed men and women by shooting and hanging them at center field. We are told that such people are Muslim extremists or fundamentalist Muslims, but they are simply carrying on the culture and religion of the past hundreds of years. The word is control, total control of a populace. When Islam takes control, they control every facet of life.

Terrorists are following Mohammed and the dictates of the Koran. For "moderate" Muslims to deplore the actions of the "fundamentalists" is simply an attempt to make themselves more comfortable in a radical, undemocratic, despotic religion. "Moderate" Muslims must not only condemn terror, they must repudiate the Koran and stop funding terror while they condemn it! Until that happens, I refuse to believe their sobbing sentiments and will insist they are America's Trojan Horse.

TEARS AND BLOOD

Liberals love to castigate England, Belgium, France, and Germany for their colonial activities in India, Africa, and the Caribbean, blaming them for all the ills of those areas without admitting that the colonial powers drained swamps, built highways, laid railroad tracks, and built hospitals and schools while making many people rich. But if we agree with the critics of colonialism, wonder why those same critics don't effuse profusely over the same kind of colonialism perpetrated by Islam? In fact, Islam did not add much to the nations it conquered, as did the Europeans. But European colonialism is bad, very bad, but Islamic colonialism is good, very good!

Kateb Yacine, who died in 1989, was an Algerian writer whose assessment of Islam is destructively insightful. In a famous radio interview he said, "Islam does not develop with sweets and roses, it develops with tears and blood. It grows by crushing, by violence, by contempt, by hatred, by the worst humiliation a people can support. We can see the result."[12] Muhammad Hisham Kabbani is head of the Islamic Supreme Council of America and seems to be a reasonable, sincere, and capable man. He said that extremists have taken over 80 percent of the mosques in the U.S.[13]

ISLAM ON THE MARCH

Mohammed may have been an illiterate barbarian but he was a charismatic and dynamic leader who unified the Arabs of Arabia into a nation and inspired his followers to take Islam to much of the world. By 661, the Muslim capital was in Damascus, not Medina, and Constantinople was in their sights. However, the Muslim victory was outside their grasp mainly because of a secret weapon called "Greek fire." Used by the Muslims' enemies, this was a liquid containing quicklime that ignited on contact with water and could only be extinguished by vinegar or sand.[14] Frustrated, the Muslims abandoned their efforts to conquer Constantinople, thereby permitting the Byzantine Empire, such as it was, to survive until they finally took it in 1453. After taking the Arabian continent, Mohammed's followers, within twenty years of his death, like burning sagebrush on a prairie, conquered the Persian Empire and within a hundred years ripped around the fringe of North Africa, jumped across the Straits of Gibraltar into Spain, and were eventually stopped in 732 by Charles Martel at the Battle of Tours. The Muslim capital was later moved to Baghdad.

In the 1000s, a fierce tribe from Central Asia, the Seljuk Turks swept through Persia and controlled the caliphs of Baghdad. Then in 1071 the Seljuk Turks (having converted to Islam) made the Byzantine Empire bleed at the Battle of Mangirert. They now occupied Asia Minor and began to harass Christian pilgrims traveling to Jerusalem. The Byzantine emperor in Constantinople pled for Pope Urban II to help; the Roman Catholic Pope was eager to please, consequently he decided to preach the First Crusade. After significant losses in the First Crusade, the Muslims began to slowly but steadily recover the Holy Land.

STILL MARCHING

It is said that Islam progressed as much in a century as Christianity did in seven.[15] However, those fawning historians don't add that Christians did it with teaching, while Islam did it with terror.

At one point, Muslims were within a day of the gates of

Paris, and they seemed invincible. Islam ruled Western Europe for over 500 years before they were repelled. The barbarian camel-driver had made an impact on the world!

The Catholic Crusades had many debilitating effects on Europe and the Middle East, one being the mauling of the Greek Orthodox Byzantine Empire headquartered in Constantinople. When the Byzantine Empire fell, nothing was standing in the way of Muslim control of the Balkans, and Islam was at the gates of Vienna in the 1680s. They would have taken Vienna were it not for some freak thunderstorms that forced them to back off their attack.

In 2002, Muslims were illegally surging across porous borders into Spain and Italy at an alarming rate, consequently those Catholic nations will become Muslim during this century! This push is similar to what happened to the Roman Empire in the fourth and fifth centuries, as Alaric and his Visagoths sacked mighty Rome in 410 followed by the Vandals in 455. In 476, the haughty Western Roman Empire came to an end.

Truly, Islam is on the march around the world–the world they really expect to conquer. The former Director of the Islamic Cultural Centre of London, Dr. Zaki Badawi, declared: "A proselytizing religion cannot stand still. It can either expand or contract. Islam endeavors to expand in Britain. Islam is a universal religion. It aims at bringing its message to all corners of the earth. It hopes that one day the whole of humanity will be one Muslim community, the Umma."[16] If that happens, how will it affect our American way of life? Is there some way we can predict the results of an Islamic America? Just look at the past. In the fourteenth-century, Ibn Khaldun lived in Tunis and observed that the Arabs created the deserts in which they lived. He wrote that civilization "always collapsed in places the Arabs took over and conquered." He reported that settlements became depopulated "and the very earth there turned into something that was no longer earth."[17]

I have traveled through various Muslim countries and even their major cities are dirty, the food in the best hotels is miserable, and thievery abounds. You see a different world if you travel from Rome to Athens to Jerusalem then to Damascus or Amman or Cairo. Beirut used to be an exception, but at that time it was not dominated by Muslims.

MUSLIM CONTROL OF U.S.

Don't be deceived–Muslims plan to control America some day. Do you want to live in a Muslim-controlled society? They may not be successful, but there is no doubt that they are sincere. Look at Britain where Muslims are taking over. Patrick Sookhdoe is a former Muslim who said in a speech recently: "I think we face a much greater threat from Muslim communities within our own countries than we realize....In Britain today, where Islam controls the inner cities, we have major social exclusion and the development of *sharia* (enforcement of Koran law). We have had churches burned, Christians attacked, and a mission center destroyed. The media has deliberately kept everything off the air. This plays into the hands of Muslims ultimately."[18]

So, why are Bush and his administration skirting the Muslim issue? He doesn't want to antagonize Islamic governments and give cause for a Muslim uprising, especially in the "moderate" states such as Egypt and Jordan. So he kisses the moderates while he kicks the extremists. The fact is that all Muslims, if they believe what they profess, would climb into bed with the terrorists. If not, they should renounce their "holy" book.

Why haven't you heard Bush, Blair, and Company demand accountability from Islamic states that persecute Christians? If we are to have foreign aid (state welfare), how can it be justified when **all** Muslim states permit persecution of Christians? A simple statement could be sent to each Muslim government: "No more trade between our nations and no more welfare checks will be sent until we have guarantees that all persecution of Christians has stopped. The slave trade in Sudan must stop now, and all slavers must be brought to justice."

BUSH, BLAIR AND COMPANY WILL BACKPEDAL

How can any world leader sit down with Muslim terrorist Arafat when his hands drip with the blood of innocent Jews and Arabs? How could sane people award him the Nobel Peace Prize? Of course, one doesn't **have** to be a socialist, totalitarian, or one-worlder to qualify for the Prize, but it seems to help! After all, other socialists, communists, and one-worlders such as Nelson Mandela, Martin Luther King, and Kofi Annan of the U. N. are prize winners.

No, President Bush was wrong, and while I commiserate

with the position he is in, I refuse to commend his policy. I wonder if we will ever see U.S. government officials commiserating with Bible-believing Christians as they do with Muslims? Don't hold your breath unless you like the color of blue.

Bush, Blair, and Company have a coalition of many countries including some from the Islamic world, but they had better understand that the Muslim leaders don't sleep well at night. Uneasy rests the head of the kings because they know that Muslim terrorists can get to them rather easily. So, while Islamic leaders are impressed with our gun power, our money, and influence, they are more fearful of fellow Muslims. Those leaders must walk a very thin line—or else.

Watch for the U.S. coalition to soften then disintegrate if the U.S. aggressively goes after terrorists in Muslim nations. The "moderate" Muslim leaders will start to pull away (and many have never totally climbed aboard) until the U.S. coalition is totally non-Islamic. Even as I write, it is almost totally American and British. From the Muslim nations, we get talk, and it is time for "moderate" American Muslims to take a stand with the U.S. against their buddies in Baghdad and other Islamic states.

Also watch for Bush, Blair, and Company to backpedal.

1. *Encyclopedia of Religion*, eds, Paul Meagher and Thomas O'Brian, Consuela Aherne, Washington D.C., Corpus Pub., 1979, 1:117.

2. Henry P. Smith, *The Bible and Islam: or, The Influence of the Old and New Testament on the Religion of Mohammed*, New York, Charles Scribner's & Sons, 1897, p. 102.

3. E. M. Wherry, *A Comprehensive Commentary on the Quran*, Osnabaruck, Otto Zeller Veriag, 1973, p. 36.

4. Norman Cantor, *The Civilization of the Middle Ages*, HarperCollins Publishers, 1993, p. 134.

5. Belerime Topalli, column on *Heal the World* web site, Crescentlife.com, 10-5-01.

6. Daniel Pipes on Daniel Pipes.org, Nov., 2001.

7. Ibid.

8. Shamim A. Siddiqi, *New York Post,* 11-12-01.

9. *WorldNetDaily*, "Islamic studies required in California district," 1-11-02.

10. Jamie Glazov, *FrontPageMagazine*, 10-19-01.

11. *Independent,* 7-7-92.

12. Interview on Radio *BEUR*, 4-20-94, Quoted in *Why I am not a Muslim,* p. 352.

13. Speech at an Open Forum at U.S. State Department in January, 1999 from The Root and Branch Ass'n Ltd., web site.

14. C. W. Warren, *Medieval Europe: A Short History,* Hollister, 7th Ed., McGraw-Hill, 1994, p. 75.

15. Norman Davies, *A History of Europe,* Oxford Press, 1996, p. 253.

16. Cited in *Why I Am Not a Muslim,* p. 352.

17. Tom Bethell, *The American Spectator,* Nov./Dec. 2001.

18. *Christian News,* 1-28-02.

Chapter Seven

The Mavericks

Black Muslims in America

Are Black Muslims a part of the traditional Muslim community, poor second cousins, or what? I asked that question of leaders at the Indianapolis mosque during an interview on April 25, 2002. A leader dismissed Black Muslims with the wave of his hand as mavericks "who use Muslim terms." In other words, they are Blacks but not Muslims. However, other Muslims have told me that Black Muslims are a part of Islam. Seems as if they are as confused as the mainline "Christian" denominations.

Muslims around the world talk about Christianity being the "White man's religion" while Islam is the religion of "everyone," and they are loath to admit that Mohammed was a white man as evidenced by many references in the Koran and the Hadith. He was a "white" man who kept slaves as Hadith vol. 6, book 60, no. 435 reveals: When a man came to Mohammed's home he saw a "black slave of Allah's apostle sitting on the first step." Mohammed often referred to blacks as "raisin" heads as seen in vol. 1, book 11, no. 662 and other places. It is also a fact that Muslims were slavers long before Europeans got involved in that dirty business. But it is unkind for me to mention that!

As to Mohammed's "whiteness," vol. 1, book 3, no. 63 says, "When we were sitting with the Prophet in the Mosque, a man came riding on a camel. He made his camel kneel down in the Mosque, tied its foreleg and then said, 'Who amongst you is Muhammad?' At that time the Prophet was sitting amongst us (his companions) leaning on his arm. We replied, 'This white man reclining on his arm.'" Further references as to Mohammed's "whiteness" are found in Hadith vol. 2, book 17, no. 122 and vol. 2, book 17, no. 141. For those who always wanted to know, vol. 1, book 8, no. 367 reveals that his penis was white! (Some translate "penis" as "thigh.")

EARLY BLACK LEADERS

A Black Nationalist movement seems to have begun in the early 1800s with Paul Cuffe, a black sea captain who tried to establish a Black American colony in Africa; however, after transporting a few dozen Blacks to Africa, his effort fizzled. Then along came W. E. B. Du Bois, the first Black to earn a Ph.D. from Harvard, who leaned decidedly to the left, and late in life became a Communist. He developed a sophisticated Pan-African plan to join Blacks in Africa and America. Another fizzle.

Marcus Garvey who started the United Negro Improvement Association (UNIA) in 1914 followed Du Bois. His goal was to organize Black Americans as a nation that would be oriented toward Africa. He purchased various businesses including ships, hotels, grocery stores, etc., but because of mismanagement at the very top and antagonism of Whites, that too fizzled. The *Encyclopedia Britannica*, among other sources, gives Garvey credit for some ideas later advocated by the Nation of Islam, known by many as Black Muslims.

FIRST BLACK MUSLIMS

There was little Muslim influence in America until the early 1900s when the Moorish Science Temple Divine and National Movement of North America was founded in 1913 at Newark, New Jersey, by Timothy Drew, also known as Noble Drew Ali. Then in 1925, the name of the sect was changed to the Moorish Temple of Science. Drew Ali taught that Allah had ordained him as his prophet to the dark people of America. Ali taught that people of color should not be called Negro, Black, Colored, Ethiopian, etc. He only experienced nominal success in reaching Blacks and died in 1929. A struggle ensued between two of his followers who loudly claimed to be the reincarnation of Drew Ali! And with the reincarnation went the crown of leadership and the checkbook, of course.

One of those disciples was Wali (Wallace) D. Fard, a **white** man with Middle East origins (some say Turkey, while the *Encyclopedia Britannica* says it was Saudi Arabia) who called himself "Prophet Fard" and "the savior." His real name was David Ford. The "savior" had a part-time job selling African clothing door-to-door.

He told Blacks to renounce their American names and adopt Muslim names. Furthermore, he told them to dress as people in Muslim nations do, and he just happened to have the necessary clothing to sell them at special discount prices!

WHITE DEVILS

The prophet also preached that Blacks were gods and white men were devils, and it seems no one asked him to reconcile the fact that he, the prophet, was a white devil! It is amazing what people will believe when they don't believe the Bible. Fard was thought to be Allah in person! He founded the Temple of Islam in Detroit, Michigan. This "savior" had all the answers for the problems that faced the Blacks of America. Fard was a charlatan who passed himself as black. Like all religious quacks before him (and all after him), he used the Bible to confuse and convert many uninformed and gullible Blacks. Later he used the Koran to further confuse them.

Fard, like many contemporary black leaders was a demagogue. He used the Bible and the Koran to control people. He used religion to gain influence over disadvantaged, discouraged, and downtrodden Blacks. He told them that white people (like himself?) were devils and that Blacks must be separated from them and not dependent on the white devil. As he got them into the Koran, he told them that Christianity was a tool that the white slave masters used to control Blacks.

ELIJAH MUHAMMAD

Between 1930 and 1933, Fard recruited about 8,000 followers among Detroit Blacks, and the sect exploded in numbers so that Fard needed associates to help tend the growing flock. He tapped an unemployed auto worker named Robert Poole to be an assistant "savior." Poole, son of slaves, changed his name to Elijah Muhammad and became chief minister of the Temple of Islam. Poole was the son of a Baptist preacher and eventually succeeded Prophet Fard.

Elijah Muhammad (Poole) moved to Chicago in 1932 and founded Temple #2, at about the same time Fard went to prison. Upon his release, Fard joined Elijah Muhammad at the Chicago Temple, but he was soon arrested there as well. Fard eventually mysteriously disappeared in June of 1934 after he began referring to himself as "the Supreme Ruler of the Universe!" Maybe James

111

Hoffa, Elvis and the Supreme Ruler of the Universe are sitting under a cabana, sipping cold drinks on a South American beach at this minute! Judge Crater who disappeared in 1930 under strange circumstances may even be with them!

There was a disagreement and a power struggle; Elijah Muhammad came out on top of the heap. He would tell anyone that Fard was Allah in person, and he did so without smiling. The surprise is that his listeners did not fall to the floor holding their sides with laughter. He affirmed, "You must forget about ever seeing the return of Jesus who was here 2000 years ago. Set your heart on seeing the one that He said would come at the end of the present world's time (the White race's time). He is called the 'Son of Man', the 'Christ,' the 'Comforter.' "[1] To think they killed a tree to print such tripe!

HAWKERS OF HATE

Elijah, like Fard, was an angry, hostile man who despised anything associated with Christ. He declared that Christianity was the cause of the black man's problems. Furthermore, he ridiculed the Bible teaching of loving your enemy. He and his brood were hawkers of hate who infected that generation of Blacks and fomented anger, resentment, and hatred of Whites that is still festering today.

Elijah Muhammad exposed his racist soul and ranting mind whenever he spoke or wrote about race. He taught that the Black race came into existence about 78 **trillion** years ago (evidently Elijah was not a young earther!) and they all lived a good life until Whitey was created. He wrote that the Father of the White race was a mad, **black** scientist named Yakub from Mecca who created the white devils (about 6,000 years ago) to war against the black race and bring them into subjugation for about 6,000 years! It seems that Allah exiled his enemy, Yakub, along with 59,999 of his followers to the island of Patmos. Muhammad ranted: "The white man is Mr. Yakub's idea...his made-man whom he would teach to rule the Black man. He taught his made-man (white race) the method by which a peaceful (Black man) could be overcome and ruled until One Greater Than, Mr. Yakub, Come [sic] to our rescue. (Allah, God, Who Came in the Person of Master Fard Muhammad, to Whom Praises are due forever.)"[2]

112

BLACK KKK

All right, so it isn't the greatest prose in literary history, but he reached deep into the souls of thousands of unemployed, uneducated, and unsophisticated Blacks in Detroit, Chicago, New York, etc. One wonders how any sane person could stomach such blather, but they did. And they still do. It is incredible that no one ever asked Elijah how white people could be blamed for evil if a black man created him or her that way! That would mean, dare I say it, that a black man is responsible for all evil in the world!

Elijah also said, "EVERYWHERE the white man may be, even in Europe, the earth belongs to the Black Man."[3] He taught that Blacks created and own the entire earth. He stated that no black man would be accepted by God as long as he believes in the white man's religion.[4] On the back page of any issue of *Muhammad Speaks,* his weekly diatribe, the "prophet" made clear what he demanded: a separate state or territory of their own "either on this continent or elsewhere."[5] And all their needs must be met for the next 20 to 25 years. He demanded that all black felons in all Federal prisons be released. Furthermore, all Blacks must be freed from the obligation to pay **any** taxes. But that's not all. He also demanded that black teachers in their own schools teach black children. Boys and girls should be taught separately with all expenses paid by the government, with no government oversight. Then he demanded that intermarriage or race mixing should be prohibited. Sounds to me as if we have a Black Ku Klux Klaner here. I suppose they wore black sheets instead of the standard white.

MALE DOMINANCE

Young black men flocked to this black cult in large numbers (unlike black and white congregations in the mainline denominations where one can shoot a shotgun and not hit any male older than 13). Elijah purchased numerous small businesses that provided organizational funds and employment for his followers.

This male-dominated black movement attracted other men (and even women) who liked seeing men take some responsibility. To their credit, the Nation of Islam insisted in having strong, consistent male leadership in the home with women being protected and respected as homemakers. This has resulted in very little juvenile delinquency among them.[6] I tip my hat to them in this regard. At one point, however, Elijah Muhammad (Poole) told young men of draft age that they should not register for the draft or fight in a white man's war; consequently, he spent 1943-1946 in prison. A later black convert, Muhammad Ali, also refused to enter the military and fight in Vietnam.

It seems that women did not resent the male dominance but really liked the strong, religious male image in the home. Black Muslim women were not to have contact with white "devils" either male or female. They were taught that white men, by their very nature, can not have any honorable intentions toward any black woman. They were also taught that white women are by nature very immoral.

MALCOLM X

Elijah does not get credit for the explosive growth of the movement during the 1950s. That credit goes to Malcolm Little (another Baptist pastor's son) who, while serving a prison sentence in Massachusetts in 1948, came in contact with the teachings of Elijah Muhammad and was converted. Little grew up in Lansing, Michigan, and saw his house burned down at the hands of the Ku Klux Klan. Two years later his father was murdered, and his mother was carried off to a mental institution. The following years Malcolm spent in detention homes, and as a teenager moved to Boston to live with his sister. Upon release from prison, Little, a former strong-arm man, thief, pimp, drug pusher, and numbers man, began preaching the gospel of the black cult in Detroit. Attendance at Temple #1 exploded; Elijah Muhammad took notice of his new convert and changed Little's name to Malcolm X.[7]

This former felon hit the big time in black circles and was soon known by Whites across the nation. He was a spellbinding orator with an ability to capitalize on poor Blacks and their hopelessness. Soon, he was speaking to groups in many colleges and in ghetto storefronts. There were Malcolm X buttons, sweat shirts, posters, and his autobiography sold 800,000 copies! He was even called "St. Malcolm" by some as he spewed his hymn of hate whenever he had the opportunity.[8] Organizationally, he was the Black Muslims' Apostle Paul.

As a reward for his loyalty to Elijah, his stunning success in bringing in converts, and his innovative ideas, he was appointed as national spokesman for the Nation of Islam. Detroit, Chicago, Boston, Philadelphia, and New York City always supplied a goodly group of Blacks to hear him. The Black Muslims could boast of a membership of 40,000, due mainly to the efforts of Malcolm X. Malcolm took justified credit for establishing Black Muslim temples in many of the major cities.

Malcolm was in great demand and became an international figure, and some leaders of the movement thought he was gaining too much prominence at the expense of Elijah Muhammad. Malcolm was often reprimanded for making statements not authorized by Elijah. In a speech at the Cory Methodist Church in Cleveland, Ohio, on April 3, 1964, Malcolm stated "If we don't do something real soon I think you'll have to agree that we're going to be forced either to use the ballot or the bullet. It's one or the other in 1964. It isn't that time is running out–time has run out!"[9] He added that Blacks out there don't intend to turn the other cheek any longer. At this time, he had announced that he would leave the Nation of Islam and form his own movement that would be closer to orthodox Islam. Elijah was not thrilled to have competition from this young, talented zealot.

DADDY ELIJAH

Relations between the two leaders became even more tense when two former employees filed a paternity suit against Elijah Muhammad. (Elijah had 13 illegitimate children!) Malcolm X decided to discover the truth for himself about the allegations and eventually questioned Elijah himself. "I'm David," Elijah Muhammad replied. "When you read in the Bible how David took another man's wife, I'm David....You read about Lot who went and laid up with his own daughter. I have fulfilled all those things."[10] Malcolm was disenchanted and severed all connections with the movement. Elijah had five affairs going at the same time usually telling the women about his "divine seed." Among all his affairs one was incestuous! Some prophet!

It didn't help Malcolm when he saw Elijah living in an 18-room mansion and owning two Cadillacs and a Lincoln Continental! I suppose he didn't consider Elijah was "suffering for Allah" while he lived in such luxury. Malcolm gave an interview to the *Village Voice* saying, "Muhammad is the man, with his house in Phoenix, his $200 suits, and his harem. He didn't believe in the black state, or in getting anything for the people. That's why I got out."[11] He's not the only one who got out. Others started bailing out, including two of Elijah's sons and a nephew!

Malcolm continued to live in the house purchased by the Nation of Islam and refused to vacate it when ordered by Elijah. In September of 1964, the Black Muslims got a court order to evict him (since they had retained title to the house), but he refused to obey it. On Feb. 14, his home in Queens was firebombed, but Malcolm and his family escaped unharmed. The next day, Malcolm charged that his home was "bombed by the Black Muslim movement on the orders of Elijah Muhammad."[12] Things were heating up!

Malcolm had visited Mecca in April of 1964 and saw black and white people worshipping together without rancor or racism and in returning to the states, he mellowed. He and one of Elijah's sons had begun to question some of Elijah's teachings, especially that Fard was Allah himself. Malcolm began to see that Blacks and Whites need not hate each other. In fact, they could work together for a common cause! Then in October of 1964, he confessed that he had been converted to orthodox Islam after seeing all races worship together in Mecca.

BLACKS KILL MALCOLM X

My assessment of Malcolm X is that he was sincere and had been genuinely rehabilitated without Bible regeneration. He developed into a strong family man and hard work advocate. The different Black Nationalist groups in Harlem and elsewhere considered Malcolm X a potential liberator, "a man on a black horse who would someday lead them in a revolutionary struggle against the hated whites."[13]

On February 21, 1965, Malcolm was speaking to a group of about 500 people, almost all Blacks, in the Audubon Ballroom in New York City when several gunmen opened fire on him from the front few rows. Police had made many offers to station policemen at the doors but were rejected. It is also true that no one was searched for weapons. Three former members of the Nation of Islam were convicted of the murder. One of them, Talmadge Hayer (alias Thomas Hagan), confessed and implicated the other two. Later he claimed that these two men were innocent, but that four active members of the Nation of Islam had actually helped him. All three were sentenced to life in prison. Police said that seven bullets hit Malcolm from two different kind of guns along with shotgun pellets. Black men in a black community, before a virtually all black audience, murdered Malcolm X.[14] No sensible person says that any white man had anything to do with his murder.

By this time Black Muslims were no longer perceived as a small, unknown group of cultic fanatics. With the murder of Malcolm, Americans were making judgments about the radical movement. Supreme Court Justice Thurgood Marshall, a black liberal, said that Elijah Muhammad's organization was "run by a bunch of thugs organized from prisons and jails and financed, I am sure, by Nasser [Gamal Abdel Nasser of Egypt] or some Arab group." He added that followers of Mr. Muhammad were "vicious" and a threat to the Federal Bureau of Investigation and state law enforcement agencies.[15]

One of my favorite writers was black conservative, George Schuyler, a columnist for The Pittsburgh *Courier*; his view was different from the above. He wrote: "Mr. Muhammad may be a rogue and a charlatan, but when anybody can get tens of thousands of Negroes to practice economic solidarity, respect their women, alter their atrocious diet, give up liquor, stop crime, juvenile delinquency and adultery, he is doing more for Negroes' welfare than any current Negro leader I know."[16]

LOUIS FARRAKHAN

After Malcolm's murder, Elijah Muhammad restored Warith Deen (his son who had left the movement) back into the Nation of Islam in 1969 and back into the Black Muslim ministry in 1974. Then, on February 25, 1975, Elijah Muhammad died in fulfillment of Hebrews 9:27: "It is appointed unto men once to die but after this, the judgment." The following day Warith D. Muhammad was appointed the new leader with the support of a "rising star" named Louis Farrakhan. With Elijah and Malcolm now dead, the movement began to sputter if not to a stop, at least to a crawl. The Nation of Islam discovered that dead leaders can't lead. And those who aspired to leadership positions didn't have the leadership qualities of the early founders, except for a young man from Boston who had been mentored by Malcolm X himself, Louis Farrakhan.

117

Warith D. Muhammad led the Nation of Islam to become an orthodox community of Sunni Muslims and restored Malcolm X to a position of honor. The name of the organization was changed to the Bilillian Community and later to the World Community Al-Islam in the West (WCIW). Although Warith opened the WCIW to all races, its membership remained predominantly black. Warith also repudiated the overt racism and the deification of Fard.[17] He called Fard, a "wise" man, but not Allah. It seems the apple fell far from the tree in Warith's case. While still a heretic, he was far more reasonable than his father was.

SPLINTERING

The Warith group (WCIW) continued to be known as Bilillians after an Ethiopian Muslim who was born about 600 AD.[18] In 1975, the group was accepted by orthodox Muslims and even decided that whites were not devils. The group is now known as the American Muslim Mission. The move away from the teachings of Elijah Muhammad toward orthodox Islam angered many, including Louis Farrakhan who broke with Warith Deen in 1977, forming his own Nation of Islam. It's getting confusing, isn't it!

The Nation of Islam had big problems in 1970, toward the closing years of Elijah Muhammad's leadership, and it started to splinter into various groups. Warith Muhammad had tried to make concessions and theological adjustments, but the factions within the Bilillian Community remained. They resisted the changes and stayed faithful to the teachings of Elijah Muhammad.

In 1976, Silas Muhammad, splintered off from Warith's group and founded the Lost, Found Nation of Islam. He restored all of Elijah Muhammad's myths and teachings. The leader of the third splinter group was a former national spokesman for the WCIW, Louis Adul Farrakhan, who now refers to himself as the national spokesman for the Honorable Elijah Muhammad, and his group is almost identical with Elijah Muhammad's original group.

The leader of the fourth splinter group was John Muhammad. In 1978, he broke with Warith Muhammad and founded another Nation of Islam.[19] The fact is that there have been too many splits and splinters to discuss here, and there is no need to do so.

UNDISPUTED LEADER

Louis Farrakhan, born Louis Eugene Walcott in New York in 1933, is the undisputed leader of U.S. Black Muslims. He grew up in Boston, became an honor student and accomplished musician who attended the Episcopal Church. He attended Winston-Salem Teachers College for two years, dropped out and afterward found work in nightclubs as a calypso guitarist-singer known as "Calypso Gene." He recorded an original song, "A White Man's Heaven is a Black Man's Hell," and wrote plays that were performed in mosques. He assisted Malcolm X at the Boston Mosque and became minister when Malcolm moved to New York City. Farrakhan is an articulate, charismatic orator and an excellent organizer.

It is interesting that Farrakhan also succeeded Malcolm X as Nation of Islam minister at the Harlem Mosque #7, the most influential mosque outside Chicago and wrote just before Malcolm's murder: "Malcolm shall not escape." He declared that "such a man is worthy of death," and within two months, Malcolm was killed! It should be noted that Farrakhan later expressed regret for making any contribution for a climate of antagonism that led to Malcolm's death.

Farrakhan lives very well off the backs of Blacks. So what's new? Don't most black "leaders" do that? Louis has a 77-acre country estate in addition to two posh Chicago homes. And you thought Elijah Muhammad lived above his upbringing!

DISTORTED THEOLOGY AND DANGEROUS POLITICS

Louis derides Christ's virgin birth, saying that since Allah is a man, he had sexual intercourse with Mary resulting in Christ's birth. After all, Fard was Allah, **then** Elijah became Allah, **now** Louis is Allah!

At the 1991 Savior's Day celebration, Farrakhan was introduced as the fulfillment of Isaiah 9:6-8. Not Christ, but Louis Farrakhan was proclaimed as the "child who would be born" and the "son who would be given" because he was "Wonderful, Counselor, the Mighty God, the Prince of peace."[20] During that service Farrakhan told the crowd that he saw a huge plane shaped like the wheel in the book of Ezekiel with thousands of people looking out the windows. Not only did he see the huge plane, he was taken for a ride in it. While inside he heard the voice of Elijah Muhammad, so he was still alive! Farrakhan did not tell them if he also saw Elvis, but had he done so, the crowd would have believed him. After all, god cannot lie. Louis told the crowd that the "wheel" ship would one day destroy the white man and bring Blacks into power. He also assured the adoring crowd that 1500 smaller planes from the giant "wheel" follow him at all times.[21]

In February, Farrakhan was sponsored by two large black denominations as speaker in Los Angeles! Why would "Christian" leaders **pay** to have a cult leader spout distorted theology and dangerous politics to thousands of gullible citizens? It only proves that many black religious leaders are as uninformed and unprincipled as their members. Or, maybe they are simply unconcerned about Truth. Farrakhan told the "Christians" they should rethink their Christianity (well, maybe so) and their allegiance to Israel. Even the city fathers got into the act and waved most of their enormous fees for the use of the convention center. Wonder if they would do that for a bunch of white Baptists?

INFLAMMATORY RHETORIC

Farrakhan often bellows about how Blacks lost their Muslim religion during slave days and he deplores American society; yet, few Blacks would be willing to go back to their ancestral home land in Africa or any of the 50 plus Islamic states. Maybe some of us could sponsor **Farrakhan** to move to one of those Islamic nations! I'll give the first thousand dollars!

Farrakhan has a reputation for his inflammatory rhetoric such as calling Hitler a "great man." He said Jews followed a "gutter" religion, and some of his top people are vicious Jew-haters. His top aid and National Spokesman for the NOI, Khalid Abdul Muhammad (who grew up as a Methodist), spoke at Kean College in Union, New Jersey on November 29, 1993, where he called Jews "hook-nosed, bagel-eatin', lox-eatin'" imposters. As to the Pope, he said, "somebody need to raise that dress up and see what's really under there." But it got worse. He showed his hatred for all white people when he said: "[W]hen we gain enough power from God Almighty to take our freedom and independence [in South Africa], we give [Whites] 24 hours to get out of town by sundown. That's all. If he don't get out of town before sundown, we kill everything white that ain't right that's in sight in South Africa. We kill the women. We kill the children. We kill the babies. We kill the blind. We kill the cripples. We kill them all. We kill the faggot; we kill the lesbian. We kill 'em all. You say why kill the babies in South Africa? Because they're gonna grow up one day to oppress our babies, so we kill the babies. Why kill the women? Because they lay on their back. They are the military or the army's manufacturing centre. They lay on their back and the reinforcements roll out from between their legs. So we kill the women too.

"You gonna kill the elders too? Kill the old ones, too. [Expletive deleted] if they have a wheelchair, push em off a cliff in Cape Town. How the hell you think they got old? They got old oppressing black people. I say kill the blind; kill the cripple; kill the crazy, [expletive deleted], and when you get through killing them all, go to the [expletive deleted] graveyard and dig up the grave and kill em [expletive deleted] again, cause they didn't die hard enough." Well, that did it. Liberals in New York went ballistic and demanded an apology. Louis said he agreed with the content of the speech but not the manner it was given. However, later Farrakhan gave a speech in Harlem and at that time he embraced his bigot aid on stage.[22] The following year, Louis fired his top spokesman who died in an Atlanta hospital on February 17, 2001, at age 53.

In February, 1996, Louis did a five-week tour of the world's most despotic nations. In Iran he was reported to have said "You can quote me: God will destroy America by the hands of Muslims.... God will not give Japan or Europe the honour of bringing down the United States; this is an honour God will bestow upon Muslims." (See Anti-Defamation League's web site and many others.) Question: Why is that loose cannon not sitting in a prison cell for treason?

It must be emphasized that many people do not consider Black Muslims true Muslims. Many traditional Muslims consider them an aberration or cult. The Federation of Islamic Association, the official Muslim organization in this country, has repudiated the Black Muslims, claiming that it is not affiliated and is not recognized as truly Muslim. That is supported by my Indianapolis interview with traditional Muslim leaders who consider Black Muslims as mavericks.

H. RAP BROWN

However, criticism of Black Muslims stops when it encounters us "infidels." Case in point is former Black Panther, Hubert Rap Brown, who was recently found guilty by an Atlanta jury for the murder of a Black policeman. Rap became infamous in the 1960s when he boasted, "We're gonna burn America down." Instead his mob only burned two city blocks in Cambridge, Maryland. He was the "Minister of Justice" for the Black Panther Party and was wounded in an attempted robbery in New York City. That resulted in his spending five years in the slammer where he was converted to the Dar-ul Islam movement of Islam. (Most prisons are simply recruiting stations for Black Muslims.) Rap took the name of Jamil Abdullah al-Amin.

Jamil (Rap) ended up in Atlanta in the 1980s where he became active in the Dar-ul Islam community; however, the group fell apart and in 1981, he organized some members from the group as the National Islamic Community. Many authorities consider Jamil's group to be the country's third largest behind those led by Warith Deen Mohammad and Nation of Islam leader Louis Farrakhan. Jamil's movement, which has formed 36 mosques around the nation, helped revitalize run down areas in inner cities.

In 1995, Brown was arrested for shooting a drug dealer four times in the legs and a year later was investigated for more than a dozen murders.[23] Not the normal southern Sunday school boy, this Rap. (By the way, violent rap music got its name from this dude! Enough said?) When two sheriff's deputies approached Brown in March of 2000, he pulled two guns and fired, killing one deputy and injuring another. The jury found him guilty on 13 counts including murder. He was sentenced to life in prison without possibility of parole. You can bet the farm that he will not spend his life in prison. I have been amazed in doing my research that some in the media and academia have presented him as a noble figure: a "religious leader," "author of *Die, Nigger, Die,*" "spiritual advisor," "defender of oppressed Blacks," *ad nauseam.*

TRADITIONAL MUSLIM SUPPORT

Even traditional Muslim groups have supported this convicted killer! The Council on American-Islamic Relations characterized him as one of the "leading figures" of American Islam, and the American Muslim Council called him "a leader in the American Muslim community." Four major Muslim organizations issued a statement in Brown's defense that would gag a buzzard: "The charges against Imam Jamil are especially troubling because they are inconsistent with what is known of his moral character and past behavior as a Muslim."[24] Hand me a barf bag! His violent actions are symptomatic of his life of crime.

Brown often spoke at traditional Muslim affairs and now Muslims are rallying to his defense, even raising large sums of money and petitions for his defense. Farrakhan and the Executive Director of the Council on American-Islamic Relations have visited him in his cell. I would think they would be demanding justice for those Brown attacked rather than sitting in his cell holding his hand. Why not raise money for the families of those he killed and injured?

Black Muslims, like Middle Eastern Muslims, have a propensity for violence and crime as exemplified in H. Rap Brown. But recently the world saw another example of terror perpetrated by a Black Muslim follower–the two snipers in the Washington, D.C. area during the fall of 2002.

WASHINGTON D.C. AREA SNIPERS

In October of 2002, there was a series of sniper killings in the Greater Washington D.C. area that grabbed the attention of the nation. One person after another was shot at random: young and old; black and white; male and female; etc. The "experts" all said that it had nothing to do with terror. It was probably an "angry white male," maybe one who had poor potty training or was "whapped" on his rear when he was a child; or one who grew up deprived of the latest toys while his friends seemed to have everything. Throw in a few rats and maybe even extreme religious training and you have a mental mix that finally exploded in multiple shootings. But it turned out to be two black dudes, the elder being a member of the Nation of Islam! I suppose it is possible to be an "angry **black** male."

Some newspapers reported that the terrorist thugs, John Allen Muhammad and Lee Boyd Malvo had "possible ties to 'skinhead militia' groups." What! A black dude with his hairdo, being associated with skinheads! The media were so disappointed that the sniper wasn't an angry white male active in the NRA with "cutesy" bumper stickers all over his old pick up truck. Sample: "A gun in the hand is better than a cop on the phone." Or, "If guns cause crime, then pencils cause misspelled words." Or, "Guns only have two enemies: rust and liberals." Or, "Gun control is not about guns but about control." Or, "If guns cause crime, then matches cause arson." But, surely you get the belabored point, don't you? No, the sniper was not an angry white male, but I am one angry white male who demands that top law officers start looking at those most likely to be terrorists– whatever their race or religion.

The media would have been thrilled if the shooter had been a white, fundamentalist Christian who, when apprehended had pockets full of gospel literature providing the way to heaven, anti-abortion information, a 1968 copy of *The Sword of the Lord,* and a copy of the *Protocols of the Elders of Zion* in his rusty, pick-up truck. No, we must never leap to a conclusion, but it seems that the media always lunges **away** from any connection if a Muslim (or any minority) is caught in an incriminating situation. John Allen Muhammad's ex-brother-in-law, reported that at the mention of Jesus Muhammad would get very offended and told his wife, "If you ever leave me, I'll kill you and the kids." (Rob Carson, *The News Tribune,* Tacoma, WA 11-18-02.) Muhammad also expressed delight over the September 11 attack on America according to *ABC News.* So it was an angry black male with Islamic connections who was responsible for the shootings.

Hey, is it so unbelievable that the sniper might be motivated by religious hatred? Should it not be considered? Is it racist to suggest that possibility? It seems the media and many officials have been appointed to smooth out any Islamic public relations problems. What is this, Saudi Arabia? It is conceivable that the two were not connected to the Big Bad Boys in the Middle East, but we know Muhammad had a connection with the Nation of Islam. He reportedly was a security guard during the misnamed Million Man March on Washington. Whether the two alleged (my attorney made me add that word) killers acted on orders from Master Terrorists abroad or simply saw a chance to get their fifteen minutes of fame by killing innocent people, it doesn't really matter that much. At least not to those killed and their families.

The media "experts" were so sure that the killer was very smart, had an elaborate plan, and knew the area well, probably lived there. Turns out they were wrong on all counts! As to being smart, they turned out to be dumb as a box of rocks. They left all kinds of evidence behind and tied themselves to the Alabama killing! The only dumber thing they could have done was walk in on one of Chief Moose's (or is that Meese) live news conferences carrying their rifle. As an afterthought they demanded ten million dollars to stop the shootings but wanted the money put in a credit card account they had stolen! That wasn't dumb. That was super dumb! They didn't have a plan but drove around looking for victims, and as to living in the area, they lived in their car and were finally arrested sleeping in a rest area. It has recently been determined that the two alleged killers are tied in with a shooting spree that left 14 people dead and five others wounded in Washington, D.C., Maryland, Virginia, Washington state, Alabama, Georgia, and Louisiana. It looks as if Virginia will get the first chance to try them and send both killers into the arms of the dark-eyed virgins. After all, they caused "unbelievers" to live in terror for weeks. That seems to please Allah.

Of course, not all Muslims would endorse the bloody activities of Lee Boyd and John. Even Farrakhan has distanced himself from the two snipers. However, the hatred of whites and the resulting violence must be laid at the feet of Farrakhan and all who preach hatred of people simply because of their differences. But according to the practitioners of political correctness it seems only white people can be haters. Are the PC people blind or dishonest? Only Whites can be racist and hostile! Is it impossible for Blacks to be?

So it seems traditional Muslims and many ordinary Americans hold various opinions about Black Muslims in America, from embarrassment to full support of their most violent activities. About one million Black Americans identify with Islam. Make no mistake: they all accept the Koran and the seventh-century culture of the Arabian Desert. And many are in the belly of America's Trojan Horse.

1. Elijah Muhammad, *Message to the Black Man in America*, Muhammad Mosque of Islam No.2 Chicago, 1965, p. 10.

2. *Muhammad Speaks*, July 4, 1969, p. 20.

3. *Muhammad Speaks*, July 11, 1969, p. 21.

4. *Muhammad Speaks*, October 10, 1969, p. 21.

5. Any issue of *Muhammad Speaks*.

6. C. Eric Lincoln, *Black Muslims in America*, Beacon Press Boston, MA, 1961, p. 33.

7. Young, Henry. *Major Black Religious Leaders Since 1940*, Abingdon

Nashville, TN, 1979, p.75.

8. Lionel Lokos, *The New Racism*, Arlington House, New Rochelle, NY, 1971, p. 42.

9. Malcolm X, *Malcolm X Speaks*, Grove Press, New York, 1966, p. 25.

10. Clifton Marsh, *From Black Muslims to Muslims,* Scarecrow Press, Inc. Meteushen, NJ, 1984, p. 78.

11. Malcolm X, p. 194.

12. *New York Times,* News of the Week in Review, February 16, 1965, p. 18.

13. C Eric Lincoln web site, *The Meaning of Malcolm X.*

14. Lokos, p. 61.

15. *New York Times,* 2-26-75.

16. Ibid.

17. *The New Encyclopedia Britannica,* vol. 1, 15th Edition, p. 333

18. Marsh, p. 93.

19. Web site of Adam Edgily and Carl Ellis, "Emergence of Islam in the African-American Community."

20. Lincoln, p. 168.

21. Ibid. p. 165-166.

22. *Time*, Feb. 7, 1994.

23. Daniel Pipes, *American Spectator,* Nov.-Dec., 2001.

24. Ibid.

Chapter Eight

The Mistakes

Mistakes, Mishmash, and Madness

Muslims claim that the Koran is a holy book sent from Allah to Mohammed through various visions. They claim that it has been preserved **exactly** as it was revealed to the prophet with no corrections, additions, or subtractions, and that it is pure Arabic. If so, I demand to know how the Arabic in the Koran is the vocabulary and dialect of a member of the Quraysh tribe living in or near Mecca during the seventh century![1] Is it unkind to suggest that the Koran came from Mohammed's fevered mind, not the mind of an all-powerful, all-knowing God? In this chapter I will reveal the many mistakes, mishmash, and madness in the "holy" books of Islam and their many contradictions and some comparisons with the Bible.

THE HADITH

The Hadith is a collection of Mohammed's sayings, speeches, actions, etc., as attested by various relatives and followers. There is a big debate in Muslim circles whether or not the Hadith is inspired. Muslims can't agree on the issue. It is my opinion that thinking Muslims know the Hadith can't be defended to the satisfaction of sane, honest people. Those who defend the Hadith are defending a castle in ruins.

Many Muslims consider the Hadith (traditions) as "holy" yet scholars such as Schacht, Goldziher, and others have concluded that most or maybe all of the traditions were forgeries put into circulation a few hundred years after Mohommed![4] Following Mohammed's death, Islam split as Muslims opposed Muslims. The unauthorized splits managed to "find" other hadiths to support their particular doctrine! (Could that be the rationale behind the many Bible versions we have today?)

Muslims consider Sahih Bukhari (also Bukhary) the best translator of the Hadith. He considered 600,000 traditions out of which he accepted only 7,295. Since the same tradition is often repeated more than once under different chapters, the number of distinct hadiths is reduced to 2,762. All right, we have fewer than 3,000 hadiths that scholars consider authentic, while the others are unacceptable because they are unreliable or repetitious. Question: why are there so many unreliable statements of Mohammed floating around out there? For the same simple reason that there are many spurious writings of the early church leaders in Christianity. A sect arises and it needs validation for its aberrational teachings, so a "Gospel of Paul" or a "Gospel of Barnabas" is written that "substantiates" the false doctrine. It is a reasonable phenomenon when you understand the wicked heart of man. Islam started splitting immediately following the death of Mohammed; consequently, various hadiths were produced to support each faction, but there was no Koranic support for those splits. However, Muslims are told that they can accept weak hadiths if it is for a good purpose!

HADITH BACKGROUND

Rashad Khalifa revealed on his pro-Muslim web site how the hadiths came to be written: "It is well known that the first book of Hadith is that of Bukhary, who was born more than 200 years after the death of Muhammad. When Bukhary wrote his book of Hadiths, he used to visit the people whom he knew as sources. After verifying that his source is 'truthful,' and known as a man or woman of righteousness, Bukhary would ask, 'Do you know a Hadith?' The person would answer, 'Yes,' then proceed to narrate the 'Hadith' as follows: 'I heard my father, may God bless his soul, say that he heard his older brother, may God bless his soul, say that he was sitting with his grandmother, may God bless her soul, and she told him that she was having dinner one day with her great uncle, may God bless his soul, when he stated that his maternal grandfather knew Imam Ahmad ibn Muhammad alAmawy, who mentioned that his grandfather heard from his oldest uncle that he met the great companion of the Prophet Omar ibn Khaled AlYamany, and he told him that the Prophet, peace be upon him, said, ...'" Is it any wonder that honest, thinking Muslims reject the Hadith?

I interviewed three clerics at the Indianapolis mosque, and the top honcho (an Indianapolis physician) later responded to my e-mail regarding the Hadith as follows: "There is not much split on Hadith but the fact is hadith or sayings of prophet do not have same weight as Quran which we believe is word of God. Hadith were not guaranteed protection by God. Some hadith we call authentic or agreed upon as they are mentioned in all the collections. While some other, if mentioned by only one chain of narrator we call weak hadith. To those who do not consider Quran to be inspired, what difference it makes if certain hadith is inspired or not?"

The above notwithstanding, there seems to be a serious split in Islamic thinking as seen in the following statement (from his web site) by Muslim, Rashad Khalifa: "Since the socalled (sic) hadith & sunna of the Prophet have been vastly corrupted, they can never meet the criterion of divine revelation. It is an acknowledged fact that the vast majority of Hadiths are false fabrications." He also added that saying the above was like telling Christians that Christ was not the Son of God.

Khalifa gained great popularity in Islamic circles when he scientifically "proved" the Koran was without error but his life was threatened when he made his critical assessments of the Hadith. So there is a major split in Muslim circles as to whether the Hadith is a "holy" book or not.

Furthermore, the Muslim clerics in Indianapolis gave me a copy of the Koran published by the King Fahd Complex in Saudi Arabia and almost every page has one or more hadiths to help explain the confusing, convoluted, and contradictory verses in the Koran. So the official Muslim position is apparently that the Hadith is a "holy" book of Islam. So, why are American Muslims trying to distance themselves from it? Because it is impossible to defend to the satisfaction of sane, sensible people.

WHICH KORAN?

If the Koran is from God, then it must be perfect, without contradictions. A Muslim booklet, *The Amazing Quran* challenges readers to show any mistakes and contradictions. I accept that challenge with gusto! Now, we must admit that there is a difference in confusion and contradictions. So I will try to be fair, honest, and candid in this chapter dealing with mistakes in the Koran, the Hadith (their second holy book) and Islam in general.

Most Muslims are uninformed, as are most Christians, as to

their "holy" books. What the average Muslim knows about their "holy" books would fit into the navel of a flea. They don't know that the Hadith says that Uthman got the Koran compiled and sent copies to various places. Wait a minute, I thought Mohammed received a perfect text from heaven during his fits, swoons, seizures, etc.!

It is a fact that there was no definitive Koran text even as late as the ninth century.[2] That was because the sayings of Mohammed had not been collected and put in a volume. Many Muslims began to collect Mohammed's sayings and soon there were many "Korans." The third caliph after Mohammed, Caliph Uthman, tried to bring order to the disorder and clearness to the confusion by putting his stamp of approval on what was called the "Medinan Codex." He then sent copies to all the major Muslim cities with orders to destroy all other variations of the Koran. Dr. Robert Morey asks four penetrating questions about the work done by Caliph Uthman:[3]

♦ Why did he have to standardize a common text if there were already a standardized text available?

♦ Why did he try to destroy all the other manuscripts if there were no other conflicting manuscripts? Vol. 6, book 61, no. 510 reveals that Uthman tried to destroy all conflicting copies.

♦ Why did he use death threats to force acceptance of his text if that were the only available text?

♦ Why did many people reject his text in favor of the one they already had?

SCHOLARS ASSESS THE KORAN

A major **supporter** of Islam was Thomas Carlyle, yet he assessed the Koran as "A wearisome confused jumble, crude, incondite [unpolished, crude]; endless iterations, long-windedness, entanglement; most crude incondite—insupportable stupidity, in short! Nothing but a sense of duty could carry any European through the Koran."[5] That was written by a **big supporter of Islam!**

About 830 A.D., al-Kindi analyzed the Koran deciding that its "histories are all jumbled together and intermingled; an evidence that many different hands have been at work therein, and caused discrepancies, adding or cutting out whatever they like or disliked. Are such, now, the conditions of a revelation sent down from heaven?"[6] Great question!

Mohammed was not well acquainted with the Bible as his many errors proved. Obermann speaks of "gross discrepancies, inaccuracies and delusions he exhibits," whenever he makes observations about the Old Testament and often about the New Testament.[7] Numerous scholars agree.

Islamic scholar Ali Dashti assessed the Koran as "not fully intelligible without the aid of commentaries; foreign words, unfamiliar Arabic words, and words used with other than the normal meaning; adjectives and verbs inflected without observance of the concords of gender and number; illogically and ungrammatically applied pronouns which sometimes have no referent; and predicates which in rhymed passages are often remote from the subjects."[8] Translation: It's a mess!

The German scholar Salomon Reinach wrote: "From the literary point of view, the Koran has little merit...It is humiliating to the human intellect to think that this mediocre literature has been the subject of innumerable commentaries, and that millions of men are still wasting time in absorbing it."[9] The Koran is incoherent without any logical order of thought, and an Islamic reference work refers to the "disjointed and irregular character" of the Koran.[10] Ali Dashti wrote: "To sum up, more than one hundred Qor'anic aberrations from the normal rules and structures of Arabia have been noted."[11] In fact, there are more than 100 non-Arabic words in the Koran![12] I suppose it is good that Allah is multi-lingual! Middle East scholar Canon Sell revealed that there are many foreign words.[13] Many verses have been lost and even Shiite Muslims admit that 25 percent of the original verses in the Koran were left out for political reasons.[14] When you consider the mishmash in the Koran, it makes one wonder what was left out!

Mohammed used a juvenile device, although somewhat innovative, to promote the alleged miraculous nature of the Koran. Many suras (chapters) start with letters that have absolutely no meaning! One example is sura 50: "Qaf. [These letters (Qaf, etc.) are one of the miracles of the Qur'an, and none but Allah (Alone) knows their meanings]. By the Glorious Qur'an." I can just hear Mohammed say, "Now, how about **that**?" Gibberish disguised as a miracle, and to think that some people are impressed!

TREASURE OR TRASH

The above characterizations of the Koran are understandable when one discovers that the Koran was written on pieces of papyrus, flat stones, palm leaves, shoulder blades and ribs of animals, pieces of leather, wooden boards, etc.[15] The 114 suras (chapters) were collected long after Mohammed's death and were not in any logical order. They are arranged from the longest to the shortest suras. Muslims tell us that Allah is always speaking directly to Mohammed; however, that is not true. It is obvious that, at times, Mohammed is speaking. (Of course, Mohammed is **always** speaking.)

The first English translation of the Koran by a non-Muslim scholar in the West was in 1734 by George Sale. Many others were to follow, although Muslims tell us that the Koran **cannot** be translated; however, they tell us that in the **very** translation they have done! Notwithstanding, there are many translations available.

There is general agreement among scholars that the early suras were written during Mohammed's early life and the later suras were written during his days in Medina. When in Mecca during his early years, he was persecuted and rejected, but in Medina, he was in the seat of power. During those early days, he spoke of tolerance because he **wanted** tolerance. When he came to power, the early suras were abrogated (cancelled) in favor of later ones that demanded persecution of Islam's enemies. It seems Mohammed was an unprincipled opportunist. And if the Koran came from Allah, then why didn't an all-powerful, all-knowing god get it correct the first time? Dashti rightly wrote: "Evidently even the simple, uneducated Hejazi Arabs could understand that Almighty God, being aware of what is best for His servants, would prescribe the best in the first place and would not have changes of mind in the same way as His imperfect creatures."[16]

Some Muslims angrily deny the abrogation doctrine; however, some of their scholars say otherwise. In his book, *How to Perfect the Science of the Quran* (Al-Itqan), Mr. Al-Syoti, writes in volume 2, page 37; "The verse of the sword has abrogated (annulled, cancelled) one hundred and twenty four Quranic verses and all what came in the Quran on matters of forgiving and ignoring, unbelievers have been replaced (Mansookha), by the verse of the sword." **The most famous interpreters of the Koran also confirm this.** For fur-

132

ther evidence refer to the following: Kitab Al-Nasekh Wal-mansookh, Al-Hafeth Ibnu Katheer Ibin Abas. Al-Tasheel Lulum Al-Tanzeel, Al-Husain Ibn Fadl, Abu Abdullah Muhammad Ibn Hazm, Al-Muhaqiq Abu Al-Qasim Hibatullah Ibn Salameh, Al-Sudy Wa-AlDahak, and Muhammad Abdulsalam Faraj.

Most scholars have concluded that to leave the Bible for the Koran is to go from a greater to a lesser.[17] They are correct. It is going from a Treasure to trash, from the real to the ridiculous, from reality to rubbish.

MOHAMMED'S FOUL-UPS

Mohammed had a scribe named abd Allah b. Sa'd Abi Sarh, and "On a number of occasions he had, with the Prophet's consent, changed the closing words of verses. When the Prophet had said 'And God is mighty and wise,' Abd Allah suggested writing down 'knowing and wise' and the Prophet answered that there was no objection. Having observed a succession of changes of this type, Abd Allah renounced Islam on the ground that the revelations, if from God, could not be changed at the prompting of a scribe such as himself. After his apostasy he went to Mecca and joined the Qorayshites." Eventually, Mohammed had him assassinated when he took Mecca.[18]

Mohammed really fouled his nest, so much so that it stinks to this day. The problem arises with the famous "satanic verses," made famous in recent years by Rushdie's book by that title. The "stink" arose following one of Mohammed's visions. It seems he was courting the folks at Mecca, but they weren't responding, so he decided to "give a little" to get some consideration for his new religion. He, of course, received a revelation: It would be acceptable to Allah for the Meccans to worship their favorite gods, the three daughters of the moon. Prayers to them might impress Allah to answer their requests! Wow! That was an incredible concession for the "prophet" to make. But it didn't last long. He received later revelation that told him Satan had given him permission to use al-Lat, al-Uzza, and Manat as divine intercessors. It was all a dirty trick of Satan. So the early revelation was abrogated. Well, if Satan deceived Mohammed at that time, is it not possible that he was deceived many times? **All** the time?

133

IS THE KORAN RELIABLE?

The "Abrogation" (cancellation) doctrine is essential for Islam to hold together because of the contradictions. Mohammed revealed in sura 2:106: "Whatever a Verse (revelation) do We abrogate or cause to be forgotten, We bring a better one or similar to it." It is believed by scholars that there could be up to 500 such verses. Sane people want to know how an all-knowing God can revise his plans so often and why he couldn't do it right the first time![19] So how can a Muslim, with a straight face, say the Koran is totally reliable when much of it is obsolete?

Muslims affirm that Islam is a religion of peace, not violence and they expect us to wipe out 1600 years of history to make them comfortable in a "civilized" era. They point to sura 2:256 that teaches, "There is no compulsion in religion," but sura 9:5 commands them to "Kill the idolaters wherever you find them." So sura 9:5 abrogates all the "tolerate" verses.

In my copy of the Koran, given to me by Muslim clerics in Indianapolis, there are numerous examples of abrogation. The first one is sura 2:109 where Mohammed tells his followers to forgive the Christians and Jews who try to turn Muslims away from Islam. The footnote on page 21 clearly commands Muslims, "The provision of this verse has been abrogated by the (V. 9:29)." That verse commands Muslims to "fight against" the Christians and Jews.

It is very important to note that the early verses that preach tolerance are considered to be the Meccan passages and those that advocate decapitating, maiming and general killing are Medinan. Why? Because in the early days, Mohammed and his few followers were ridiculed and persecuted, so of course he preached toleration, but when he was the top honcho and ruled like an Arabian despot, toleration was a sign of weakness and aggression a sign of strength. Mohammed changed his tactics and preaching depending upon his circumstances. After all, he may have been a liar, thief, killer, child molester and desert despot, but he wasn't a fool.

After reading **all** of the Koran and studying much of the Hadith, I have found numerous errors of historical fact, scientific fact, and scriptural fact. It must be remembered that **sura locations will vary with each translation.** The desired verse may be a few verses before or after the given location.

DID MOHAMMED PERFORM MIRACLES?

We are told that Mohammed did no miracles in sura 17:90-93 and 29:50 as the latter reveals: "The signs are only with Allah, and I am only a plain warner." While Mohammed did not perform miracles according to the Koran, we know that Christ did according to the New Testament and according to sura 2:253: "And to Jesus the son of Mary We gave clear proofs and evidences...."

Herein is a contradiction because while the Koran tells us Mohammed **did not** perform miracles, the Hadith reveals many of his miracles: healing the sick, feeding a thousand people with one kid, etc. Which is it? Did he or did he not perform miracles? A few hundred years after Mohammed died, his followers were faced by Christians who spoke of Christ's miracles. So Muslims replied, "Well, Mohammed **also** performed miracles," Then they proceeded to write hadiths that revealed miracles performed by Mohammed!

Following are some of the miracles allegedly performed by Mohammed: Vol. 4, book 56, no. 779 tells that as Mohammed ate food, the food shouted praises to Allah and the Prophet! When he multiplied the bread, he had the people come in groups of ten. (Sound familiar? Christ, in Luke 9 had them sit down in groups of fifty.) Mohammed healed a man with eye trouble by spitting in his eyes according to vol. 4, book 52, no. 192 and vol. 5, book 57, no. 51; vol.7, book 71, no. 641 and 642, reveal that Mohammed could heal all kinds of diseases with his spit. Holy spit! In fact, vol. 4, book 56, no. 777 and vol. 5, book 59 nos. 471, 472 reveal that Mohammed spat a mouthful of water into a well and satisfied 1400 men and their camels! The Hadith tells us that Mohammed's spit, his quoting the Koran, and waving his hand over a wound healed all kinds of illnesses including scorpion stings and snakebites. There is power in spit!

Mohammed cursed the tribes of Mudar because they rejected him, and within a year they were eating hides and dead animals. Another time he prayed for rain, and it rained! How about **that**?

When Mohammed was asked to perform a miracle to prove he was a true prophet, he pulled his sword and cut the moon in half according to Hadith vol. 4, book 56, nos. 830-832; vol. 5, book 58, nos. 208-211 and vol. 6, book 60, nos. 387-390. Desert Arabs thought the moon and sun were about the size of a basketball! When Muslims needed water, Mohammed rode to the rescue. He called for a bowl and water flowed from his fingertips into the bowl until each person could perform his ablution (vol. 1, book 4, nos. 170, 194; vol. 4, book 56, nos. 773-779). How many people were satisfied? Well, it depends on which hadith you read! No. 774 says it was 70; no. 775 gives 80, then no. 772 says it was 300, but no. 776 and vol. 5, book 59, no. 473 give 1500. Well, you don't expect a holy book to be **exact** in every respect do you?

WHAT THE KORAN TEACHES

In sura 4:106; 40:55; and 47:19 we discover that Mohammed was a sinner. Of course that is no surprise because all men are born sinners. Informed people are aware that he kept slaves, killed people, tortured people, etc., and most people would agree that he was a sinner. However, we know that Christ was sinless but became sin for us according to II Corinthians. 5:21: "For he hath made him to be sin for us, who knew no sin; that we might be made the righteousness of God in him." I Peter 2:22 reminds us of Christ "Who did no sin...." and sura 19:19 speaks of Christ as being a "righteous son."

The Koran affirms that Jesus was **not** God in sura 3:59, 62, and 4:171. The New Testament clearly teaches that He **was** and **is** God. Jesus said in John 10:30: "I and my Father are one." And in John 14:9: "he that hath seen me hath seen the Father." John 1:1, 18; 20:28; Romans 9:5; Titus 2:13; and Hebrews 1:8, 10:12 all affirm His deity. Jesus may not be the Son of God in sura 4:171 but then He is if you continue to read 19:17-21. It seems Allah just couldn't make up his mind. That's bad for a god!

According to sura 4:157-158, Christ did not die on the cross. "Yet they slew him not, and they crucified him not, but they had only his likeness." We are told that God substituted someone else (many say it was Judas!) in His place. Wonder why a sovereign God has to use subterfuge to accomplish His purpose? And what would be His purpose in deceiving the disciples, the authorities, and the religious leaders? Philippians 2:5-8 clearly states that Christ died for all mankind and verse 9 says He is exalted far above every name. That would include Mohammed. John 19:32-33 tells us that when the soldiers came to break the legs of the three crucified men, they did not break Christ's legs because "he was dead already."

The Hadith also teaches Christ's virgin birth, perfect life, and His miracles. The Koran supports the Bible teaching that Christ was born of the Virgin Mary in sura 3:47. "How shall I have a son when no man has touched me?" Other translations end with, "when I am a virgin…?"

The Koran attacks the Trinity in sura 5:75: "The Mesiah (Jesus), son of (Mary), was no more than a Messenger…." In sura 5:116 Allah really got confused when he said, "And when God shall say, 'O Jesus son of Mary hast thou said unto mankind, 'Take me and my mother as two Gods besides God?'" The highly acclaimed Muslim commentator al-Baidawi said that Christians made the Trinity consist of God, Christ, and **Mary**! And over a billion Muslims are trusting their eternal souls to that holy book! I John 5:7 clearly teaches the Trinity.

ISLAM CONFUSES BIBLE TRUTH

Mohammed tried to use people and incidents from the Bible to clothe Islam with some respectability and give Islam a historical past that it does not have. He put words in the mouths of the Old Testament characters that were Biblically untrue and often ludicrous. He created a history that never happened. Maybe he was the first to take advantage of "creative" writing.

We are told in sura 5:78 that David and Jesus cursed the children of Israel because they disobeyed Allah. Well, the Jews sure disobeyed God but David and Jesus did not curse them for it.

The Koran's tale regarding Joseph and Potiphar's wife is unintelligible. Joseph wants to sin with her, but he sees a vision [of his father] at the window. Many women laughed at Potiphar's wife because of her longing for Joseph, and she invited them to see him for themselves. When they came, they were so impressed with him that they cut themselves with knives! Was that a desert declaration of devotion?

The Koran tells us that Haman lived in Egypt during the days of Moses and he worked for Pharoah in building the Tower of Babel, but most Christians know Haman lived in Persia working as the flunky of King Ahasuerus. (See suras 28:38; 29:39; 40:24.) Mohammed was only off by a thousand years and a thousand miles!

And Pharaoh did not build the Tower of Babel! Not just mistakes but massive mishmash!

In sura 9:30, Mohammed made another mistake about Jews believing that Ezra was the Son of God. And we discover in Hadith vol. 6, book 60, no. 380 that the angel Gabriel has 600 wings according to the Prophet. Well, that's always good information to know. But it gets better! We also learn that demons helped Solomon build the Temple, and Solomon had the ability to talk with birds. If Solomon talked to the birds, he spent too much time at his wine cup!

We discover in sura 7:10-12 that Allah told the angels to bow to Adam at his creation but Satan (Eblis) refused and was cast out of Paradise. We also discover from Hadith, vol. 4, book 55, no. 543 that "The Prophet said, 'Allah created Adam, making him 60 cubits tall.'" Then no. 544 informs us that wives in paradise all look alike and will also be 60 cubits tall! Does any Muslim with an IQ equivalent to his hat size really believe such poppycock?

Sura 19:28-29 reveals that after the birth of Christ people came to Mary and said, "O Mary, now you have done an extraordinary thing! O sister of Aaron! Your father was not a bad man, nor was your mother a whore!" Mohammed confused Mary, the mother of Christ, with Miriam, the sister of Moses and Aaron! Sura 3:46 tells of baby Jesus speaking from the cradle, and 3:49 reveals the old fable that Christ gave life to birds of clay! Mohammed couldn't even come up with unique fables!

Sura 19:10 (also 3:41) informs us that Zacharias could not speak for three days before John was born, but Luke 1:20 tells us he did not speak for the entire time of the pregnancy.

Muslims teach that Ishmael, not Isaac, was taken to be sacrificed (sura 37:100-112) and the Land of Promise belongs to Ishmael's descendents. They also teach that Abraham's father's name was Azar in sura 6:74. Abraham lived in Mecca according to sura 14:37, not in Haran (and later in Hebron). Furthermore, in sura 21:68-69 we discover that Abraham was thrown into the fire by Nimrod. Mohammed didn't know that Nimrod lived hundreds of years before Abraham!

Mohammed tells us in sura 20:87, 95 that Aaron made the golden calf in the wilderness at the suggestion of "the Samaritan." There were no Samaritans until hundreds of years later!

Gabriel, who Mohammed taught was the Holy Spirit, opened Mohammed's chest and washed his insides then took wisdom and faith and poured them into his chest (vol. 1, book 8, no. 345). I'm not sure whether Gabriel or an assistant closed.

Such confusion is not unusual since Mohammed could not read, according to most historians, and picked up bits and pieces of Bible stories as he heard them around the caravan campfires.

ISLAM CONFUSES SCIENTIFIC FACTS

Mohammed didn't know any more about science than he did the Bible! In sura 27:61 he taught that the earth is a fixed object and in 16:15 he "revealed" that the mountains are there to provide stability to the earth "lest it should shake with you." But he becomes even more confused in 18:86 where he taught that the sun sets in a "spring of black muddy (or hot) water." In 36:40 we discover that the sun will not "overtake the moon." He thought the sun and moon traveled around the earth. While the moon does, the sun does not.

I'm sorry, but it does get worse! In 67:5 we learn that Allah created the stars to adorn "the nearest [lowest] heaven," and they are missiles "to drive away the devils...." Of course, the stars are not in the lowest heaven and no sane person believes they are used to pelt "the devils." Mohammed did not know that the moon was not in the midst of the stars, and is less than 250,000 miles from earth. He would be shocked to discover that our nearest star is 100 million times farther from earth!

INCONSISTENCIES IN THE KORAN

We are told in sura 54:49-50 that Allah created everything "in the twinkling of an eye" then in 41:9 and 12 we discover it took a little longer–"two days." But it gets worse because in 41:10 it took "four days" then in 7:54; 10:3; and 32:4 it took "six days." It seems Allah didn't remember how long it took him to create everything. Seems as if the longer you read the more time it took! Sura 77:20 tells us that Allah created man from semen and then sura 21:30; 25:54; and 24:45 tell us that all living things were created out of water. Speaking of water, Mohammed has the Flood taking place during the time of Moses, not Noah! (See sura 7:137.)

The Koran forbids wine in sura 2:219, yet sura 16:67 permits drinking wine, and we are assured there will be plenty of wine in Paradise.

In sura 24:2-4, Allah requires 100 lashes for fornication for unmarried persons (although slaves received half, only 50): "The woman and man guilty of fornication, flog each of them with a hundred stripes; let not pity move you in their case." Muslims have required stoning for centuries for married people contrary to the Koran. Furthermore, according to sura 4:3, a Muslim may cohabit with any female slave and sura 4:24 permits any Muslim to take a married woman if she is a slave. Christ told us not even to lust after a woman!

SOCIAL LIFE

Mohammed tells us in sura 3:106-107 that only white people will be saved. Blacks are damned! Yet Black Muslims insist that Christianity is the white man's religion and Islam is the black man's religion. Wrong! Muslims have been buying and selling black slaves for centuries. The Hadith often refers to Mohammed as being a white man, and Mohammed called Blacks, "raisin" heads in vol. 1, book 11, no. 662. There are various references to Mohammed owning black slaves, and need I remind everyone that Christ came to set men free? And it was white Christians in England and America who set the slaves free!

Mohammed had very definite ideas about what to do about drunks, and it was not to talk them out of drinking or drying them out. He thought it best to beat drunks!

Bukhari vol. 8, book 81, no. 772:

Narrated Abu Huraira: A drunk was brought to the Prophet and he ordered him to be beaten (lashed). Some of us beat him with our hands, and some with their shoes, and some with their garments (twisted in the form of a lash). When that drunk had left, a man said, "What is wrong with him? May Allah disgrace him!" Allah's Apostle said, "Do not help Satan against your (Muslim) brother."

The Prophet would chop off the hand of his daughter if she stole something! Of course **he** was a thief, but that was different.

Bukhari vol. 8, book 81, no. 778:

Narrated 'Aisha: Usama approached the Prophet on behalf of a woman (who had committed theft). The prophet

140

said, "The people before you were destroyed because they used to inflict the legal punishments on the poor and forgive the rich. By Him in Whose Hand my soul is! If Fatima (the daughter of the Prophet) did that (i.e., stole), I would cut off her hand."

It is dangerous to look into a Muslim's house. In fact, one could lose an eye.

Bukhari vol. 9, book 83, no. 38:

Narrated Sahl bin Sa'd As-Sa'idi: A man peeped through a hole in the door of Allah's Apostle's house, and at that time, Allah's Apostle had a Midri (an iron comb or bar) with which he was rubbing his head. So when Allah's Apostle saw him, he said (to him), "If I had been sure that you were looking at me (through the door), I would have poked your eye with this (sharp iron bar)." Allah's Apostle added, "The asking for permission to enter has been enjoined so that one may not look unlawfully (at what there is in the house without the permission of its people)."

Animal lovers of PETA (People Eating Tasty Animals) will not be thrilled with Mohammed since vol. 4, book 54, no. 540 reveals: "Allah's Apostle ordered that the dogs should be killed."

It is one thing to have animal lovers angry with you but to purposely antagonize women is close to suicidal! Sura 4:34 states: "Men are the managers of the affairs of women....Those you fear may be rebellious—admonish; banish them to their couches and beat them." "Beat" means to "scourge them." Muslim television programs give explicit instructions on how to beat a wife, where on her body to beat her, and what to use in the beating.

Women are ideal in the bedroom and kitchen but bad news elsewhere according to Mohammed. One hadith has him saying, "Three things can interrupt prayers if they pass in front of someone praying: a black dog, a woman, and an ass."[20] Mohammed commands that "The woman should never refuse her husband even on the saddle of a horse" or another version says, "on the top of a burning oven." Hey, a wife should seek to satisfy her husband (as he should seek to satisfy her), but on top of a burning stove!

According to vol. 1, book 2, no. 28, vol. 1, book 6, no. 301, and vol. 2, book 18, no. 161 "The Prophet said, 'I was shown the Hell-fire and that the majority of its dwellers were women." Mohammed didn't think women had much chance for Paradise and he didn't help make their earthly existence much of a paradise either. He didn't think a woman had much of a mind. In vol. 3, book 48, no. 826, "The Prophet said, 'Isn't the witness of a woman equal to half of that of a man?' The women said, 'Yes,' He said, "This is because of the deficiency of a woman's mind."

Homosexuality is condemned in the Koran, yet it has been practiced in Islam for hundreds of years with only sporadic times of punishment. Sura 7:80, 81 is rather blunt: "And Lot said to his people: Do you commit indecent acts that no nation has ever committed before? You lust after men in preference to women. You really are a degenerate people." Well, I didn't say Mohammed was wrong **every** time he opened his mouth! Again in sura 4:16: "If two men among you commit indecency, punish them both." Sura 26:165-166 and sura 27:55 further condemns perversion; however, sura 52:24 seems to sanction perversion to faithful Muslims: "And there shall wait on them young boys of their own, as fair as virgin pearls." We do know that some of the early Muslim leaders (caliphs) were homosexuals (even the famous Saladin in the twelfth century) while other caliphs executed homosexuals.

SUPERSTITIONS

The Koran is littered with seventh-century Arabian superstition such as the evil eye! Mohammed was asked, "O Prophet, the family of Jafar are affected by the baneful influences of an evil eye; may I use spells for them or not?" Mohammed replies, "Yes, for if there were anything in the world which would overcome fate, it would be an evil eye."[21]

In sura 18:8-26, the old legend of the seven sleepers is retold as a revelation from God! Edward Gibbon says that Mohammed probably heard this tale many times during his trading days with the caravans. It seems that seven youths fled to a cave to escape persecution and their pursuers sealed up the cave. However, the youths survived and walked out about 300 years later unharmed! This is a famous tale that Mohammed treated as his own.

Vol. 5, book 58, no. 200 reveals something that I've always wondered about: the spirits or jinn eat dung and bones. Now **you**

142

know!

ABSURDITIES

Muslims learn that Mohammed has given explicit instructions on when and how to urinate. He said:

> One of the major sins is not to protect oneself [one's clothes and body] from one's urine [i.e., from being soiled with it]. Once the Prophet, while passing one of the graveyards of Medina or Mecca, heard the voices of two persons being tortured in their graves.

> The Prophet then added, "yes! (they are being tortured for a major sin). Indeed, one of them never saved himself from being soiled with his urine" (vol. 1, book 4, no. 215).

Mohammed's rules for taking care of the daily personal needs that everyone has: don't face Mecca when urinating or defecating. Don't use your right hand to hold or clean yourself. And wash all your private parts after taking care of these personal chores. (See Hadith vol. 1, book 4, nos. 146-157.)

Mohammed was obsessed with urine, yet he told his followers to drink a concoction of camel's urine and milk! (See Hadith vol. 1, book 4, no. 234.) My grandkids would say that Mohammed was a weird-o. I concur. Remember that Muslims are bound by what the Koran and Hadith teach. A Muslim leader's ideas don't matter. What matters is the teaching from the Arabian Desert of the seventh century.

Mohammed warned people that if they slept during the mosque service or did not get up for morning prayers Satan would urinate in their ears! Yes, read vol. 2, book 21, no. 245. Mohammed also revealed something that eye, ear, and nose specialists still don't know: that Satan stays all night in the upper part of the nose according to vol. 4, book 54, no. 516. Don't look at me like that. I don't explain them, I only report them!

Vol. 1, book 8, no. 436 promises us that the angels ask Allah's forgiveness for anyone who passes wind while he is at his praying place. At another place, we are told, "When he enters the mosque he is considered in prayer as long as he is waiting for the prayer and the angels keep on asking for Allah's forgiveness for him and they keep on saying: 'O Allah! Be Merciful to him, O Allah!

Forgive him, as long as he keeps on sitting at his praying place and does not pass wind." (See vol. 1, book 8, no. 436.)

Faithful Muslims are promised that they will be protected from poison or major powers if they eat seven dates every morning. (See vol. 7, book 65, no. 356.) Do intelligent Muslims really believe such poppycock? Do they really **know** the poppycock that is taught in the Koran and the Hadith?

HATRED IN THE HOLY BOOKS

There is much hatred in the Koran and the Hadith, with love almost absent. Love for fellowmen is absent. Allah doesn't do much loving, but there is much about who he (Allah) does not love. He does not love the unjust (3:57; 3:140); nor the extravagant (6:141); nor those who "exceed the limits" (7:55); nor the proud (16:23); nor the ungrateful (22:38); nor mischief-makers (28:77); nor unbelievers (30:45). My Bible tells me in many places that God loves the world.

Allah showed his hatred in sura 5:60 where he changed people into apes and hogs: "They whom God hath cursed and with whom He hath been angry—some of them hath He changed into apes and swine...." In sura 7:163-166, Mohammed regurgitates the old Arabian fable of a village whose citizens were turned into apes because they fished on the Sabbath! Mohammed's fables and heresies weren't even original!

INTOLERANCE OF ISLAM

Muslims leaders have told me that Muslims have the right to decide what they wish to believe of the Hadith; however, that is modern propaganda developed because Islamic truth would turn all thinking people away from Islam. The following quotations prove the intolerance of Islam:

Bukhari vol. 9, book 84, no. 57: Narrated 'Ikrima: Some *Zanadiqa* (atheists) were brought to 'Ali and he burnt them. The news of this event, reached Ibn 'Abbas who said, "If I had been in his place, I would not have burnt them, as Allah's Apostle forbade it, saying, 'Do not punish anybody with Allah's punishment (fire).' I would have killed them according to the statement of Allah's apostle, 'whoever changed his Islamic religion, then kill him.' "

Bukhari vol. 9, book 84, no. 58: Narrated Abu Burda:

Abu Musa said, "I came to the Prophet along with two men (from the tribe) of Ash'ariyin, one on my right and the other on my left, while Allah's Apostle was brushing his teeth (with a Siwak), and both men asked him for some employment. The Prophet said, 'O Abu Musa (O 'Abdullah bin Qais!).' I said, 'By Him Who sent you with the Truth, these two men did not tell me what was in their hearts and I did not feel (realize) that they were seeking employment.' As if I were looking now at his Siwak being drawn to a corner under his lips, and he said, 'We never (or, we do not) appoint for our affairs anyone who seeks to be employed. But O Abu Musa! (or 'Abdullah bin Qais!) Go to Yemen.'" The Prophet then sent Mu'adh bin Jabal after him and when Mu'adh reached him, he spread out a cushion for him and requested him to get down (and sit on the cushion). Behold: There was a fettered man beside Abu Muisa. Mu'adh asked, "Who is this (man)?" Abu Muisa said, "He was a Jew and became a Muslim and then reverted back to Judaism." Then Abu Muisa requested Mu'adh to sit down but Mu'adh said, "I will not sit down till he has been killed. This is the judgment of Allah and his apostle (for such cases) and repeated it thrice. Then Abu Musa ordered that the man be killed, and he was killed. Abu Musa added, "Then we discussed the night prayers and one of us said, 'I pray and sleep, and I hope that Allah will reward me for my sleep as well as for my prayers.'"

The Koran is full of inconsistencies, superstitions, absurd stories about genies, fables from Arabian folklore, tales from numerous apocryphal works, Jewish Talmud, etc., yet the gullible believe that it came from the throne of a holy God! Their "holy" books are filled with mistakes, mishmash, and madness. How could anyone in his or her right mind trust their eternal souls to the "holy" books of Islam when they are aware of the mistakes, mishmash, and madness?

1.   *The Concise Encyclopedia of Islam,* ed. Cyril Classe, London: Stacey Inter., 1989, p. 228.

2.   Cited in *Why I Am Not a Muslim,* 154.

3.   Robert Morey, *The Islamic Invasion,* Harvest House, Eugene, OR, 1992, p.

125.

4. Ibn Warraq, *Why I am Not a Muslim,* p. 170.

5. Quoted by H. A. Gibb in *Mohammedanism, An Historical Survey,* Mentor Books, NY, 1955, p. 37.

6. Cited in *Why I am Not a Muslim,* p. 113.

7. Julian Obermann, "Islamic Origins: A Study in Background and Foundation." In *The Arab Heritage.* Nabih Faris, ed. Princeton, 1944. P. 94.

8. Ali Dashti, *Twenty-three Years: A Study of the Prophetic Career of Mohammed,* London, 1985, p. 50.

9. Salmon Reinach, *Orpheus: A History of Religion,* New York: Livercraft, Inc. 1932, p. 176.

10. *The Concise Encyclopedia of Islam,* p. 231.

11. Ali Dashti, p. 50.

12. Arthur Jeffery, *The Foreign Vocabulary of the Quran,* Baroda: Oriental Institute, 1938, no. 79.

13. Edward Sell, *Studies in Islam,* (Diocesan Press, London, 1928). P. 226.

14. John McClintock and James Strong, *Cyclopedia of Biblical, Theological, and Ecclesiastical Literature* Baker, Grand Rapids, 1981, V:152.

15. *The Concise Encyclopedia of Islam,* p. 230.

16. Dashti, p. 155.

17. Morey, p. 115.

18. Dashti, p. 98.

19. Ibid. p. 155.

20. Warraq, p. 301.

21. Ibid., p. 49.

Chapter Nine

The Motives, I

Holy Hatred of Christians

Television pundits have been talking incessantly about terrorism, but few are talking about motives. So I will. What could make people hate America so much that they would fly a plane into a building and kill themselves and innocent people? First of all, many of them don't hate **Americans** but they hate our Government. There is a difference, you know. But why don't they hate other governments as they do ours? Most countries usually don't meddle in the affairs of other nations. (Muslims do have some hatred toward Americans because of our "corrupting influence" of their culture.)

Following the September 11 disasters, a militant Islamic group in Pakistan held up a sign that was flashed all over the earth: AMERICANS, THINK! WHY YOU ARE HATED ALL OVER THE WORLD. Inquiring minds want to know the answer.

Sheikh Omar said of the terrorist attacks: "The question is not who did it, but why America creates more enemies than friends." No, we must know **who** did it but the sheikh asks a good question. Are the pundits correct when they tell us that the Muslims envy our success and covet our "good life?" If they covet our "good life," they don't get it by driving planes into buildings or other acts of terror.

AMERICA HAD IT COMING

One conservative wrote that the U.S. is a target for terrorists "because we are powerful, rich and good." Well, why don't they blow up buildings in France, England, and Australia? Sheikh Omar Bakri Mohammed, founder and leader of the radical Al Muhajiroun group, told *The Times of India*, "Yes, it is Muslims who have done this. There is no one else who would feel that much anger against

147

America." A London Muslim cleric added, "America had it coming."

No, we didn't have it coming, but **we should have seen it coming**! What else could we expect after 15 years of bombing Arab cities and aspirin factories, (boycotting them resulting in over a million civilian deaths in Iraq), and the U.S. knee-jerk support of their enemies? Example: Former U.S. Ambassador to the U.N., Madeleine Albright told Lesley Stahl of *CBS* that 500,000 dead Iraqi children, killed by U.S. sanctions, was morally justified to get Saddam! She said, "We think the price is worth it." Muslim mothers may think that their children might as well die as martyrs as to die by mortars. Sure it is warped thinking, but hearing the Koran every day for a lifetime and other contributing factors could lead to that kind of thinking. I have yet to hear any politician successfully justify killing innocent children on a massive scale. Can you justify the deaths of more than 500,000 children who are loved as much as yours? Dare I write that God loves Arab babies as much as He does Israeli babies! Now, surely **that** makes me an anti-Semite! Or, maybe simply a Christian?

U. S. POLICIES

The American Government is hated because of such policies and because our policies over the past 50 years have not been even-handed. George Washington warned us about getting involved with other nations, but we have totally disregarded his warning. Thomas Jefferson said, "Peace, commerce and honest friendship with all nations; entangling alliances with none." Jefferson did not believe in expanding the U.S. Empire to Europe.

America has not followed Jefferson's advice. An obvious example is our involvement with Israel. We have not been even-handed in the treatment of Israel and the Arab states. We have almost given Israel a blank check since her founding over 50 years ago. We are now giving them over 3 billion dollars per year! I think it is time for Israel to pay its own bills. Does **that** make me anti-Semitic?

I have been to Israel and the Arab states about 13 times since 1970. Sharon, Begin, Peres, and other Jewish leaders have briefed me, along with about 50 other U.S. religious leaders. I have often walked the streets of Jerusalem, Jericho, Tiberias, and even

Beersheba and Hebron, without apprehension, except in Hebron. I have walked upon the Golan Heights amid the bunkers and other defenses even before the landmines had been removed following one of their wars. I have seen young Arabs throw stones at Americans (including my vehicle) and wondered how they developed such hatred so young. Now I know. The U.S. helped promote animosity by our policies, but promoting animosity is not the same as producing terrorism. Some Islamic leaders are doing that right here in America!

Israel has a right to exist. I am thrilled that they are a nation, but I don't want to continue funding them. I also refuse to assume that what they do is justified by the circumstances. It is a fact that Israel has a policy of torture, holding people for months without trial, carrying out political assassinations anywhere in the world, and over-reacting to rock-throwing youths by responding with bullets and tanks!

ISRAELI POLICIES

I have been in the homes of Israeli **and** Arab friends. One long-time friend is a Christian businessman in Jerusalem who is a Christian Arab from a wealthy family. The Israelis took his father's prime property in Jerusalem without compensation. I always thought that was thievery. If it happened to your family, you would consider it thievery, but the Israelis got a pass. Why? Well, because they are God's chosen people, but what does that have to do with anything? Do "God's chosen people" not have to abide by the Ten Commandments? How about the rule of law?

My Arab friend loves Americans but hates our government because we have permitted Israel to operate outside normal parameters. Furthermore, I need to remind my Christian friends that Israel is a socialist state where it is illegal to witness for Christ. I will not surrender my right and responsibility to hold Israel to the same standard I demand of other nations, even if bigots and non-thinkers call me an "anti-Semite."

I am not a pacifist. I believe in self-defense personally and nationally, but I don't believe it is wise to get involved in every beer-hall brawl in town. We must permit Israel to form its own policies, fund its own military, and fight its own battles. The U.S. has no legal right to assume the position as policeman of the world. In fact, if we are consistent, we have no more right than the smallest nation in the world. We must respect the sovereignty of every other nation and defend our sovereignty against every incursion, including that coming from the United Nations. Of course, we have every right, even an obligation to hunt down, try, convict, and execute all perpetrators of the terrorist attacks against us, but we must keep in mind that some of our policies for the last fifty years are part of the equation as we try to find an answer for such dedicated terror against innocent people.

ISLAM WAS THE FUTURE

Many Muslims all over the world have been anti-American for fifty years because they perceive us as the supporter, sustainer, and supplier of Israel. They consider Saudi Arabia holy ground since it is the land of Mohammed and is the location of their main mosque in Mecca. That foreign troops (infidels) are stationed in Saudi Arabia inflames them further. Muslims, in general, have hated the West for hundreds of years because of the Crusades and for sundry other reasons.

One reason for Muslim hatred and resentment of the U.S. is our success, but it is more than that. Muslims remember that they were on the march during the Middle Ages. Europeans lived in squalor except for the lords of the manor. Europeans were bathing every few months when Muslims bathed daily. Muslim ships, loaded with trade goods from afar, plowed the open seas and provided the best the world had to offer. They built libraries, universities, and mosques all over the Middle East and Europe. Their armies seemed invincible. They were the future. Then something happened: the Crusades occupied much of their time for more than two hundred years. One Crusade after another was fought seeking to dislodge Islamic rule from the Middle East. Huge numbers of "Christians" traveled to the Middle East to "fight the Turks" and consequently were exposed to other cultures, inventions, opportunities, and goods. While the Muslims had many great military victories, they also were humiliated many times. Then something else happened.

MUSLIMS AS LOSERS

Columbus discovered America. Other mariners discovered ocean routes to exotic places. Gold, silver, ivory, and other trade goods were brought to European cities. Universities, hospitals, and other institutions were established in all the major European cities. Armies and navies were built and the Muslim tide began to recede. "Christian" Europe was on the march, and momentum was no longer with Islam but with Christianity.

Muslims watched in horror as their place in the world slipped from first to last, or almost last. Their great achievements were no longer remembered, and they have watched as America became the world leader in the past hundred years. Muslims are looking at their "glorious" past as they and the whole world are aware of their galling inferiority. They dwell on their "glorious" past until they are jerked back into their gloomy present. They recognize themselves as losers while we are winners. They realize that America saved the world from Germany in 1914 (when Muslims supported Germany) and we went on to pull England and France from the grip of Nazi Germany in 1945. In recent years, they watched as Communism was discredited, though not decapitated, and the Berlin Wall came down because of America.

Muslims see in the U.S. all that they should have, could have, and would have been–only if! While they hate Israel, they also hate our way of life, freedom, success, money, power, arrogance, and materialism. As they wish to drive Israel into the sea, they would also like to bring America to her knees. September 11 was part of their Trojan Horse Project to accomplish that objective.

U.S. OUT OF THE MIDDLE EAST

Muslims also want us out of all Middle East countries, and with that I concur. They consider Saudi Arabia holy land, and they believe "infidels" are camping there today. Bin Laden has made it very clear that we are trespassing on holy land with our troops in Saudi Arabia, and he (along with other Muslim leaders) want us out of "their" land. Even so, I'm convinced that he and others want to dislodge the royal family and make Saudi Arabia a pure Islamic state. He is not unmindful of the petro-dollars that will flow into the treasury from the oil fields. I believe bin Laden could march through the major cities of Saudi Arabia and take the nation without firing a shot! Literally! I am fearful that if the U.S. goes after a terrorist state such as Iran or Iraq, killing thousands of innocent people, it will inflame and unite the whole Arab/Islamic world against us. I'm convinced that there will be a last ditch effort to use weapons of mass destruction against the U.S. or Israel.

BIN LADEN'S CRUSADE

Osama bin Laden has used inflammatory rhetoric to energize Muslims around the world to his political and religious philosophy:

> Despite the great devastation inflicted on the Iraqi people by the crusader-Zionist alliance, and despite the huge number of those killed, which has exceeded 1 million...despite all this, the Americans are once again trying to repeat the horrific massacres, as though they are not content with the protracted blockade imposed after the ferocious war or the fragmentation and devastation.

> We–with God's help–call on every Muslim who believes in God and wishes to be rewarded to comply with God's order to kill the Americans and plunder their money wherever and whenever they find it. We also call on Muslim ulema, leaders, youths, and soldiers to launch the raid on Satan's U.S. troops and the devil's supporters allying with them, and to displace those who are behind them so that they may learn a lesson.

> The ruling to kill the Americans and their allies–civilians and military–is an individual duty for every Muslim who can do it in any country in which it is possible to do it, in order to liberate the al-Aqsa Mosque and the holy mosque [Mecca] from their grip, and in order for their armies to move out of all the lands of Islam, defeated and unable to threaten any Muslim.[1]

Bin Laden issued a holy war against Israel, America, and her allies until Islam is supreme. Note his use of "crusader." It is not only a clash of cultures, but also a clash of religions. In a video delivered to Pakistani TV in early November of 2001, bin Laden said the conflict in Afghanistan was "primarily a religious war" between Christianity and Islam. Of Bush's "crusade," he said, "it is a certain fact that Bush carried the cross high....Whoever stands behind Bush has committed an act that stands as annulment of their Islam." Here again the master terrorist referred to "crusade" and the "cross" and "a clash of religions." The Muslim terrorists are still fighting the Catholics of the Crusades!

You may remember that President Bush originally used "Crusade" in giving a name to his war on terrorism! Bad choice of words as the following chapter will support.

FOUNDATION FOR CATHOLIC CHURCH

Most people think that the Roman Catholic Church started with the Apostle Peter with each succeeding pastor taking the title of Pope. Others think the Roman Catholic Church began on a Monday morning at 9:00 on a given day. Not so. It all happened very slowly. In fact, there were some good preachers (priests) in the Church for a long time.

During 68 A.D., Rome was in turmoil. The city had burned, resulting in Nero's suicide. Vespasian was now on the mighty Roman throne and sent Titus to Jerusalem to put out some political fires in that irascible city where 600,000 rebels had gathered. Titus arrived in February of 70, at the head of 80,000 troops. He also had thousands of war machines (I would call them "wallbusters") to wage war against a city. General Titus sought their surrender but was met with ridicule and had massive stones and hot oil hurled at his army.

Each day the Romans crucified hundreds of Jewish prisoners in full view of those Jews on the walls. Soon the black horse of famine galloped through the streets of the holy city and mothers ate their own dead children. Josephus said that the streets were clogged with the dead. The Temple was torched and as it burned, the defeated, desperate, and defiant Jews fell on their swords and others jumped into the flames. Josephus reported that 1,197,000 Jews were killed in the siege and its aftermath.[2] Durant wrote that no people in history fought so tenaciously for liberty as the Jews nor had any people fought against such odds.[3]

Following the destruction of the Temple and the fall of Jerusalem, Judaism hid in fear while its offspring, Christianity, went out to witness about Christ to the world.[4] The churches had dark periods of bloody persecution; however, their numbers continued to increase. Churches were established all over the land and extended their influence throughout Asia Minor and into Europe.

The greatest drama in human history was to see a relatively small group of Christians (hated, scorned, libeled, jailed, and tortured by numerous Roman dictators) bearing all their troubles, tests, and trials with tenacity, yet multiplying amid all the oppression, and finally overcoming and outlasting the mightiest state that had ever existed. Durant aptly wrote: "Caesar and Christ had met in the arena, and Christ had won."[5]

By 590 A.D., the situation changed relating to Christian churches. Whereas each pastor (bishop) had been equal to all others (whatever the size of the church and city in which it was located), now there was an organizational hierarchy and papacy of the Roman Catholic Church. In 445 A. D., the Roman Emperor recognized the primacy of the Roman bishop and Leo I, who ruled from 440 to 461, was the first Roman bishop to take the title of pope. (No, it was not Peter!) Leo claimed that as the Bishop of Rome, he had authority over all other churches. When Rome fell in 475 A. D., the Dark Ages began. Alaric attacked and seized Rome in 410, and the Roman legions withdrew from Britain to protect the city. By 425, barbarians settled into the Roman provinces in southern Spain (Vandals), in Dalmatia (Ostrogoths), etc. Rome was crumbling. By 436, the last Roman troops had left Britain to return home, but without providing necessary protection to the Imperial City. In 455, the Vandals sacked Rome and the citizens were in panic. Mighty Rome was only a ghost of itself.

CHRISTENDOM SPLITS

The Roman Church experienced many heresies and grew wealthy but weak. Cyprian complained that the Christians were "mad about money, that Christian women painted their faces; that bishops held lucrative offices of state, made fortunes, lent money at usurious interest, and denied their faith at the first sign of danger." While Christianity "converted" the world, it seems the world converted Christianity![6] The corruption got progressively worse until the Reformation in the 1500s.

Power shifted from Rome to Constantinople, the capital of the Eastern Roman Empire (Byzantine), and while Europe was in the throes of the Dark Ages with trade, invention, etc., almost at a standstill, the Byzantine Empire was booming. Constantinople was becoming the center of world trade.[7] When London and Paris were small towns, Constantinople was the largest, richest city in medieval Europe.[8]

The remnant of the old Roman Empire was ruled from what

is now Istanbul in Turkey. First known as Byzantium, then Constantinople, the Byzantine Emperors abandoned Roman Catholicism for what is now known as the Eastern Orthodox Church. The great Byzantine cathedral of Sophia was the spiritual center of the Byzantine Empire **until** the advance of Islam.

Christendom formally split like a ripe watermelon into east and west in 1054 A.D. They became the Greek or Eastern Orthodox Church in Constantinople and the Roman Catholic Church in Rome. Their split was over very **serious** issues such as: What type of bread should be used in communion? Must the priests wear beards? Is a weekly fast required? Much like today! It also involved the normal power play: should the top honcho in Constantinople (the Patriarch) be forced to recognize the Pope as supreme ruler of the churches? Like most splits, the two preachers (Pope and Patriarch) kicked each other out of their respective churches! In 1453, Constantinople and the Eastern Roman Empire (Byzantine) fell to the Muslims.

MILITANT MUSLIMS ON THE MARCH

By this time, the Muslims had been on the march for hundreds of years. Within 20 years of Mohammed's death (632), the Muslims erupted out of the Arabian Peninsula and conquered Iraq, Syria, Palestine, Egypt, and western Iran. Then Muslim ships sailed the "Roman lake" (Mediterranean Sea) and took Cyprus in 649, Carthage in 698, Tunis in 700, and Gibraltar in 711. From there they ripped into Spain in 711-716 and on to France in 720.[9]

Islam advanced into Europe via the Iberian Peninsula (Spain and Portugal) in 711, and fighting continued between Muslims and Catholics for hundreds of years. By the middle of the eleventh century, "Christian" forces managed to retake about half the peninsula, and the Pope got into the act. He told citizens of other nations to come to the aid of their fellow "Christians" and drive the Muslims out of Europe. To make it palatable to them, he offered them limited indulgences (forgiveness of sins) to fight for the cause. This reconquest is known as Reconquista and is considered by some to be the unofficial "first" Crusade.

In 1009, the Muslims ordered the destruction of the Church of the Holy Sepulchre in Jerusalem. Some 30,000 Christian buildings are said to have been destroyed at that time. In 1076, Seljuks Turks occupied Jerusalem. They came from the borders of China and had been converted to Islam, and they followed Mohammed by persecuting Christians and Jews.

CATHOLIC CHURCH CORRUPTION

During those years, the Roman Catholic Church was festering with corruption from the lowest, uneducated, unsophisticated, unconcerned priest to the pompous pugilistic popes squatting on the plush throne in Rome (or wherever). In our day, the Roman Church is in one of the worst crises of its existence: homosexual clergy who have preyed on helpless boys for more than 30 years with subsequent cover ups by the higher ups have been exposed. Even Boston's Cardinal Law was forced to resign in December of 2002 because of his unethical, unlawful, and unscriptural handling of homosexual priests who preyed on young boys and his subsequent cover-up. Some major Catholic leaders will go to jail if there is any justice left in the U.S. Of course, any clergyman (Catholic, Baptist, or whatever) who abuses males or females should go to the clinker for 25 years or more!

Manchester quotes Abbot Johannes Trithemius' evaluation of his own monks thusly: "The whole day is spent in filthy talk; their whole time is given to play and gluttony....They neither fear nor love God; they have no thought of the life to come, preferring their fleshly lusts to the needs of the soul....They scorn the vow of poverty, know not that of chastity, revile that of obedience....The smoke of their filth ascends all around."[10] It was not unusual for women who came to the confessional to be offered absolution in exchange for sex in the very cramped booth! There is documentary evidence of priestly immorality in almost every town in the Italian peninsula, according to Manchester.

With the incredible priestly immorality, including the selling of priestly positions, appointing **children** to official religious office, and other corruption, the Roman Church in Europe was in convulsions. The stage was now set for the Crusades, probably the greatest tragedy in church history.

CATHOLIC CRUSADES

The Crusades were also one of the most unnecessary events in history. The Muslims were harassing Christian pilgrims in the Holy City and on their travel route; that distressing news disturbed the Roman pontiff. When the timid emperor, Alexius Comnenus, thought Constantinople might fall, he appealed for help to none other than the Pope himself. Pope Urban was ready and willing to commit to a crusade. Urban, the Roman Catholic pope, thought his help in defending the Eastern Empire in Constantinople might ingratiate himself to the Greek Orthodox Patriarch and at the same time take the city of Jerusalem from the infidels. A crusade would become a unifying cause for all "Christians." How could he lose? It was a win-win situation. His attempt to help the top honcho in Constantinople would also strengthen the Pope's weak position.

The Roman Pope was "heartbroken" over the church split in 1054, and thought his calling for a crusade against the Turks would establish his long-time claim as Pope of all "Christians" in the East and West. He would show that Greek Patriarch a thing or two with a trek into the heart of the Muslim world with his army of "Christians." (And no doubt there were some Christians in the crowd.)

It was in 1095 that Urban called a council in central France and urged all his bishops and abbots to bring their respective secular lords and knights to the meeting. Urban touched all their "buttons" during his sermon. He described the Holy City and Holy Sepulchre in infidel hands. He talked of the land of "milk and honey" and of carving out their own kingdoms in the Holy Land. He promised that the families of those who "took up the cross" would be protected and debts would be suspended during the crusade. Finally, he took a page out of Mohammed's own book when he promised plenary indulgence for their sins! Heaven for martyrdom! If they lived, they would be little kings in the Holy Land. If they died, they would go straight to Heaven. The only thing missing was 72 dark-eyed virgins waiting for each crusader!

Witnesses reported that the crowd yelled, "God wishes it. God wishes it." And a cardinal fell to his knees in convulsive trembling. (It must have been a very effective sermon!) Prominent lords and common people rushed forward "at the invitation" to take up the cross. They grabbed red cloth and cut crosses and sewed them on the fronts of their tunics. All over Europe "Christians" made plans to "take up the cross" to do battle with the hated Muslims.

The First Crusade (of eight) was the only one that could be called a success. And it was successful not because of the fighting ability of the Crusaders but because the Muslims had been getting weaker for many years. As the Crusaders advanced toward Jerusalem, they killed 8,000 Jews in their trek through the Rhineland, after all the Jews were unbelievers too! After battles along the way, they finally took Jerusalem and quickly slaughtered 70,000 civilians in cold blood!

There were eight major crusades to free Jerusalem from the pagan Muslims, and all were disgraceful, laying a foundation for Muslim hatred of all things "Christian."

1. Bin Laden's statement issued Feb. 23, 1998, by the World Islamic Front, "Jihad Against Jews and Crusaders."

2. Will Durant, *The Story of Civilization,* Book 3, 1944, p. 545.

3. Ibid., 542.

4. Ibid., 549.

5. Ibid., 652.

6. Ibid., 657.

7. *The Record of Mankind,* fourth ed., Roehm, Buske, Webster, and Wesley, D.C. Heath and Co., Lexington, Mass., 1970, p. 125.

8. Ibid., 125, 126.

9. *The Oxford History of Islam,* ed., John L. Esposita, Oxford University Press, 1999, p. 71.

10. William Manchester, *A World Lit Only by Fire,* Little, Brown and Co., Boston, 1992, pp. 128, 129.

Chapter Ten

The Motives, II

Crusades: Preached by Popes and Punished by God

Christopher Columbus was convinced that God had chosen him to lead a Crusade against the Muslims who controlled the Holy Land in the early 1400s. He did not see that dream fulfilled; however, those who had already fought in the Crusades discovered the dream was, in reality, a nightmare. The Crusades forever changed the face of the world and set the stage for the Reformation in the sixteenth century and the nightmare of terrorism the free world faces today.

The Crusades were one of the darkest periods in the history of man. They were preached by popes, promoted by priests, planned by potentates, and will someday be punished by God. Most of the Crusaders were no better than the Muslims who were the objects of their hatred. They called the Muslims "unbelievers," but most of the Crusaders were also unbelievers, as well as being thieves and killers.

How could a church even consider the slaughter of innocent people? While I am not a pacifist, I also don't believe in butchery and cruelty. I do believe Christians have a right to defend themselves and an obligation to defend the family even at the cost of another's life. A rapist or thief needs to realize that getting shot is an occupational hazard of being a rapist or thief. That principle of defense of family carries over to the defense of one's country. I have no respect for those who refuse to fight for their freedom, while others do fight and die so all of us, including cowards and pacifists, can be free and safe.

A JUST WAR

Isidore of Seville, five hundred years before the Crusades,

stated: "That war is lawful and just which is waged upon command in order to recover property or to repel attack." You would think that anyone would agree with that statement; however, many limp-wristed sissies tell us it is better to be Red than dead, and then they try to appeal to the Bible for support of their warped doctrine.

Isidore continued: "There are four types of war: that is just, unjust, civil and more than civil. Just war is that which is fought after the enemy was warned concerning the unjust loss of holdings or for the sake of fending off enemies. Unjust war is that which is begun from wrath rather than lawful reason. Cicero speaks of this in his *Republic* (3,35): 'Unjust wars are those begun without a reason. For there is no just reason for war outside of just vengeance or self defense.' And Cicero added this shortly afterward: 'No war is to be considered just unless it was openly announced and declared, unless reparation has first been demanded.'"[1]

In 1209, Pope Innocent III encouraged the King of Denmark to go a step or two further. He was not only interested in recovering property and repelling attack, he wanted him "to extirpate the error of paganism and spread the frontiers of the Christian faith." The king would also share in the Indulgences if he managed to spread the Pope's religion. Indulgences provided forgiveness of past and future sins and were granted for favors done to and for the Roman Catholic Church, or for money given to the Church.

INDULGENCES

In return for a sum of money or for service to the Church, the Pope would grant a dispensation or license either to excuse or to permit an action which was sinful. Furthermore, if anyone had been to the confessional and had been given a very heavy penance to absolve his sins, he could pay the Church money instead of carrying out the required duty to pay for his offences. These practices made the Church very prosperous and the commoners very poor.

These indulgences were one of the major reasons for Luther's break with Rome. The church had become a money-machine as indulgences were sold all over Europe. Tetzel, a Dominican friar, promised poverty-stricken villagers, "I have here the passports...to lead the human soul to the celestial joys of Paradise."[2] So a person could purchase his way to heaven and even guarantee that the dead in hell could escape eternal torment. Tetzel promised relatives of dead loved ones, "As soon as the coin rings in the bowl, the soul for whom it is paid will fly out of purgatory and straight to heaven." What concerned person would refuse to give his last coin to release his beloved relative from the flames of "purgatory"? It was a powerful tool but it backfired on the church in later years.

So, if a king, knight, or common citizen went on a Crusade, he received total forgiveness of all sins, past and future. Those guilty of robbery, rape, or murder would receive total forgiveness of sins and at death pass by Purgatory right into heaven! They thought it was a good deal.

NOT FIGHTING BUT FOOLERY

St. Bernard forbade any truce with the pagans "until such time as, with God's help, they shall be either converted or wiped out." Convert 'um or kill 'um–a choice of being baptized or buried. So we see a progression from the legitimate use of force to its illegitimate use to "spread the frontiers of the Christian faith." Pope Innocent IV, in the middle of the thirteenth century, tried to justify the Crusades by affirming that the Holy Land was Christian property and the Crusades were actions to recover land that rightfully belonged to Christians.

There was another reason war with the Turks was acceptable to the general population. The Muslims were dangerous people and they harassed Christians and refused to permit preachers of the "gospel" to preach in their lands, so war was acceptable and even desirable with them. Later, schismatics were considered a **greater** threat to the Church than the threat of the Muslims in the Holy Land, so it was all right to behead, to burn at the stake, and to persecute Christians who dared disagree with Rome! (This was before the first ecumenical council!)

A pope or one of his designates would preach a Crusade asking all strong, able-bodied people to join in the "noble" cause to "take the cross." To persuade knights to "take up the cross," Pope Urban ridiculed the old knight (who stayed home) and compared him with the knight who left all to "fight for Christ." He said, "Let those who, for a long time, have been robbers, now become knights. Let those who have been fighting against their brothers and relatives now fight in a proper way against the barbarians. Let those who have been serving as mercenaries for small pay now obtain the eternal reward."[3]

St. Bernard continued the thought when he said: "For how long will your men continue to shed Christian blood, for how long will they continue to fight amongst themselves? You attack one another, you slay one another and by one another you are slain. What is this savage craving of yours? Put a stop to it now, for it is not fighting but foolery. So to risk both soul and body is not brave but shocking, is not strength but folly. But now O mighty soldiers, O men of war, you have a cause for which you can fight without danger to your souls; a cause in which to conquer is glorious and for which to die is gain."[4] (Sounds like they took their cue from the Muslims.)

RELIGIOUS RABBLE ROUSER

Bernie's teaching is not much different from the Muslims who taught that if a man were to die in battle against infidels (those who were not Muslims), he would, upon entering heaven, experience a thousand sexual climaxes in one! Anyway, Bernie and his Catholic friends were preaching a "Holy War" against the hated Muslims.

They were offered full salvation and forgiveness of all sins if they took a vow to go on the Crusade. This is the oldest religion in the world, the false religion of works. Listen to St. Bernard whip up the crowd: "Go forward then in security, knights, and drive off without fear the enemies of the Cross of Christ, certain that neither death nor life can separate you from the love of God which is in Jesus Christ.... How glorious are those who return victorious from the battle! How happy are those who die as martyrs in the battle! Rejoice, courageous athlete, if you survive and are victor in the Lord; but rejoice and glory the more if you die and are joined to the Lord. For your life is fruitful and your victory glorious. For if those who die in the Lord are blessed, how much more so are those who die for the Lord."[5]

How could Bernard, whom Martin Luther called a "God-fearing and holy monk," use his talent as a "stem-winding" speaker to rouse the rabble (and the nobles) to such an ignoble cause as the Crusades? Bernard also wrote the hymn, "Jesus, the Very Thought Thee," but Bernard was not thinking of Jesus when he called the "faithful" (and some were no doubt faithful) to "take up the Cross" and take the Holy Land for Christ. In fact, Bernie wasn't even thinking when he got involved with a corrupt pope to baptize Europe and the Middle East with blood.

SOME WERE SINCERE

When a man took the public vow to go on a Crusade, he was to sew a cross on his clothing and he was legally bound to fulfill that oath. If he could not keep his oath because of sickness or death, his son was expected to keep it. If a man simply refused to keep it, he was threatened with excommunication. His vow was legally binding upon him and his family. Those who stitched a red cross on their clothing were promised that their family would be protected (if left behind) and any debts or legal problems would be delayed for the years they would be on their "Holy Land" trip. Some were glad to be away from the little woman and others were pleased to escape debts and other problems. Others were excited about the possibility of a good fight and the promise of free estates after the victory. Still others were sincere people who were only following the leader of the Roman Catholic Church.

Of course it needs to be said that sincere people died in the blood and mud of a hot battle fought at the gates of some unknown city, while the pope and his prelates lived well, warm, and worldly in a secure palace hundreds of miles away from the tip of the longest shot arrow.

FIGHTING BISHOPS KISS AND MAKE UP

The "Christian" world had split like a ripe watermelon in the eleventh century. Emperor Alexius who was also the Bishop of Constantinople excommunicated the Bishop of Rome (the Pope), who in turn excommunicated him! Christendom was divided between the Roman Catholic Church and the Byzantine Empire. In 1071, the Turks defeated the Byzantine warriors at the Battle of Manzikert, leaving Constantinople exposed to Muslim attack. Meanwhile, Christians were being ambushed during their "Holy Land trip" to Jerusalem.

There was no longer one Holy Roman Empire, and with the Byzantine Empire in Constantinople under threat from the Turks, the Emperor Alexius swallowed his pride and requested help from Pope Urban II in Rome. This plea for help was a good opportunity for Pope Urban to regain some influence over Constantinople and to also fulfill his obligation to protect the rights of Christendom. He couldn't lose. But the fact is, he couldn't win.

Pope Urban started the Crusade ball rolling when he personally preached the First Crusade throughout France. He did so after the appeal from the Byzantine emperor for help in defending the Church against the Turks who were almost at the gates of Constantinople. He believed that cooperation might also help draw the Latin and Greek churches closer together, but it could also liberate Jerusalem from the hands of the pagans. I can hear Pope Urban say to the Crusaders at their going away party, "Now fellows, after you protect Constantinople, run over to Jerusalem and take it away from a handful of Turks."

WHAT A SERMON!

Pope Urban spoke to the Council of Clermont (France) on November 27, 1095, and later from a platform to 10,000 church leaders and peasants. As he preached on the final day of the council, the people sat on the grass outside of town. Urban was surrounded by his Italian Guard and about 200 bishops and hundreds of priests. It was **some** denominational conclave, that's for sure.

There are various reports of his sermon, and one of the most famous is by Fulcher of Chartres: "On this account I, or rather the Lord, beseech you as Christ's heralds to publish this everywhere and to persuade all people of whatever rank, foot-soldiers and knights, poor and rich, to carry aid promptly to those Christians and to destroy that vile race from the lands of our friends. I say this to those who are present, it is meant also for those who are absent. Moreover, Christ commands it." I would like to know how the Pope knew that "Christ commands it." O, the crimes that have been committed in His name!

The "infallible" Pope went on and on and on: "Let those who for a long time, have been robbers, now become knights. Let those who have been fighting against their brothers and relatives now fight in a proper way against the barbarians. Let those who have been serving as mercenaries for small pay now obtain the eternal reward. Let those who have been wearing themselves out in both body and soul now work for a double honor. Behold! On this side will be the sorrowful and poor, on that, the rich; on this side, the enemies of the Lord, on that, his friends. Let those who go, not put off the journey, but rent their lands and collect money for their expenses; and as soon as winter is over and spring comes, let them eagerly set out on the way with God as their guide"[6]

ARROGANCE AND AUDACITY

To his credit, the Pope threatened strong sanctions against anyone who did any evil to the women, children, goods, or properties of anyone engaged in the Crusade; however, he was not very concerned about those who were **not** involved in the Crusade. Various church leaders did try to protect Jews in different cities along the crusade route, usually without success.

Urban was considered as a heavenly (wrong direction) trumpet, summoning the sons of the Holy Roman Catholic Church from several parts of the world to free the Eastern Church. Those who refused to take up the sword for Rome were ungrateful wretches who would face the pope on Judgment Day. Each pope, issuing a call for holy warriors, wrote: "We firmly state on behalf of the Apostle that they should know that they will have to reply to us on this matter in the presence of the Dreadful Judge on the Last Day of Severe Judgment."[7] What arrogance and audacity! I don't believe the "Apostle" would appreciate the pope's speaking for him, and I am sure the pope will be too occupied in giving an account for himself at the Judgment to hear the excuse of some peasant for not picking up a rusty sword and going after the Turks.

Remember that the Roman Church recognized no boundaries. The power of the pope transcended nations, languages, and customs. The popes often ordered kings around. In the middle of the eighth century, Pope Zacharias removed King Childeric of the Franks from the throne, and Pope Gregory humiliated King Henry IV by making him stand (barefoot) in his (the Pope's) courtyard for three days in January before he would see him! How could a pope effectively command a king and make it stick? He could launch a Crusade against him or threaten interdiction which is to excommunicate **all** the people in the nation!

HATE THE TURKS

The popes were often not very successful in raising men to spill their blood in a "holy war" or to spend their funds (and years of their life) in the liberation of Jerusalem. Sometimes the hatred of one king for another king was more intense than his fear (or respect) for the pope. The kings were too busy fussing and fighting each other to care about fighting the Muslims. Pope Innocent III thought that was a dirty shame and seethed with what he would call righteous indignation. In his preamble to the encyclical of 1198 (proclaiming the Fourth Crusade), he self-righteously said: "Now indeed...while our princes pursue one another with inexorable hatred, while each strives to vindicate his injuries, suffered at the hands of another, there is not one who is moved at the injury suffered by the Crucified One....Already our enemies insult us, saying, 'Where is your God, who cannot free himself or you from our hands?'"[8] Ironically, he was saying that the kings and princes should be ashamed for the hatred they had for each other–they should hate the Turks instead. This bloody pope was a self-righteous tyrant who used God to consolidate his own power, and for him to criticize the kings for their hatred of others was like a skunk telling a rabbit that the rabbit has bad breath.

PREACHING THE CRUSADE

The popes **finally** (they were slow learners) realized that the mere publishing of a papal bull would not raise an army or fill their coffers with gold. So, they sent out priests to raise money for an attack on innocent women and children, calling it the "preaching of the cross." The popes even granted Indulgences for those who **listened** to the sermon of the vicars of violence. Things were so bad, the popes resorted to taxing the churches and priests, and that idea was no more popular then than it is today. Two things were sure: death and taxes, but death was far more prevalent and more permanent than taxes.

A Roman Catholic clergyman usually preached a Crusade, following orders from Rome, trying to convince the locals to leave home for an exciting journey to Jerusalem. Those accepting the responsibility were supposed to be fighting men or men who could make a contribution to the "cause." Each man must also have his wife's permission since he would be gone for a long time (usually forever) and she would be deprived of her "marital rights." Pope Innocent III got so desperate for troops in the thirteenth century that he no longer insisted on a wife's permission.

There is no doubt that many courageous, sincere men went on a Crusade, especially the First Crusade; Constantinople **was** be-

166

ing threatened, and the Turks were among the most cruel and vicious people alive. Escaping a life of backbreaking toil (without possibilities of improvement) motivated others to join the Crusade. There were many examples of great courage and little honor–great devotion to a cause and little understanding of concepts. Idealism was besmirched by voracious greed and unbridled cruelty. The gentle voice of the Savior was unheard as the bloody sword was unsheathed. T. S. Eliot said of them, "Among [them] were a few good men, Many who were evil, And most who were neither, Like all men in all places."[9]

FIRST CRUSADE

Peter the Hermit accepted Pope Urban's challenge and went throughout France "preaching the cross" and raised an army that was scheduled to leave on August 15, 1096, in the First Crusade. The wealthy made elaborate plans for departure and the poor sold their few belongings and waited for that fateful day in August. The leadership of the First Crusade was made up of several high nobles and a papal legate (the pope's envoy). The best known of these leaders included Bohemond of Taranto, Raymond of Toulouse, Hugh of Vermandois, Godfrey of Bouillon, Baldwin of Boulogne, Robert of Flanders, and Robert of Normandy. The papal legate was the Bishop of Le Puy, Adhmar.

How pathetic to see thousands of poor people with ox-drawn, two-wheeled carts bearing all their worldly goods while their small children asked at every walled city if this were Jerusalem. The rich often took their families, servants, and food, while the poor ate what they found. Soon they were all starving together. Through rain, mud, pain, and sickness, they pushed with "hell licking at their heels" at every step. They had to keep going if they wanted to earn forgiveness of sins and a good seat in Heaven, and they were sure of Heaven (Didn't the Pope, priests, and prelates tell them so?), as long as they kept decapitating the infidels with a dull blade. The duller, the better. However, they started their slaughter long before reaching the Middle East. Since Jews were infidels, did they not qualify to be put to the sword? That's what Pope Urban had preached, so whop, whop, and off went numerous Jewish heads in villages throughout Germany.

HOLY MISSION

By now, they had attracted 40,000 "Crusaders" each with a red cross stitched onto his clothing. In Cologne, the Archbishop opened his palace to protect the Jews, but the dedicated mob broke down the doors and slaughtered everyone inside, killing over 10,000 in that one incident. The Jews were given an opportunity to be "converted" just before they were beheaded and the prettiest Jewish girls were raped by those who had "taken the vow."

When this slow-moving pack of vermin reached Hungary, it was altogether different in every way. The large, beautiful cities were behind them and now they only saw small villages of thatched huts that housed, for the most part, cattle-raisers. However, the peasants were glad to share what they had with the "pilgrims." The cattle-raisers did have fields and barns rich in foodstuffs, food that the pilgrims assumed belonged to them since they were going to fight a "holy" war. The looters took what they wanted, then set fire to the wheat stores while their kind hosts watched in dismay and unbelief. Then they took what women they wanted, and if a sensitive conscience whimpered a cry of protest, it was stifled, for after all, they were on a "holy" mission and a "holy" mission justifies everything. Besides, the pope, Constantinople, and Jerusalem were far away.

Peter the Hermit cautioned them to act like Christians, but they ridiculed him and moved on to Moysson which they planned to sack as they had the other villages. But the timid citizens had learned their lesson, and they ambushed the butchers and pushed them back into a flooded river to perish. The hungry survivors trekked back to France to be mocked by their own people (who had wisely stayed home).

NEXT STOP: CONSTANTINOPLE

Of course, there were many groups of pilgrims who were headed for Constantinople at the same time. Some were more disciplined than others, but few made it. Henry Treece wrote: "Of a total of 300,000 Crusaders who had started off in such haste, only a third survived the first stage of the journey. Those who struggled on into Constantinople were like walking corpses, brutalized beyond all measure and no longer Christians of even the most primitive sort. Behind them a train of bones reached back to the Rhineland and to France"[10]

During July of 1096, this tattered "army" started straggling into Constantinople and was treated graciously by the Emperor who had invited them to make the journey. They were given lodging outside the city and after satisfying their hunger, they went on another rampage setting fire to the palatial homes, looting the churches, and slaughtering all who tried to stop them. Even the most crude and brutal among them knew this was wrong because the safety of Constantinople was one of the reasons they were there, but no cause to fret; didn't Pope Urban promise forgiveness of all sins? So, on with the murder and mayhem.

The Emperor could have set his troops upon his "friends," but instead he ordered the Crusaders to attack the Turks of Kiliz Arslan. Finally they would get a chance to put the Muslims to the sword and dispatch them to meet their already departed leader, Mohammed. So, 100,000 peasants crossed the straits into Roum. They found a deserted castle (a trap laid by the wily Turks) and took it without any bloodshed. The Turks then surrounded the castle that was gorged with European peasants who thought they had won an easy victory. It was a dry "victory" because there was no water and after eight days of torment, the "Christian" mob surrendered to the Turks with the understanding that all prisoners would be spared. After the surrender, all the Crusaders were butchered or sold into slavery. Muslim archers used those who were not acceptable as slaves for target practice. The Turks celebrated their victory by erecting a monument of bones that was "most conspicuous in height and breadth and depth." So ended the first wave of the First Crusade to defend Constantinople, to bring the two church groups together, and to liberate Jerusalem from the Muslims. Yes, the dream had become a nightmare.

CONSTANTINOPLE THEN ANTIOCH

The next wave of Crusaders was not composed of peasants but of great noblemen and princes who got started late and did not arrive in Constantinople until May of 1097. There were about 600,000 experienced soldiers who expected victory over the Muslims and a lot of loot for their trouble. However, since they were of such mixed nationalities, they could not decide on a leader, so they broke up into four divisions, each with its own general. When those four armies reached Constantinople, the Emperor convinced three of the generals to swear allegiance to him for he knew he could not withstand a battle with the Turks **and** the four armies of "liberation."

Next stop, the gates of Jerusalem. Well, not exactly the **next** stop, for there were a few problems such as a desert and a mountain range to cross, then Antioch to take, **then** Jerusalem. Antioch was a city of silk, gold, silver, and beautiful works of art, and the noblemen wanted their share before taking Jerusalem. They surrounded the well-defended city and lived off the fruit and grain they discovered while waiting for the siege to begin. However, the food ran out and a couple of the leaders took a force of 20,000 men to search the countryside for food. While they were gone, the Turks attacked the weakened force, inflicting them with great harm.

The Crusaders stopped all food supplies from entering Antioch and after the numerous battles with thousands killed on both sides, they made a bargain with one of the Turkish leaders to betray the city. The traitor opened the gate one night and permitted the Crusaders to commandeer the outer wall. Although the Crusaders had promised safety to the Turks, they massacred everyone they could find—soldiers and civilians. Other Turks escaped to a citadel on a hill. Three days later Kerboga of Monsul arrived with 200,000 Muslims to continue the struggle with the Crusaders. The Crusaders had kept food from the city and now they occupied it and they were hungry again. They ate their horses to stay alive. Then 200,000 angry, well-fed Muslims who were anxious to avenge the slaughter of the soldiers and citizens of Antioch surrounded them. "Pope Urban, where are you when we need you?"

TELLER-OF-TALL-TALES

A meek priest, Peter Bartholomew, accompanying the Crusaders told them that he had seen a vision where Christ warned them about having intercourse with Muslim women. Tancred, the Crusade leader, then swore that he would assault the gates of Jerusalem if he only had forty knights. The priest had another vision from St. Andrew informing him that the actual lance used by the Roman soldier that had pierced Christ was in the Church of St. Peter in Antioch. That lance would guarantee victory to the side that raised it in battle. The Roman lance transformed the Crusaders as they marched through the gates into battle with the Turks. They were so hypnotized that they marched and rode through a shower of arrows not even aware of being pierced. The Turks were panic-stricken. The

Crusaders pointed toward the mountain and "saw" thousands of soldiers led by St. George coming to rescue them. Of course, no soldiers were there, but it worked. The Turks turned their horses and fled pursued by the "nobles" from Europe. The Syrians and Armenians (of that area) rode to the mountains and cut off the retreating Turks and killed all they could.

The Crusaders re-entered the city to discover that the Muslims who had fled to the citadel on the hill had surrendered and some even became "Christians." The others were permitted to leave the city unharmed. The Norman faction of the Crusade had a hunch that the priest was not so much a see-er-of-visions but a teller-of-tall-tales. They accused him of planting the lance and telling a false story to whip up emotions. They made the priest run through two large fires twice to prove that he was Someone Special. To the surprise of the priest and the crowd, he survived the test of fire and that made him a very special person, one to be admired and sought after. And they sought after him, all at once. The crowd rushed him to get a "holy relic" from him that might protect them in the following battles. They pulled out his hair, tore off his burned clothes, and, heedless of his cries, almost tore him apart. As the soldiers walked away with their relics, the priest lay dying on the ground, a sacrifice to the mad mob.

ON TO JERUSALEM

Finally, nothing stood between the mob and Jerusalem! Most people assume that Jerusalem was populated by Jews but not so. Palestine and Syria were within the boundaries of the Roman Empire and became mainly "Christian." The Jewish population of Jerusalem had been largely dispersed by pagan Roman authorities following the Jewish anti-Roman revolts of A.D. 66-70 and 132-135, and few Jews remained in the area.

When Titus took Jerusalem on September 8, 70 A.D., over a million Jews were slaughtered and 97,000 were taken captive. Josephus reports that the streets were clogged with bodies and during the famine, mothers ate their own children. He reports that one Mary took her infant son, knowing he would become a slave, and killed him. Then she roasted him and ate half his body, "hiding away the rest." When thieves arrived at her door, having smelled the meat cooking, they demanded the food. When shown what she had to offer, they recoiled in horror. She taunted them "for being weaklings who couldn't bring themselves to do what a woman had done."[11] The Temple and other buildings were burned with thousands dying within them. The escaping Jews dispersed all over the Empire, while others were put to work in the Roman mines.[12]

So the Jews were not in great abundance even in the eleventh century. Arab Muslims had governed the Holy City for many generations and the Christian and Jewish inhabitants lived as second-class citizens with their Muslim masters. ("Christian" Crusaders wanted to take the city from the Muslims and the few Jews that were there.) As the Crusaders approached the city, all the Christians were expelled from the city in preparation for the inevitable siege.

SIEGE OF JERUSALEM

The battle for Antioch had lasted almost nine months, and after a five-month rest, the army (now only 25,000 of the original 600,000) moved upon the Holy City. The siege of Jerusalem began on June 7, 1099, and after a lengthy battle, the "Christians" broke into the city and the maddened maniacs ran through the streets of Jerusalem, driving all before them into a temple where they were butchered. Of course, the Crusader's "noble" motive was to kill a Turk for Christ, as if Christ had anything to do with the whole Crusade movement. They slaughtered men, women, and children throughout the day and well into the night. As the sun rose, they discovered about 6,000 Jews who had fled to the synagogue for refuge. They torched the synagogue and burned the people alive. The surviving Muslims had fled to the Mosque of al Aqsa in the southeastern quarter of the city. The Crusaders broke down the doors and slaughtered an estimated 30,000 Muslims.

Such acts of brutality can not be defended in any way; however, an explanation for it could be the brutality that had accompanied the Muslims in their conquests from the Arabian Desert into Spain. While the "Christian" brutality was deplorable, it also is a reminder of the Biblical truth that men, families, and nations reap what they sow.

So ended the battle for Jerusalem and immediately a king was chosen establishing the Kingdom of Jerusalem. The Holy City was now in the hands of the Roman Catholic Church. The final result of the First Crusade was the establishment of four Latin "states" or "kingdoms" in the Middle East: the County of Edessa, the Principality of Antioch, the County of Tripoli and the Kingdom of Jerusalem. Jerusalem exercised an ambiguous political control over the other three.

CONTINUING CRUSADES

In 1144, the Turks had regrouped and took the northern outposts of the Kingdom of Edessa. So, guess what. Another Crusade was preached by St. Bernard in 1146 and led by King Louis VII of France and Emperor Conrad III. Again, this Crusade was not successful and St. Bernard's reputation lost its luster. Though disgraced, he was honored by the Church for his "faithfulness" to the cause–killing Muslims.

A few years later Saladin united the Muslim world from Cairo to Baghdad, and he preached a "Holy War" against the Christians. Fair enough. If a Roman Catholic Pope can preach hatred, who says a Turk can't do the same? In 1187 the Turks took Jerusalem again. It was now time for Crusade number three, led by Emperor Frederick I, King Philip Augustus, and King Richard. They were determined to retake Jerusalem but failed, so why not try crusade number four? Pope Innocent III was now the Man In Charge at Rome, and he was the first pope to claim a divine supremacy over all civil rulers! That was one of Europe's darkest days.

The Fourth Crusade never reached Jerusalem, but in 1204, the Crusaders did make it to Constantinople (the greatest city in Christendom) which they attacked and burned, resulting in Emperor Alexius III fleeing the city and his imprisoned brother's replacing him. Pope Innocent III had forbidden the Crusaders to sack the city (after all they were "Christians"), but the Crusade leaders refused to obey the most powerful man on earth!

To his credit, Pope Innocent III had already excommunicated all the Crusaders, but that didn't help the citizens of Constantinople. Remember that the protection of Constantinople was one of the reasons for the First Crusade. The result of this Crusade affects the Roman Catholic and Greek Orthodox Church to this very day. It erected a massive iron door that some say will never be opened between those major divisions of "Christianity."

CHILDREN'S CRUSADE

There were many Crusades for many more years but the most shameful one was the Children's Crusade in 1212. There were two groups: one from France, another from Germany. Thirty thousand children gathered in a French market and started their journey of tears without food, maps, or supplies. Under the leadership of a French peasant boy, Stephen of Vendôme, thousands of boys and girls, many less than twelve years old, traveled to Marseilles. Those who were not drowned in shipwreck were betrayed, starved, and butchered or sold into Egyptian slavery. Others were taken to Baghdad, where eighteen of them were beheaded for refusing to become Muslims. Only **one** of the 30,000 French children ever returned home. A few of the 20,000 German children straggled back over the Alps to their villages to be ridiculed for their altruistic motives. Surely, if any Crusade had sincere motives, this one did; however, sincerity didn't keep it from being foolish, and in the end, tragic.

CRUSADE AGAINST HERETICS

The Crusades continued to evolve from being arguably highly motivated (First Crusade) to the Children's Crusade to a Crusade to "cleanse" the Church of "heretics" in the thirteenth century. The Albigensians (arising in southern France) were people who followed the principles of modern-day Baptists emphasizing:

- a membership of born-again people.
- baptism by immersion only.
- total separation of church and state.
- the Priesthood of all believers.
- the Bible as the sole authority.
- independent, self-governing churches; not dependent on any other church.

Pope Innocent III has been called (well, a lot of things) but he is known as the most powerful man who ever lived. He had that reputation because he had the power to boot **everyone** in a nation out of the Church (thereby damning every soul), if the kings of Europe disobeyed him. Innocent was alarmed with the exploding growth of independent churches and tried to persuade them, but they only wanted to discuss what the Bible had to say about the above distinctives. The Pope became alarmed at the growth of the movement and tried persecution since persuasion didn't work. Eventually, Innocent III declared a Crusade against these "heretics," making the Albigensian Crusade the first against internal enemies of the Church instead of external ones.

Of course, persecution only made these independent churches grow even more until a Roman Catholic historian suggested that about one-third of Europe's population "identified with independent churches!"[13] Innocent also ordered vicious campaigns against the Jews and even threatened European kings with interdiction (excommunicating all citizens) if the kings did not destroy the independent churches within their jurisdiction.[14]

LEGACY OF CRUSADES

However, the independent churches continued to grow as did the Roman Churches' hatred for all "unbelievers." This culminated with the Inquisition of the Middle Ages where Roman Catholic Church tribunals "tried" thousands of Christians and Jews for heresy. Thousands of people were burned at the stake, stoned, drowned, flayed alive, etc. But the independent churches continued to grow until the explosion in the sixteenth century known as the Reformation.

After a hundred or so years of Crusades, some people in Europe (with an I.Q. equivalent to their hat size) began to ask; "If the Pope is infallible why are the Crusades such abysmal failures?" Why, indeed!

The Catholics preached peace and came with a sword while the Muslims preached peace **by** the sword. One was a hypocrite, the other a heretic, and both were unbelievers and deserve our pity and scorn. Catholics would say that the Crusades were the long-term result of the Muslim terror, while Muslims would admit that much of their hatred goes back to the Crusades. I say, "A pox on both their houses."

After two hundred years, the Crusades finally sputtered out, and surviving Crusaders returned to their home ports after many months' absence. They staggered off hired ships with their swords, souvenirs, spices, and exaggerated stories of violence, virtue, and valor. As they disembarked from the ships into the arms of their loved ones, no one noticed black rats, infested with disease-laden fleas, running down the tie ropes to the dock. Europe was going to face the Bubonic Plague for hundreds of years, a menace far more vicious than the Muslim hoard.

1. Isidore of Seville, *Encyclopedia of Greco-Roman Culture in the 7th century.*

2. William Manchester, *A World Lit Only by Fire, Little, Brown & Company,* Boston, 1992, pp. 134-135.

3. Pope Urban's speech at the Council of Clermont, 1095, according to Fulcher of Chartres.

4. Quoted by Don Boys in *Pilgrims, Puritans and Patriots,* Good Hope Press, Indianapolis, 1983, p. 43.

5. Ibid. pp. 43-44.

6. Edgar Holmes McNeal, eds., *A Source Book for Medieval History,* New York, Scribners, 1905, pp. 513-517.

7. Pope Urban's speech at Council of Clermont.

8. Boys, p. 45.

9. T. S. Eliot, *Collected Poems 1909-1962,* San Diego, 1984, p. 165.

10. Boys, p. 49.

11. F. Josephus, *Josephus Thrones of Blood, A History of the Times of Jesus,* Barbour publishing, undated, p. 223.

12. F. Josephus, *The Works of Flavius Josephus,* vol. 1, trans. William Whiston, Baker Book House, 1974, p. 469.

13. Quoted by Phil Stringer, *Faithful Baptist Witness,* Landmark Baptist Press, Haines City, FL, 1998, p. 86.

14. Ibid., p. 87.

Chapter Eleven

The Menace, I

Diseased, Damaged, and Dead!

If civilized people do very wicked, harmful things in time of war, what can we expect the bad guys to do? U.S. General George Patton told his troops that their mission was not to go out and die for their country, but to make the enemy go and die for **his** country! (Cleaned up version!) He was saying that war is an all-out effort to win. He was also saying that the purpose of war is to advance your nation's cause. And many believe it should be done at **any** cost. However, decent, reasonable people can debate that. Some activities are beyond the pale, even for wartime.

Did you know that the British government manufactured 5,000,000 cakes loaded with anthrax bacteria to be fed to German cows during World War II? The *Sunday Herald*[1] of London reported on "Operation Vegetarian" that was to wipe out the German beef and dairy herds with the possibility of killing "perhaps even millions" of German innocents. Why didn't the English do it? Because the Allied success on the battlefields made it unnecessary. But the plan was in the works–to kill innocent civilians with anthrax! Could mass killing like that happen in the U.S.? Such a thought would have been un-thinkable until September 11. U.S. authorities are now telling us that it is a good possibility, while others say, "It **will** happen here." Are we ready?

EXAMPLES OF TERROR

We already have other examples of terror during time of war. During the French and Indian War in 1763, the British infected the Indians with smallpox by giving them blankets and handker-chiefs taken from infected patients. Approximately 95% of the Indi-ans that were exposed died of the disease. During the Middle Ages, infected bodies of the enemy were dropped into wells especially in dry, desert areas. They also catapulted diseased, rotting bodies over walls into cities and on ships. By the time the ships entered home-port, often the whole crew was dead or dying.

It was recently reported that famous Nobel Prize winner, Sir Macfarlane Burnet of Australia, recommended to the government that they develop biological weapons to use against Indonesia and other nations that were "overpopulated" in Southeast Asia! This No-bel Prize winner, note it was the Nobel "Peace" Prize, suggested that the Aussies target the crops of other countries with biological chemi-cals and seek to infect mass populations with infectious diseases! This 1947 report was discovered in 1998, and remember that it was suggested by the "good guys" in white hats.

But many Americans would say that the U.S. Government would never try something so inhumane nor get away with it if they did. Wrong on both counts, as the following incredible information clearly shows.

U.S. ADMITS USE OF TERROR!

The Pentagon made an incredible admission in May of this year that is mind-numbing: In the 1960s the U.S. military used two kinds of nerve gas in experimental tests on military personnel serv-ing on Navy ships! The deadly agent sarin, known as VX, was one of the gases used according to Defense Department officials. The tests were conducted on barges, ships, etc., to test the weapons, pro-tective gear, and decontamination procedures. The *Associated Press* reported: "The tests were among 113 conducted as part of a project called SHAD, or Shipboard Hazard and Defense. The Penta-gon has acknowledged using chemical and biological simulants be-fore, but has not admitted using the actual weapons agents them-selves."[2]

You may remember that sarin was the deadly gas used by a religious cult that killed 12 people in a Tokyo subway in 1995. The U.S. military used the same gas **against** the U. S. military in a 1994 test code-named Flower Drum Phase I near Hawaii! The gas was injected into the ship's ventilation system, but the exposed crew wore gas masks and those crewmembers who worked with the gas also wore protective clothing.

Let's see if I understand what the authorities have admitted:

U.S. military officials purposefully exposed U.S. military to deadly gas in order to test its effectiveness, also to test the protective gear the hapless sailors were wearing, and to look at their decontamination procedures following the tests!.I think the officers of those experiments should go to prison for 20 years.

But it gets worse!

REPUBLICAN TERROR PLAN

It was 1959 and Republican Dwight Eisenhower was the U.S. President in his second term. Cuban President Batista had fled Cuba for the Dominican Republic as Fidel Castro shot his way to power in Havana. Castro soon began to take over various industries and expropriating American-owned businesses, proving to be the Communist he denied being. Of course every informed person (except most Federal officials and the editors of the *New York Times*) knew he was a Communist from his youth. Americans were horrified: Here we had a Communist nation less than a hundred miles off our Florida coast!

The confrontation between Communism and the Free World was exacerbated in 1960 when the Russians shot down a U-2 reconnaissance plane piloted by Gary Francis Powers who was captured, tried, and sentenced by a Russian court. He was later exchanged for a Russian caught spying by the U.S. Very recent information proves that Eisenhower himself ordered Powers' over flight of the Soviet Union, yet the president lied about it to the American public. Furthermore, we now know that he ordered his cabinet to lie about his knowledge of the over flights! It is incredible that they obeyed and no one resigned! One member even lied under oath to protect the President! (We also know that many spy planes had been shot down costing America about 200 of its best pilots! Their families had no idea how they died until recently.)

Eisenhower, in the waning days of his administration, wanted to do something about Communism in Cuba, a laudable desire, but he wanted a pretext to justify his invasion of the island! The Joint Chiefs of Staff Chairman, Army General Lyman Lemnitzer, and the Joint Chiefs proposed an attack on America's Naval Base at Guantanamo Bay, Cuba! They would then blame Cuba and bang, we would have our justified War in the Caribbean! After all, who would believe the protestations of innocence by a Communist despot who had been lying all along? And surely everyone would believe top U.S. military and civilian officials! General Lemnitzer gave his approval of the plan only hours before Eisenhower left office on January 20, 1961. As Kennedy came into office, the clandestine plan was put on ice.

NSA: NO SUCH AGENCY

Enter the massive super-secret National Security Agency, so secret that Washington insiders call it No Such Agency. They started to work on their plan to justify an invasion of Communist Cuba.

Keep in mind that in the early 1950s we had fought the bloody Korean War with some help from a few UN countries against Red China, Russia, and other Communist nations. The war was never won. It just came to an end. Communism was "on the march" all over the world, especially in Southeast Asia. Senator Joe McCarthy had made a big splash with his anti-communism crusade, but he was censored and silenced by his soft colleagues in the U.S. Senate. Julius and Ethel Rosenberg, American citizens, had been executed for spying for the U.S.S.R., and other high officials had been arrested for treason. Consequently, Americans had no love for Communists of any color, race, or nationality, and now we had a Communist nation off our shores, but a "plan" was cooking.

So what to do? Well, U.S. Joint Chiefs of Staff under Kennedy produced a proposal code-named "Operation Northwoods" (the old Eisenhower plan) with the title of "Justification for U.S. Military Intervention in Cuba." The Joint Chiefs of Staff gave this recommendation to Secretary of Defense Robert McNamara on March 13, 1962. Many Americans will not believe this is possible, but our government wanted an excuse to invade Cuba and made plans to foment actions that would provide them the cover to carry out such a plan! They would develop a false, Communist-Cuban-terror campaign in south Florida and even in Washington, D.C. In the event that John Glenn's orbital flight was unsuccessful, resulting in his death, our government planned to accuse Castro of sabotage, using fabricated evidence.

The plans that had been made during the last days of the Eisenhower Administration to attack Cuba were implemented (except for the promised U.S. air support) in April of 1961, during the beginning of John Kennedy's term. However, it turned into a rout with Castro killing and capturing the invaders who had fled Cuba during the revolution. Kennedy had promised the courageous Cuban refugees that he would send air support for this Bay of Pigs invasion, but he did not keep his commitment, resulting in one of the worst disgraces in U.S. military history. Kennedy rejected the provocative "Northwoods" plan (concocted under Republican Eisenhower) because he did not want a covert U.S. attack upon Cuba, and he did not want an **overt** attack either as proved by his failure to keep his word, resulting in the deaths of hundreds of brave men. But it's politics as usual.

INCREDIBLE U.S. TERROR PLAN

James Bamford, investigative reporter and former *ABC News* producer, in *Body of Secrets,* reveals this amazing incident. He reported the plan called for "innocent people to be shot on American streets, for boats carrying refugees fleeing Cuba to be sunk on the high seas, for a wave of violent terrorism to be launched in Washington, D. C....People would be framed for bombings they did not commit, planes would be hijacked. Using phony evidence, all of it would be blamed on Castro, thus giving [General] Lemnitzer and his cabal the excuse, as well as the public and international backing, they needed to launch their war."[3] They even made plans to shoot down an American charter plane full of college students or senior citizens off on a holiday or any grouping of persons and to provide "proof" that it was the work of the Communists off our Florida coast!

While most Americans would have supported an attack on Cuba to free the island from Castro's totalitarian regime and introduce a free republic, that was not the intent of the nefarious plot. The U.S. Government's plan was to imprison the Cubans in a U.S. military-controlled police state! American forces would rapidly take military control of Cuba, but continued police action would be required! I **wondered** what happened to Curly, Larry, Moe! They have been advising U.S. Presidents for the last 40 years!

NO CONFIDENCE IN GOVERNMENT

So you see, that is only one example of why we never put our confidence in princes but in God. The above scenario is a reason to fear your government, even though you love your country. We must be careful that in our pursuit of terrorists that we don't become what they are. The red, white, and blue in the flag must never blind us to the extent that we think it is unpatriotic to question government officials. In fact, patriots will demand that state and Federal authorities be chained to the Constitution.

Most people think that the American government is protecting us against all threats, domestic and foreign. So we can sleep in peace. That is not true. An "innocent one" says, "but the U.S. is guarding our boarders to protect us." Say what? Our borders are leaking like a sieve, and the U.S. isn't even guarding shipments of highly classified and dangerous weapons across the country! "Yes," says another innocent one, "but they are careful about goods and material that enter the country." Afraid not, but they do catch a few by accident!

WorldNetDaily reported a harrowing case about a terrorist who was discovered before he made his way into Canada and the U.S. The column reported, "On Oct. 18, curious sounds emanating from a cargo container on board a freighter docked at the South Italian port of Gioia Tauro brought the port police running. Opening the container, they were astounded to find a 43-year old Egyptian stowaway, identified as Rigk Amid Farid, boxed in amid the comforts of a luxury hotel suite outfitted for a three-week journey to Canada: bed, toilet, portable heater and water supply. His luggage contained a cell phone, satellite phone, computer, and cameras, and he was equipped with a Canadian passport, airport maps, airside security passes and an airline mechanic certificate, all valid for New York's JFK, Newark, L.A. International and O'Hare airports."[4]

The Italian police arrested him then released him! I suppose on his own recognizance! He has since vanished! Surprise! The container was loaded in Egypt and headed for Canada, and now the Canadians are trying to discover the party who was to have taken delivery. Over six million of those containers arrive each year in U. S. ports and only 2% are inspected. Terrorists could have smuggled into America a factory to build **anything.** A ship's container may not be a Trojan Horse but it is the same principle!

IT GETS WORSE

Now we discover that it is even worse than the above. On Sunday, May 19, 2002, Senator Graham of Florida revealed on *CBS* "Face the Nation" that 25 extremists had entered the U.S. in huge

182

containers in the last 15 days! He said that two of them had entered at a Florida port. Who are those men? Where are they now? What do they plan to do? What have the authorities done to apprehend them? Did those men have weapons of mass destruction? Inquiring minds want to know.

FBI Director Robert Mueller told the National Association of District Attorneys meeting in suburban Alexandria, Virginia that there will be another terrorist attack, adding, "We will not be able to stop it."

Most sane, sensible people cannot imagine that other humans would wreak mass destruction upon hundreds of thousands, maybe millions of innocent people. But we are living in the real world, not a world of make-believe. Those of us who have been aware of the statements of Muslim terrorists have always known that terror would strike the U.S. sooner or later. The attack on the World Trade Center has brought terrorism into every home in North America; however, that is only the beginning. We could experience a reign of terror unlike any known before. Not scare statements but statements based on facts.

We are told that no one could be so ruthless and evil as to use nuclear, chemical, or biological weapons on innocent people where millions would be killed. However, such Pollyanna personalities don't understand the blackness of the human heart without Jesus Christ. Nor do they understand that the Koran teaches Muslims that non-Muslims are the enemy to be converted or killed! Most decent people find it very difficult to understand the mentality that fosters hatred, brutality, and murder of innocents. But world leaders and knowledgeable authorities are very concerned about our future.

THINKING THE UNTHINKABLE

U.S. leaders are thinking the unthinkable! I hesitate to even write the words, but here goes: In the fall of 2001, intelligence agents were alerted to the possibility of a nuclear attack on New York City! Top agents were informed that terrorists had smuggled a Russian 10-kileton bomb and planned to detonate it in the Big Apple. Not only did they have the information from one of their sources, but also a Russian general admitted that he was missing such a bomb. *Time.com* reported that such a bomb detonated in Manhattan would kill about 100,000 people and irradiate 700,000 more and flatten everything in a half-mile diameter.[5]

Time interviewed counter terrorism experts and government officials and was told that America's luck will probably run out again, sooner or later. "It's going to be worse, and a lot of people are going to die," warned a U.S. counter terrorism official. "I don't think there's a [expletive deleted] thing we're going to be able to do about it."

Federal officials are so sure of another terrorist attack that the goverment has assigned 100 senior civilian government officials to 24-hour rotations in underground bunkers outside Washington, in a program known as the "shadow government," ready to take over the government if the next target turns out to be Washington. It is officially known as "Continuity of Operations Plan" and is based on presidential directives that go back to the Eisenhower administration.

It is interesting that Federal officials are concerned about the government's continuing but not about your and my continuing! What it means is that second-string players will govern us in the event a massive terrorist attack destroys our Federal government.

WEAPONS OF MASS DESTRUCTION

In a more ominous report the same day, the National Intelligence Council, an analytical group that advises the CIA, flatly stated that "weapons-grade and weapons-usable nuclear materials have been stolen from some Russian institutes."[6] No one knows how much or where it has gone. The article continued: "The U.S. Customs Service has dispersed 4,000 radiation-detection devices among its border inspectors to check for nuclear weapons and weapons-grade materials, Commissioner of Customs Joseph Bonner said last month. It plans to install additional X-ray and gamma-ray inspection technology, along with radiation detectors, to the northern border and at seaports in the coming year."

On October 8, 2001, President Bush created the Office of Homeland Security with Executive Order 13228. He gave its new director, former Pennsylvania governor Tom Ridge, instructions to "review plans and preparations for ensuring the continuity of the Federal Government in the event of a terrorist attack that threatens the safety and security of the United States Government or its leadership." Then in June he told Americans that he wanted to upgrade

Homeland Security to cabinet level. On November 25, 2002, that became reality when Bush signed it into law providing for the Department of Homeland Security. That could be one of the biggest mistakes made in modern political history. Or it may save millions of lives. Obviously, Federal officials think we are going to experience a massive attack from Muslim terrorists in the near future and are making plans, if not to thwart it, at least to survive it.

Tony Blankley wrote, "In 1996, General Alexander Lebed, former Yeltsin national security adviser and candidate for president of Russia, came to the United States to warn us that Russia had lost more than a dozen nuclear suitcase bombs. Each of those bombs, the size of a pineapple and weighing 100 pounds, if detonated would utterly obliterate an area four miles square."[7] Many are concerned about the suitcase bombs that are floating around the world. Can anyone even calculate the disaster if a small plane carrying one of those bombs flew into a nuclear power plant?

On October 2, 2002, *WorldNetDaily* published a column revealing that Paul L. Williams, a former FBI agent has declared that Al Qaeda purchased twenty nuclear suitcase bombs in 1998 from Russian KGB agents for thirty million dollars. Williams also affirms in his book, *Al Qaeda: Brotherhood of Terror,* that Al Qaeda has anthrax spores, plague viruses, including Ebola and salmonella, botulism biotoxin and sarin on their shelves. Sleep well tonight! It's good to know that God is still in control!

U.S. NOT READY

The media reported in May of 2001, that Attorney General John Ashcroft admitted that the U.S. Government is preparing city officials in 120 metro areas for the coming attacks: "We are now in the process of completing training and exercises for the nation's largest 120 cities under the Domestic Preparedness Program."[8] What are they doing? They are preparing them to handle the horrible aftermath of an attack, including how to clean up the dead and dying, how to seize control of vital industries and utilities, how to limit panic, and how to enforce public curfews.

The editor of a paper of Hamas, a Muslim terrorist organization, has recommended in a letter that anthrax be put into the U.S. water supply! After all, we are the enemy to be humiliated and conquered. We know that chemical bombs have already been used in

Israel according to Israeli Intelligence. Hamas first added poisonous chemicals to homemade bombs in 1997. They used pesticides and other poisons that are relatively easy to acquire. Authorities are concerned that terrorists are trying to procure sarin and other nerve gases. Pesticide-packed bombs have been used in recent terrorist attacks in Israel. Will that happen in the U.S.?

U.S. Army Colonel David Franz told Diane Sawyer and Sam Donaldson on *ABC*'s PrimeTime, "The likelihood of a biological attack in the U.S. is now extremely high." Dr. Michael Osterholm, of the Minnesota Department of Public Health told PrimeTime: "I can tell you it is not a matter of **if** this will occur. It's a matter **when**...and how much panic and how much death are we willing to accept at the time that it occurs...It will be the closest thing to a living hell that I could imagine."

When asked, in 1998, about obtaining chemical or nuclear weapons, bin Laden said, "Acquiring such weapons **for the defense of Muslims** [is] a religious duty." (Emphasis added.) Note that he admitted his motive was in defense of Muslims and was a part of his religion. Of course it is. *Reuters* published a story from Pakistan in which Osama bin Laden (giving his first interview to a journalist since the September 11 terrorist attack) admitted that he had biological and nuclear weapons that he would use as a deterrent.[9] World authorities also believe he and others have them and would use them especially if they saw the hangman coming to get them. *Insight* magazine reported high-level sources revealing that the terrorist alerts have been based on the growing conviction of U.S. intelligence agencies that the bin Laden network "definitely" has a nuclear weapon of some type "in this country."[10]

Anthony Loyd reported that he found partly burned blueprints for a "Nagasaki bomb" that were left by fleeing al-Qaeda terrorists. The column reported that: "Intelligence sources told *The Times* last month that bin Laden and al-Qaeda had acquired nuclear materials illegally from Pakistan. And at least ten Pakistani nuclear scientists have been contacted by agents for the Taleban and al-Qaeda in the past two years, according to reports."[11]

IRAQ INVOLVED IN TERROR

Furthermore, it is commonly known (and disputed by some) that Mohammed Atta, one of the September 11 terrorists, met with

186

Iraqi diplomats before that date and that those diplomats disappeared from their various European posts after the World Trade Center attack. Atta was also seen with Saddam Hussein's agents this year in Spain, Italy, Germany, and the Czech Republic. There are reports that Atta received anthrax spores in April while in Prague meeting with the Iraqi consul. Intelligence agents cannot interview the consul because he was booted from the country just after his meeting with Atta.

It is also believed that Saddam Hussein has been working hand-in-glove with al-Qaeda's terrorists' groups. An Iraqi defector told intelligence agents that Saddam established a terrorist training school outside Istanbul to practice hijacking passenger airplanes! Could Iraq be the state sponsor of the September 11 attacks? *Reuters* reported that an Iraqi defector admitted he had helped renovate clandestine facilities for "biological, chemical and nuclear weapons in private villas, wells and under a Baghdad hospital as recently as a year ago." In a Baghdad interview with the *New York Times*, Adnan Ihsan Saeed al-Haiden, a civil engineer, confessed that he had worked for Saddam Hussein's government. U. S. Government agents have interrogated him twice and think his information is credible.[12]

The American Sentinel (September, 2002) reported on a study done by the Center for Strategic and International Studies that revealed that Iraq admitted the manufacture of: 22,457 gallons of Anthrax; 100,396 gallons of Botulinum toxin; 581 gallons of Aflatoxin; and 200 tons of VX nerve gas and 350 tons of Sarin! Plus, it is alleged that Saddam has huge guns that are 300 yards long that can lobe a shell all the way to Italy! Can you imagine guns with barrels 300 yards long? A Canadian who died under very strange circumstances designed them.

FOOD AND WATER TERROR

Keep in mind that the main purpose of a biological or chemical attack would be to render as many Americans (as well as our animals) diseased, damaged, or dead. Such an attack would leave our infrastructure unharmed and usable. One major risk is to our food supply. Since everyone must eat, food production is a likely target for terrorists. America's food supply is at greater risk than ever because of the various trade treaties. America gets about one-third of its fresh fruit and 12 percent of its vegetables from other nations, and much of that produce is eaten raw. But, we are told that the U.S. Government will protect us; however, less than 2 percent of imported food is inspected by the Food and Drug Administration.

Similar to the food problem is the threat to our water supply in every city. How many cities do you think have adequate protection against terrorists? How difficult would it be to contaminate a water supply with chemical or biological agents that could infect and kill a population in hours? We know that terrorists have been experimenting with biological weapons such as smallpox, anthrax, and others.

We do know that four Moroccan terrorists in Rome were arrested after discovery of a powdered, cyanide-based substance in their possession along with maps of Rome's water supply.[13] Carl Cameron of *Fox News* reported on July 30, 2002, that Federal officials arrested two terror suspects who were found with documents about how to poison U.S. water supplies!

HEALTH OFFICIALS NOT READY

How sophisticated must terrorists be to infect a city with unseen, undetectable, deadly bacteria, and are we ready for such an attack? Dr. Stephen Cantrill of the Denver Health Medical Center testified to a Senate committee on terrorism that U.S. hospitals lack the "surge capacity" to handle thousands of potential victims of biological terrorism. He said, "A true biological weapon attack would not be handled well," adding, "The lay public have abundant faith in the medical community's abilities, but they would be deeply disappointed."[14] So we can't depend on the government (city, state, or federal) to protect us. Now we discover that our hospitals are inadequate, and can not be expected to handle thousands of patients in a single day!

There has been much speculation about smallpox and other viruses being used as weapons of mass destruction (WMD) by various terrorists groups. The officials at the Centers for Disease Control and Prevention are training physicians to recognize the disease, and they have vaccinated health experts to deal with any outbreak.[15] Evidently, health officials are very serious about the possibility of such an attack and plan to rush to any part of the country when necessary.

In the fall of 2002, the media reported that President Bush was considering making the decision to vaccinate every American against smallpox even though all health experts admit that the results would be thousands getting ill or dying from the vaccines. Health officials confess that the risks are real and the benefits are doubtful. In December of 2002 President Bush told us that the military would be vaccinated for smallpox then health care workers then the rest of Americans would get the shots. We were assured that they would be voluntary. We shall see!

INCOMPETENT FEDS

The terrorists don't have to slip bombs, missiles, etc., into the U.S. since they are easily available right here! The *New York Times* reported that "security for domestic shipments of surface-to-air missiles, cruise missiles and other explosives has been so poor that terrorists could easily obtain them for use in an attack in this country, according to a classified government report and other confidential records." The General Accounting Office discovered incredible lapses in the system for shipping military explosives throughout the United States by truck. The GAO characterized those lapses as posing "substantial national security or public safety risks," according to the column.[16]

Some results of the study in the *Times* article are:

♦ Terrorists could obtain U.S. military weapons that are moved and temporarily stored in private trucks with little difficulty.

♦ The U.S. military, unlike Federal Express, often cannot even identify where weapons and explosives are after they have been shipped.

♦ Investigators found that a shipment of 192 Stinger missiles was left in a civilian storage area without the knowledge of the military or the contractor who shipped them.

♦ Trucking companies transporting weapons are allowed to leave trucks in commercial-carrier terminals with few safeguards from intruders.

♦ Investigators were able to access missiles and rockets in storage terminals by simply flashing phoney Defense Department credentials.

♦ Gates protecting dangerous materials were left

unlocked.

- ♦ A site responsible for storing Hawk surface-to-air missiles had its garage door left open.

- ♦ Five sites containing a full military arsenal–including cruise missiles, SAMs, anti-tank rockets, 72 bombs, 14,000 rounds for howitzers and other explosives and munitions–were accessible.

It is amazing that this article did not cause Americans to storm the Capitol! Hey, I thought Government was supposed to protect us. I thought we could depend on government regulations to protect us! Who was in charge of those shipments? Are they still on the same job? Government, by its very nature, cannot be trusted to protect its citizens; that has been true in all ages.

The fact that the U.S. Federal authorities have been incompetent is obvious to everyone in 2002 except those living in caves. Another example: on July 10, 2001, FBI agent Kenneth Williams, working out of the Phoenix office, warned FBI headquarters that flight schools should be investigated for possible al Qaeda infiltration. Only middle level agents read the memo and no one was impressed by it until September 11. But that wasn't the first suggestion that Arabs might fly planes into national buildings. Two years before September 11, a report prepared by the Library of Congress for the National Intelligence Council (which advises the President on threats to the U.S.) suggested that "Suicide bomber(s) belonging to al-Qaida's Martyrdom Battalion could crash-land an aircraft packed with high explosives...into the Pentagon, the headquarters of the Central Intelligence Agency (CIA), or the White House." All right, how can any Federal official say that no one could have imagined that an attack on Federal buildings using airplanes was even a possibility? Someone's asleep at the switch.

Then, the scene changes to Minnesota. Zacarias Moussaoui was reported acting strangely at a Minnesota flight school. He had no flying skills and was not interested in learning to land a passenger plane. An FBI agent speculated, in an internal memo, that Moussaoui might have intended to smash a plane into the World Trade Center. No one in Washington thought it worth following up. But maybe the most shocking fact is that the plot to fly planes into U.S. buildings was known back in 1995, but nothing was done about it.

Project Bojinka (big bang), uncovered by Philippine officials with full information going to the FBI, was an al-Qaeda plot to fly loaded jet passenger planes into public buildings. I am aware that the FBI has been very active in recent years running all over Waco, running all over Ruby Ridge, literally stealing a large Baptist church building from its congregation, etc. But, surely they could have found time to read a memo, put the dots together and think: terrorists with flying skills with access to planes can mean death to thousands of people.

WHAT THE FEDS HAD

Some may suggest that such an experience (in far away Philippines) had no connection with terror in the U.S. Even so, a high school student could put it together because authorities knew that Terry Nichols had made frequent trips to the Philippines and met with an Islamic group with connections to bin Laden! We also know that Tim McVeigh had a collection of important Iraqi telephone numbers. So here's what Federal authorities had:

- ◆ Two American white boys with connections to Middle East terrorists: one with Iraqi phone numbers; one making repeated expensive trips to the Philippines to meet with known terrorists.

- ◆ The two white boys blow up the Alfred P. Murrah Building in Oklahoma City (with help from Middle East men, as suppressed evidence will show).

- ◆ An explicit report from a Federal agency two years before the September attack clearly suggested the possibility of terrorists using planes as missiles into Federal buildings.

- ◆ A terrorist plot to fly planes into buildings uncovered in the Philippians in 1995.

- ◆ Numerous Muslim men taking advanced flying lessons in various cities.

- ◆ One Muslim with very little flying skills not interested in landing a plane, only steering it.

FBI AGENT BLOWS WHISTLE

Coleen Rowley, a 21-year veteran of the FBI, put her job on

the line when she wrote a 13-page letter to the FBI Director, alleging that the FBI headquarters in Washington is not much help in stopping terrorism and charging the Director with covering up FBI mistakes. In fact, she blistered them for incompetence in handling the Zacarias Moussaoui and Phoenix incidents. Moussaoui had been arrested on an immigration charge three weeks before the attack on the Pentagon and the World Trade Center. He was charged with being the "20th hijacker" in the September 11 attack. Rowley asserts that if the FBI had been alert (does that mean awake?), the September 11 attack might have been thwarted. Moussaoui had been in custody for at least three weeks before the terrorist attack, yet the FBI did not even get a search warrant. Rowley accused the special agent in Washington of "consistently, almost deliberately, thwarting the Minnesota FBI efforts." Wait a minute! I thought they were all on the same team in the war on terror.

Even on September 11, after the attacks, the FBI supervisor ordered Rowley to not pursue action against Moussaoui, since his seeking flight training was probably a coincidence! Very thoughtful of him. FBI Director Mueller said, "The fact that there were a number of individuals that happened to have received training at flight schools here is news, quite obviously." Mueller said on Sept. 15: "If we had understood that to be the case, we would have-perhaps one could have averted this." Mr. Director, the FBI had that knowledge as early as July of 2001, but the careerists in Washington didn't act on it. Heads should have already rolled all over Washington.

THE ATTACK IS COMING

We are daring to think the unthinkable: that Muslim terrorists are planning an even worse attack upon America! Nuclear explosion! Massive biological attack! U.S. authorities think it is coming. Many people who stumble through life not wanting to be bothered with the facts, especially disturbing facts, will suggest that I am screaming wolf, that it is all exaggerated; however, Vice President Dick Cheney does not think so. On May 19, 2002, he admitted on *NBC* "Meet the Press" that a massive attack was going to happen. He said, "it's not a matter of if but when it happens." So top officials in our government are expecting a massive attack and making plans to thwart it or respond to it. The problem is they don't know when it will come, where it will hit, or whether it will be a nuclear bomb, chemical or biological attack, or whatever. But the attack is coming.

Did you know that our government has deployed "bomb-sniffing" trucks (which look like fire trucks) around New York City and other major U.S. cities to locate any "dirty bombs" carried in or assembled by terrorists? Elite teams of specialists are ready to disarm the bombs and other weapons of mass destruction that may be discovered.[17] The founder of the Islamic Supreme Council of America (ISCA), Shaykh Hiham Kabbanii, reported that al-Qaeda has purchased from the Russian mafia more than 20 nuclear warheads that are carried in suitcases![18] Are some of those in the U.S. at this time?

On June 13, 2002, the *Associated Press* reported that Federal officials have authorized the purchase of 350,000 potassium iodide pills to protect Americans from cancer caused by radiation poisoning emanating from a nuclear blast! A spokesman for the Office for Homeland Security admitted the pills were being stockpiled "in case of a nuclear event."

But that's not all! Bill Gertz reported in May of 2002 that shoulder-fired, anti-aircraft missiles are now in the U.S. The Russian-made and U.S.-made missiles were obtained from sources in Afghanistan. The U.S. Stinger, a surface-to air missile, has a five-mile range and can hit an aircraft at 10,000 feet.[19] I am going to write the unthinkable, unspeakable, and "unwritable": Was a shoulder-fired, surface-to-air missile used to blow TWA flight 800 out of the sky July 17, 1996, as it departed Kennedy International Airport?

Will we see a U.S. passenger plane blasted from the sky in the next few weeks? It wouldn't take much for the following scenario: A couple of terrorists drive to the glide path of any major airport and wait for their target. They pull the Stinger out of a van, fire it, and leave. They are pulling into traffic by the time the plane hits the ground. Airlines were notified on May 22, 2002, of the danger. The friendly skies have turned into frightening skies, courtesy of Muslim terrorists and your local terrorist cell. After I wrote the above paragraph, the Paradise Hotel in Kenya was bombed on November 28, 2002, killing thirteen people and only minutes before, a passenger plane with Israeli tourists was fired at by two shoulder-fired missiles. Both missed. Will they miss the next time?

OUR RESPONSE

How will we respond when we experience a major biological, chemical, or nuclear attack upon America? And will the authorities be as inept, incompetent, and irresponsible as others have been in times of major threats? We have been assured that our government is ready for a massive attack on U.S. cities, but no one really believes that. Remember that politicians are called that because they are concerned about the politics involved in any given situation. Not being critical, only factual. Authorities are fearful of a stampede, and not without reason. I think there will be mass confusion and panic as everyone tries to exit the same door at the same time.

The first people on site of a massive attack on an American city will be ordinary citizens such as you and me, that is if we survive. In a few minutes the police, firefighters, and medical personnel will arrive. Hours later Federal officials, along with the military, will arrive with emergency orders to implement Federal guidelines for emergency situations. They will also provide body bags for the dead. Then the politicians will arrive for photography sessions and will make promises to "catch the terrorists."

My point is that you must take control of your own life. Make what preparation you can in event of a nuclear, biological, or chemical attack that all officials say is coming. In event of a small-pox contamination, the disease could be in many states before it is known that anyone has been exposed to it. A dozen terrorists, infected with smallpox could be circulating, as I write, in some major cities at sporting events, churches, on airplanes, etc. As they breathe, cough, and sneeze, they spread the disease. It will be days before anyone recognizes the disease. In fact, your physician has never seen a case of smallpox. He will identify the first symptoms as flu, not as deadly smallpox.

Just as average citizens are wondering how authorities will react, the authorities are wondering how the military and civilians will react to a massive attack and the aftereffects. If human nature has not changed, you can count on massive problems. The following chapter may portend the future for each one of us when massive attacks are made against the U.S.

1. *Sunday Herald* of London, 10-14-01 and *American Free Press,* 11-5-01.

2. Matt Kelley, *Associated Press,* 5-23-02.

3. James Bamford, *Body of Secrets*, Doubleday, New York, 2002, p. 83.

4. *WorldNetDaily,* 11-30-01.

5. *Time.com*, 3-3-02.

6. *Seattle Post-Intelligencer,* 2-28-02.

7. *Washington Times,* 9-26-01.

8. Attorney General John Ashcroft's statement at the U.S. Senate Appropriations Committee on 5-9-01.

9. *Reuters News Service*, 11-10-01.

10. *Insight* magazine, 11-01.

11. Anthony Loyd, *The Times,* 11-15-01.

12. *Reuters News Service*, 12-20-02.

13. *BBC News*, 2-30-02.

14. Stephen Cantrill's testimony before the U.S. Senate Committee on Appropriations, 5-10-01.

15. *New York Times,* 11-3-01.

16. *New York Times,* 10-4-01.

17. Larry Celona and Niles Lathem, *New York Post,* 1-12-02.

18. *Newsmax.com* and *Zion of Judah,* November, 2001.

19. Bill Gertz, *The Washington Times,* 5-31-02.

Chapter Twelve

The Menace, II

Desperate Days of Death

Decaying corpses were stacked all over the burial ground and the streets were littered with the dead. When trains arrived at railroad stations, they had to be cleared of the dead and dying passengers. Five million people died in the nation of India! The killer was Spanish influenza of 1918-19. In the U.S., about 500,000 people died![1] This plague started in a Kansas army camp and within a week it was in every state! It then jumped the Atlantic Ocean to cut down millions. Total world deaths are estimated to have been up to 25 million people!

From the dawn of history, mankind has experienced times of sickness, sorrow, and suffering. Often, times of pestilence were mysterious, sudden, and without remedy. Lack of knowledge, superstition, and poor sanitary conditions often contributed to the progress of the pestilence. Men often felt that God was visiting them with plague to punish their evil ways. The disease was usually dreadful, deadly, and devastating, and often left as quickly and mysteriously as it appeared. Now, we face a more deadly possibility: modern terrorists with the ability, equipment, funds, and commitment to wreak destruction, disease, and death on a massive scale.

Throughout history people often reacted out of fear and ignorance, and that only compounded the problem, extending the pestilence. They ran from the towns, but found that when they arrived in a safe haven they were met by the same pestilence! Of course, the pestilence had been a traveling companion. Hopefully, this chapter will give some insight as to the mistakes made in the past that should not be repeated in the future. Our present threat could come from a nuclear blast, poisoned water or food supply, or biological agents sprayed over a metropolitan area.

BACK INTO HISTORY

The further one goes back into history, the less reliable are the numbers of dead, and the less assurance we have of the pestilence that took them; however, it is a fact that mankind has suffered far more from bugs than from battles.

I will use the word, "plague" as a general term for any deadly epidemic disease, since even the experts can't identify some of the major plagues of the past.

We know that malaria hit Italy in the first-century B.C., and that the dead were in all the houses, and the streets were crowded with funeral processions. Many who had mourned a stricken relative died themselves with such rapidity that they were burned on the same pyre as those they had mourned.

An epidemic that lashed the whole world started in Verus' Roman army, while his troops were fighting in the East in A.D. 165. According to Ammianus Marcellinus, the original infection came from a chest in a temple which Roman soldiers had looted.[2] God warned about those who are greedy for gain in Proverbs 1:19, reminding us that it would cost the lives of the greedy souls. The results of this thievery cost the lives of millions of innocent souls. Verus' army carried the disease homeward, scattering it everywhere, and by the time they reached Rome, the disease had spread "from Persia to the shores of the Rhine," a world plague. Zinsser quotes Orosius' report that deaths were so many that some cities in Italy were abandoned and fell into decay. There was so much terror of the disease that no one dared nurse the sick and dying. It even killed Marcus Aurelius, the Emperor of Rome, among the 2,000 per day that died in that city.

In the epidemic of Cyprian about A.D. 251, the plague skulked through Egypt, leaving the dead and dying, then boldly attacked Rome and Greece where the daily dead rose to 5,000! It spread over the entire world, "from Egypt to Scotland."[3] It was during this plague that the custom of wearing black as an indication of mourning became common, according to Roman Catholic historian Baronius (1538-1607).

In the plague of A.D. 302, the pestilence had a companion–

famine. The people resorted to eating grass, and the deaths from famine almost matched those dying from disease. Hungry dogs fought over the bodies of the human dead.[4] Hieronymus tells us that the human race had been "all but destroyed," and that the earth was returning to a state of desert and forests.

WORLD-WIDE EPIDEMIC

The first instance of a true pandemic (worldwide epidemic) began in A.D. 542 at Pelusium, Egypt during the reign of Emperor Justinian. In sixty years it spread to all parts of the known world. The dead lay unburied in the streets and "at length ten thousand persons died each day at Constantinople.[5] The people of Constantinople became desperate with all the deaths and placed bodies anywhere they could. Bodies were placed on roofs, on top of towers, and others were burned. Some were simply left in houses to rot. It got worse as the black horse of famine galloped through the city because mills where corn was ground stopped operating.

Seibel, the eminent authority, tells us that the plague was preceded by many earthquakes, volcanic eruptions–Vesuvius, in 513, was one–and famines that dropped a blanket of terror and death over Europe, the Near East, and Asia. The worst natural occurrence was the earthquake and fire that destroyed Antioch in A.D. 526, killing almost 300,000 people.

When the plague arrived in Constantinople in A.D. 542, it stayed for four months killing so many people that it was impossible for the living to bury the dead, and by A.D. 565, half of the citizens of the Byzantine Empire had died![6] Gibbon suggested that perhaps 100 million people (in Europe alone) died of this plague!

The Plague of Justinian emptied the cities, turned the country into a desert, and made the habitations of men the haunts of wild beasts. The snake slithered and hissed, the hyena crouched and laughed, and wild beasts pawed and growled where proud and arrogant men once walked.

BLACK DEATH

In the early 1300s, the population of Europe had outrun the food supply, and in a few years, the poor were eating cats, dogs, and other animals. Some say they even ate their own children! People were dying, but rather slowly. Bubonic plague (Black Death) would prove to be more efficient and quicker than famine, much quicker.

The bubonic plague cut its way through the Far East to Italy, then to the rest of Europe. It is believed that Genoa merchants transported plague in their cargoes of spices, nutmeg, jewels, and silks. In Siena, 75% of the people were cut down like grain before the scythe, and about 75% also died at Pisa. As described in the *Cronica Senese* of Agnolo di Tura, "Father abandoned child, wife, husband, one brother, another....No one could be found to bury the dead for money or for friendship."[7]

The poet Petrarch reported about the effects of the plague on Florence: "We go out of doors, walk through street after street and find them full of dead and dying, and when we get home again we find no live thing within the house! All having perished in the brief interval of our absence."

George Astor wrote that, "Almost half of Europe died from the black death between the fourteenth and seventeenth centuries."[8] The Black Death (bubonic plague) raged into Paris in June of 1348, and about the same time it ravaged up and down the valleys of the Rhine and arrived in England, Denmark, Norway, and Sweden. In 1360-61, 50% of the people in many Polish towns died! Lubeck saw 80,000 of its people swept away by the plague. In 1477-78, 30,000 died in Venice; 18,000 died in Vienna in 1542. London saw thousands die each week in 1563, 1592, and 1599. Spain was lashed by the plague in 1596-1602, when half a million people died! When James I came to the throne in 1603, 38,000 people died in London; almost that number died in 1653.

Then the Great Plague lashed London, and more than 68,600 died out of a population of 460,000. It all started slowly in London. Just before Christmas of 1664, two men died in Drury Lane, with a few additional deaths during the remainder of the winter. The next few months were months of beautiful weather in London, but not for people! As the temperature climbed, so did the death toll. The rich and well connected began to flee the city. The College of Physicians left the city by the last of June, and the politicians and King Charles II fled in early July. In the last week of August, over 7,500 people died, and the dead carts rolled through the streets each morning picking up those who had died during the night. The dead were taken to the church cemeteries where huge holes had been dug

200

and where the dead were thrown. Daniel Defoe wrote that infected people threw themselves into the pit, and sought to bury themselves, since death was so sure and dying was so painful.[9] The plague spread from London to the rest of the country, and then disappeared after 1667.

By 1679, 76,000 people perished in Vienna and 83,000 in Prague during 1684. Moscow lost 57,000 people to the plague as late as 1771. In the mid-1800s, the bubonic plague raised its ugly head in China and skipped across the country. Almost 100,000 people died in Canton. It showed up in Bombay (six million died in ten months) and Calcutta in 1896, and in Japan and the Philippines the following year.

In 1899, the Black Death visited Hawaii, Central America, and South America. The next year saw it in Cape Town and San Francisco. Plague paid a visit to Egypt and Singapore in 1901. Bangkok played an unwilling host to the plague in 1904, Java in 1910, New Orleans in 1914, and Florida in 1922. About ten million people perished of bubonic plague between 1903 and 1921! Since then, it has only shown up periodically and has been contained, but the Black Death is on every continent of the earth at this very moment!

IMPACT OF PLAGUES

The preceding litany of deaths could be a portent of what the world faces if Muslim terrorists carry out their threats. No sane person thinks they are playing games. It is not demagoguery to suggest that the earth could become a mass graveyard. I have provided a sketch of some of the major plagues of the past, now I want to detail the impact these plagues had upon various civilizations. Then in the next chapter, we will try to see a pattern in the way men have reacted to plagues in the past and compare their actions to our present crises.

Past civilizations have experienced more devastating blows from sickness than from swords, more heartache from bugs than from bombings. During the Crimean War (1854-56), ten times as many British soldiers died of dysentery as from all the Russian weapons put together! And 50 years later, during the Boer War, there were five times as many deaths from disease as from enemy fire.

The face of the world has been changed more through the louse, the flea, and the mosquito than marching armies and flying missiles. We can now add the AIDS virus to the scourges that have smitten mankind, taking their dreary toll. (As of 2003, over 13 million people have died of AIDS and 40 million more are infected, worldwide!)

BREAKING POINT

When the daily count of the dead reached the breaking point (different in various societies and ages), responsible people became irresponsible, calm people became terrified, and the borderline paranoid became dangerous. As people fled their homes, social and political organizations disappeared, crops were left to rot in the fields, populations were displaced, civil war was fomented, and major shifts in religious thinking occurred. After major plagues mysteriously left a nation, interest in religion decreased because of the many deaths among the clergy and because of so many unanswered prayers. Of course, lost people have used unanswered prayer as an excuse for unbelief since the beginning of time. J. L. Cloudsley-Thompson wrote: "It is beyond the bounds of possibility for anyone to estimate the influence of epidemic disease on religion and philosophy. Nor can we clearly assess its influence on the material course of human history."[10]

Many historians believe that the empire of ancient Greece fell into Roman hands because of malaria attacks, not because of marching armies. Malaria was endemic throughout the Greek world by 400 B.C. The malarial parasite (passed to man by the female mosquito) killed infants, weakened unsuspecting children, forced the vacating of the best farmlands, and helped produce Greek citizens who were listless, lazy, and licentious. As a result, the power and glory of ancient Greece became a mocking memory. Greek historian Polybius (204-122 B.C.), called the most reliable ancient historian, reported that the whole of Greece had been visited in his time by childlessness and a general decline of the population that resulted in the emptying of the cities and the failure of the land to render its produce. He said that men refused to marry or if they married, refused to have children. If they had children, they would refuse to rear them. He said that men went out of their way to be ostentatious, avaricious, and indolent.[11]

Quite an indictment! Will Western civilization learn from the past or will we have the same experience? If Americans must live daily with the threat of terror (as do the Israelis) will that further erode our culture and destroy our homes and churches?

FALL OF GREECE

Some historians, in my opinion, give too much credit to the mosquito for the fall of Greece. It **was** a major factor, but men must always be held accountable for their actions. Today, a man gets drunk and kills a carload of people and pleads that he was not in control and should not be held responsible. Others tell us that sugar impaired their ability, and they lost control and should not be accountable for the results they produced. No doubt there is some truth to those claims, but we must all be held accountable for our actions. The same was true in Greece. Malaria did make them listless and lazy, but they **chose** to be licentious.

The Greeks slowly lost their brilliance which had been as the bright freshness of an April morning. This degeneration is obvious in their art and literature and other areas of creativity. W.H.S. Jones wrote: "Their initiative vanished; they ceased to create and began to comment. Patriotism, with rare exceptions, became an empty name, for few had the high spirit and energy to translate into action man's duty to the state. Vacillation, indecision, fitful outbursts of unhealthy activity followed by cowardly depression, selfish cruelty and criminal weakness are characteristics of the public life of Greece from the struggle with Macedonia to the final conquest by the armies of Rome."[12] Will America experience those results because of terror attacks?

Jones, De Sanctis, Celli, and others taught that disease has changed the condition of this world more than wars. Ancient Greece would not have fallen into the hands of Rome if it had not been for malaria. Are we not fools if we don't consider the same or similar results from possible biological terrorism we face today? If we don't learn from history, we are doomed to repeat it.

PLAGUE SMACKS ROME

Maybe we can learn from the plague of Saint Cyprian and not make the same mistakes people of that day made. In A.D. 250, the Roman Empire was in turbulence. The Goths had just won a major victory and the barbarians were at the gates of Rome. Then the plague of Saint Cyprian lashed the empire for fifteen years with wave after wave smashing the same areas. Its spread was facilitated by numerous military activities that were going on throughout the provinces. It was a time of terrible tragedy that pushed people to the brink of despair. An indication of the conditions prevalent at the time can be seen in Haeser's statement: "Men crowded into the large cities; only the nearest fields were cultivated; the more distant ones became overgrown, and were used as hunting preserves; farm land had no value, because the population had so diminished that enough grain to feed them could be grown on the limited cultivated areas."[13] Hieronymus wrote that the human race had been "all but destroyed."

Much of the face of Italy was changed because of this epidemic. Large parts of the land were depopulated and left vacant. Swamps appeared and Hieronymus reported that the earth was returning to a state of desert and forests. Disease was changing the face of the earth in every way. There were problems in the palace and bickering on the battlefields. The soldiers were often unpaid because the pestilence sapped the wealth and the cash flow slowed. Rebellious soldiers broke rank and fled into the forests, and took what they wanted from those trying to eke out an existence from the land. Military insurrections, civil disorders, and civil wars became common, and the empire continued to crack along its foundations.

DISEASE, DESTRUCTION, AND DEATH

An indication of the extent of national trouble during times of disease, destruction, and death can be seen in desperate laws passed during Diocletian's reign (ruled 285-305). Farmers were forbidden to leave the farms to take up other jobs and some occupations were made hereditary.[14] That simply meant that a son had to follow his father's trade or profession. Yes, it was tyrannical but when you are poor without much of a future, the chain doesn't seem too heavy! Just one more burden to carry.

Caesar had trouble "keeping them down on the farms" once they had been to the city. And after mutinous soldiers had robbed the country people, tax collectors had confiscated their money and crops (calling it–like today–taxes), the country people looked for other means to make a living. Those laws, forcing people to work at certain occupations, were passed because famine and epidemic had killed so many of the workers who had originally filled those positions.

The marching armies, fleeing populations, and famine all contributed to conditions that were inviting pestilence. The empire was crumbling and dying by the fifth-century with the Vandals, Goths, and other barbarians still beating at the gates of Rome. (Many were already in the Empire having crossed the Pyrenees into Spain.) The first of the barbarians to sack Rome were the Visigoths, led by Alaric in 410. Alaric's hopes of glory faded when he developed symptoms of malaria and soon died. His successful storming of the city signaled the final decline of the Roman Empire in the West, but it had been crumbling for many years from various internal problems. The mighty Alaric fell because of a mosquito bite!

In 455, the Vandals appeared at the gates of Rome, entered for a few weeks, then left the city for Carthage. Angelo Celli suggested they were driven out by malaria. Thousands of infected people threw themselves into the Tiber River to hasten death and escape lingering pain. It was a time of famine, fear, and fighting–and pestilence. At this time, as if Rome were not having enough trouble, faraway Britain experienced a relentless epidemic.

PLAGUE CHANGES ENGLAND

The barbarians had been moving in human waves from east to west during the troubled early fifth century and were now settled along the Danube–in Roman territory. They had already knocked down the gates of Rome and had settled in Italy, Gaul, and Spain. Now they were interested in Britain. Vortigern, Britain's leader, had his back to the wall as he faced the barbarians from the north, and the Venerable Bede reported that he called upon the Saxon chiefs, Hengist and Horsa, for help. Bede wrote: "...a severe plague fell upon that corrupt generation [Britain], which soon destroyed such numbers of them, that the living were scarcely sufficient to bury the dead....They consulted what was to be done, and where they should seek assistance to prevent or repel the cruel and frequent incursions of the northern nations; and they all agreed with their King Vortigern to call over to their aid, from the parts beyond the sea, the Saxon nation; which, as the event still more evidently showed, appears to have been done by the appointment of our Lord Himself, that evil might fall upon them for their wicked deeds."[15]

Apparently Britain's fighting forces were greatly depleted

by the plague. The Saxons arrived in 449 and acted as mercenary guards for the Britons. The Brits discovered that their "help" was to be another "plague" upon their island. Everything would be different because of the Saxons, who came to help but ended up being a plague. Bede recognized that the pugnacious Saxons were a curse from God because of Britain's wickedness.

Hans Zinsser concludes: "It requires little exercise of the imagination, therefore, to conclude that the history of the British Isles in all its subsequent developments of race, customs, architecture, and so forth, was in large part determined by an epidemic disease."[16] Britain would never be the same because of an invisible bug!

WAR, PESTILENCE, AND FAMINE

Zinsser, among others, believes that the Plague of Justinian was partly responsible for the demise of the Roman Empire. He wrote that the plague was "perhaps the most potent single influence— which gave the **coupe de grace** to the ancient empire."[17] A bug knocked off an empire! This plague lasted about seventy years and caused havoc in the Empire that was already bruised and bleeding. Justinian was trying to restore the ancient Empire to its former glory—like trying to breathe life into a corpse. His armies were fighting with Persia, Africa, and with the Goths in Italy, but those crude, unsophisticated barbarians had learned from former warlords the art of making war. They had learned how to organize, analyze, and cooperate. It was ever more difficult to sustain armies on far-flung battlefields, especially when there were insurrections at home and treachery and thievery in the very palace. Justinian needed, least of all, a major epidemic to compound his problems.

The Empire was in a state of confusion because of the added pressure, problems, and panic produced by the plague. Gibbon wrote: "No facts have been preserved to sustain an account or even a conjecture of the numbers that perished in this extraordinary mortality. I only find that, during three months, five and at length ten thousand persons died each day at Constantinople; and many cities of the East were left vacant, and that in several districts of Italy the harvest and the vintage withered on the ground." Gibbon continued: "The triple scourges of war, pestilence and famine afflicted the subjects of Justinian and his reign is disgraced by a visible decrease of the human species which has never been regained in some of the fairest countries of the globe."[18] Can anyone read that statement and doubt that disease has changed our world far more than wars? And will irresponsible Muslim terrorists change our world forever?

PLAGUE AND THE ECONOMY

The plague of Justinian ended about 590, but by that time most of Italy was controlled by the Lombards. The barbarians were no longer at the gates of Rome but inside the gates. The mighty Empire had crumbled, and when the Muslim armies swarmed out of Arabia in 634, the Roman and Persian forces gave only token resistance.[19]

The Black Death raged throughout Europe in the fourteenth century, wiping out from two-thirds to three-fourths of the population! This loss of population impacted the work force, but at first, only the more skilled positions. However, when the second and third wave of pestilence swept across Europe, every job was affected. Farmers, servants, tinkers, and others were in short supply. J.L. Cloudsley-Thompson wrote that, "some 50,000 persons died in London alone, so that all public business was interrupted for two years and the war with France had to be discontinued."[20]

During this time, inflation skyrocketed. Goods became difficult to obtain and very expensive because so many people had died. Serfs no longer were tied to one master; it became easy to leave one lord and be hired at high wages by another master.[21] It took between 100 and 133 years for Europe to overcome the shock and consequences of such a disastrous loss of workers! Gary North wrote: "So devastating was the plague in the north Italian region of Pistoia that the population did not recover to the 1347 level until the early 1800's, almost five centuries later. The economic effects were startling. Europe had been suffering from population growth and land hunger for a century. Overnight in Pistoia, rents fell from up to half of the harvest to about five percent. So did interest rates. There was now a labor shortage (at the old terms of labor). Wages shot upward. All over Europe governments passed wage controls. They made it illegal for people to move to new parishes. And all over Europe this legislation failed."[22]

STAY OUT OF PARIS

The educational world received high adulation from the

princes of the church and state during the fourteenth century. The University was "king," but most of the intellectuals placed blame for the pestilence, famines, and other natural disasters on the heavenly bodies! When the plague reached Paris in 1348, Philip VI called in his top medical people from the University of Paris to give him some answers relating to the origin of the pestilence that was ravaging the city. His learned academicians decided that the answer was astrology!

Their explanation was so reasonable that anyone would accept it–anyone, that is, whose I.Q. equalled, but did not exceed, his hat size. They informed his Majesty that there had been a conjunction of Saturn, Mars, and Jupiter in the house of Aquarius on March 20, 1345–at 1:00 P.M. (I'm not sure if that was Eastern Standard Time or Central Time.)

They told the king that the conjunction of Saturn and Mars meant death and destruction, and the conjunction of Mars and Jupiter released pestilence into the air. This was a Royal Con Job, and the king should have had a "You've got to be pulling my royal leg" look, but they assured him that the warm and humid Jupiter sucked up the water and nefarious vapors from the earth. Then, of course, Mars, known to be hot and dry, ignited a fire.[23] Of course. Those professionals were certified experts! The big surprise is that the king and his court did not fall down to the floor holding their sides with hysteric laughter; however, we must remember that it was an age of superstition and ignorance. At least the king got the message that Paris was not the place to spend that spring and summer.

The "Paris Medical Association" had decided the origins of the plague, so they could now give "expert" advice about how to escape being cut down like grass before the scythe: Don't eat fat meats, poultry, and olive oil. The learned doctors told their patients not to sleep past dawn, don't bathe, and forego sexual intercourse, since it could be fatal! During those days, quackery was part and partial of most of the disciplines. The quacks wore academic gowns and were a part of the intellectual brotherhood–just like today. And like today, no one dared say, "But that's quackery." After all, one might be accused of being an independent thinker! Horrors!

MANY CHANGES

A relatively small group of intellectuals ruled the world of education, and most of them, usually the oldest, were most vulnerable to the plague. Most of those leaders were mowed down when the pestilence visited Europe. In fact, four of Europe's thirty universities disappeared in 1350 as a result of plague.[24] And the effect of plague on the academic world was a major concern during those desperate days of death.

Another result of pestilence was the disappearance of Latin as the medium for writers, and the acceptance of the common language for literature. The reason is simple: the teachers and clerics who taught Latin in the schools, seminaries, and universities were buried! There was little choice about changing to the common languages, since the teachers of Latin were dead.

The plague also made a lasting impression on the Roman Catholic Church. Some of its monasteries were wiped out. All 150 monks died at the monastery near the French seaport of Marseilles and the same thing happened in Avignon.[25]

There was a scarcity of all kinds of workers so those who were still alive were worth more. They tried to unite and strike for higher wages, but the result was the Statute of Labourers of 1351 that kept wages at the 1346 level. It also prohibited workers from leaving their masters. Other laws followed that were just as bad, but the medieval economy experienced a major overhaul after a series of peasants' revolts in 1381 and 1449. The plague helped force many economic changes.

Millions of Europeans died of the plague, receiving little help from the medical establishment or the Roman Catholic Church. Consequently, the people lost respect for them and began to examine the old "truths" with an inquiring mind. They discovered that many of the old "truths" were without any foundation, so the people decided to think for themselves. At this time, the Pope gave permission for the bodies of plague victims to be dissected in an attempt to garner knowledge about the plague. This inquiring and commendable spirit and challenge to past authorities was the beginning of modern science. I salute the pope for his salutary and courageous decision.

SYPHILIS!

In 1492, Christopher Columbus pushed westward into the unknown Atlantic with three frail ships and arrived in the West Indies. He returned to Spain a hero and was quickly summoned to report to the king and queen who had helped finance his voyage. Columbus slowly rode through the streets with his gifts to his royal sponsors. The streets of Barcelona roared with the cheers from an ever-larger crowd and roses from the pretty senoritas littered the streets. But he and his men had brought more than fruits, parrots, natives, and a chest full of gold–they had brought syphilis! And the syphilis of that day was a quicker killer than that of today.

Some of Columbus' crew, infected with syphilis, became mercenary soldiers under Charles VIII of France when he invaded Italy. The Italians put up very little resistance, but the French army was so debilitated by syphilis, they absconded from Naples in a disgraceful retreat. The remnant of the army straggled back home, spreading the disease throughout Europe. In 1495, the disease struck France, Switzerland, and Germany, and the next year it reached Holland and Greece. Then syphilis sneaked into England and Scotland in 1497 and Hungary and Russia in 1499. It surely made the rounds quickly.

As syphilis smacked down peasants and princes, the local governments panicked. Each country blamed another. Travelers with syphilis were banned from some countries, and in Paris, syphilis carriers were quarantined in their homes or special syphilis centers. In London, syphilis was spread through bathhouses, and in some cities, bathhouses were closed. In 1579, William Clowes reported that out of every twenty persons admitted to St. Bartholomew's Hospital in London, fifteen were syphilis patients![26] Today, more than 50% of syphilis carriers are homosexual or bisexual men.

Columbus' "souvenir" from the New World was bad news for the Old World; it impacted the whole world, but there was a trade-off. When Columbus returned to the New World on his second voyage in 1509, his men carried the virus of smallpox, which along with Spanish swords, killed millions of Indians. W.H. Prescott tells us that Cortez did not conquer Mexico–smallpox did! Within six months of Cortez's arrival in Mexico (March of 1519), smallpox made Mexico a giant sepulcher. Some 3,500,000 Indians were wiped out–over half of the Empire![27]

WE SOW–WE REAP

This experience in Mexico tells us a great deal about the destructive power of disease, and about how men reap what they sow. It also tells us that sometimes millions of innocent people reap what uncaring, wicked men sow. God warned us that if we sow to the wind, we will reap the whirlwind. That may be where we are today–in the middle of a whirlwind, if terrorists use biological or chemical weapons to destroy our nation. Remember that the Roman Empire seemed to be impervious to any threat, but it was brought to its knees by a bug! Could it happen here?

When bubonic plague turned London into a graveyard, the impact on business and industry was devastating. You may remember that people of means fled the city when people started to die "like flies." Defoe wrote that when it seemed that few would be left behind in the city, "you may be sure from that hour all trade, except such as related to immediate subsistence, was, as it were, at a full stop."[28] Defoe goes on to list those who stopped working or who lost their jobs: all those who manufactured articles that were not essential to dress such as lace-makers, glove-makers, etc. Since no ships went down the river, all those workers were without jobs. All home-builders were out of work. After all, hundreds of homes were empty since so many people had died.

In light of the foregoing horror stories, should we expect to see similar results from the crises we face if or when terrorists strike again and again and again? As we face the possibilities of biological, chemical, or nuclear warfare, what impact will it have on your life, if you live through the events? That is the subject of the following chapter.

1. W.I. B. Beveridge, *Influenza: The Last Great Plague,* Prodist, New York, 1977, p. 31.

2. Hans Zinsser, *Rats, Lice, and History,* Little, Brown & Co., Boston, 1935, p. 135.

3. Ibid., pp. 138 and 141.

4. J. L. Cloudsley-Thompson, *Insects and History,* New York, St. Martin's Press, 1976, p. 32.

5. Edward Gibbon, *The Decline and Fall of the Roman Empire,* abridged by D. M. Low, Harcourt, B race and Co. N.Y, 1960, pp. 584-585.

6. Cloudsley-Thompson, p. 61.

7. Charles T. Gregg, *Plague!,* Charles Scribner's Sons, New York, 1978, p. 7.

8. Gerald Astor, *The Disease Detectives,* New American Library, New York,

1983, p. 151.

9. Daniel Defoe, *A Journal of the Plague Years,* London, Everyman's Library, 1908, p. 68.

10. Cloudsley-Thompson, p. 34.

11. Ibid., p. 86.

12. Ibid., p. 87.

13. Zinsser, p. 140.

14. William McNeill, *Plagues and People,* Garden City, New York: Anchor Press/ Doubleday, 1976, p. 118.

15. Bede, *Bede's Ecclesiastical History,* Book 1, Part 2, Ch. 14.

16. Zinsser, p. 143.

17. Ibid., p. 133.

18. Gibbon, p. 585.

19. McNeill, p. 127.

20. Cloudsley-Thompson, p.62.

21. Decameron web site.

22. Gary North, *Remnant Review,* 3-20-87.

23. Gregg, p.8.

24. Cloudsley-Thompson, 65.

25. Gregg, p.7.

26. Quoted by Cloudsley-Thompson, 82.

27. Ibid., p. 83.

28. Defoe, p. 106.

Chapter Thirteen

The Menace III

Reaction to Disaster

Major epidemics, famines, and natural disasters, not only have a profound effect upon the political, business, and agricultural life of a nation, they also change people. In this chapter, we will consider the possibility of horrific, adverse reactions to epidemics and disasters. These reactions have 'wrought havoc upon commerce, cultures, churches, etc., as paralleled with diseases and disasters of the past. If the next terrorist attack is biological or chemical, we could face the same experiences of people in the past when the pestilence was natural, not man made.

There is no doubt that the plague of Justinian nudged Europe into the Dark Ages, so informed people are aware of the danger posed by repeated terrorist attacks against our nation. Those attacks will affect our constitution, community, commerce, churches, and culture,

The plague of Athens is a good example of how people reacted to plague. Athens was crowded because the rural population swarmed into the city. Attica was the headquarters for large armies in 430 B.C., and conditions were perfect for pestilence. The disease started in Ethiopia and went to Egypt, Libya, and finally reached Athens, packed with people from Attica and the countryside.

Plague victims got severe headaches followed by inflammation of the tongue and pharynx. At the same time there was sneezing, hoarseness, and coughing. Then there was vomiting, diarrhea, and insatiable thirst. The patient usually died between the seventh and ninth day. Some patients lost their sight, others their memory, before dying. The Athenians were demoralized followed by extreme lawlessness. No one seemed to fear God or man. Honor was a forgotten concept.[1]

In 540, the Plague of Justinian smacked the Grecian Empire with 10,000 deaths per day! When the pestilence had passed, there was so much depravity and general licentiousness that it seemed, said Procopius, that "only the most wicked were left alive."

PESTILENCE PRODUCES PANIC

Panic was usually the immediate reaction to the appearance of pestilence. Defoe records how London reacted when the Black Death reached that city in the seventeenth century: "the richer sort of people, especially the nobility and gentry from the west part of the city, thronged out of town with their families and servants in an unusual manner...nothing was to be seen but wagons and carts with goods, women, servants, children, etc.; coaches filled with people of the better sort, and horsemen attending them, and all hurrying away..."[2]

As always, when fear rules, reason flees and intelligent people do dumb things. The "conners" came out of the closets and set up shop in proximity to the "connies." The sheep were ready to be sheared! Those people still in the city were "running about to fortune-tellers, cunningmen, and astrologers to know their fortune...and this folly presently made the town swarm with a wicked generation of pretenders to magic...."[3] The quacks had long lines of gullible people at their doors every day. Seems to be no end to people wanting to be taken.

The ministers of most denominations warned the people of the charlatans, but their warnings made little impression on the laboring poor whose fears dominated all their passions causing them to throw away their money "in a most distracted manner upon those whimsies."[4] And, as always, the people who lost their money were those who could least afford to.

Other con artists were more subtle than the astrologers, but not much. Notices were posted throughout the city inviting people to get the sure cure for a sure price. The notices read: "Infallible preventive pills against the plague"; "Never-failing preservatives against the infection"; "Sovereign cordials against the corruptions of the air"; "Exact regulations for the conduct of the body in case of an infection"; "Anti-pestilential pills"; and "Incomparable drink against the plague, never found out before." The people spent their hard-earned money for pills, potions, and preservatives, preparing themselves **for** the plague, not against it. In a later plague, infected folk sought to be cured by bathing in urine collected from people who had eaten cabbage!

TIME TO PRAY

Death was on everyone's mind. The talk among the uninfected was about the grave, dying, sickness, fevers, spots, dead carts, etc. They were not much interested in fun and games. Defoe wrote that "the gaming tables, public dancing rooms, and music-houses...were shut-up and suppressed...." He added that "a kind of sadness and horror at those things sat upon the countenances even of the common people."[5] People were not thinking of games but of the grave.

The government encouraged the peoples' devotion by days of prayer and days of fasting and humiliation. Officials asked the people to make public confession of sin and to implore the mercy of God to avert the dreadful judgment which hung over their heads. (Can you imagine the mayor of a major city taking such a position? No? Well, you can imagine him leading a gay rights parade, can't you?)

People of all persuasions embraced the occasion by flocking to the churches until one could not get near the church doors. The people were saying, "There's a time to play and a time to pray, and this is the time to pray." While many Christians got serious about living for Christ and became cautious in daily activities, Muslims were little affected spiritually by the plague. Their rigid predestination (some would call fatalism) led them to not take any unusual precautions, so they put themselves in danger by exposing themselves to plague carriers.

When people arrived at church, the parish minister was often absent. He had, well, felt "called" to the safe countryside where the prosperous and powerful had fled. The preacher in the pulpit was often a Dissenter (Independent Bible preacher) who had been outlawed a few years earlier! To be sure, some of the establishment preachers (Church of England) stayed on the job and died of plague, but many fled to safety. The people flocked to packed churches to hear the preachers preach the Word of God to a needy and confused congregation. Many people professed faith in Christ, and great crowds attended; but, when the plague took control, the churches emptied because it was not safe to be near any person who might be infected.

AWAKENED CONSCIENCES

Defoe wrote that many consciences were awakened: "Many hard hearts melted into tears; many a penitent confession was made of crimes long concealed....Many a robbery, many a murder, was then confessed aloud, and nobody surviving [in the home] to record the accounts of it. People might be heard, even into the streets as we passed along, calling upon God for mercy, through Jesus Christ, and saying, 'I have been a thief,' 'I have been an adulterer,' 'I have been a murderer,' and the like, and none durst stop to make the least inquiry into such things or to administer comfort to the poor creatures....Some of the ministers did visit the sick at first and for a little while, but it was not to be done. It would have been present death to have gone into some houses."[6]

The constant atmosphere of death and constant terror drove men to look honestly at their lives and at their religious experience. This resulted in thousands becoming more sincere and placing more emphasis on their personal relationship with Christ. It also led them away from the established churches in various countries. Of course, printing had been invented in 1450, and people were now reading the Bible and doing their own thinking for the first time in over a thousand years. They realized that church membership and church attendance did not produce personal satisfaction or personal salvation, as they had been taught. Following personal conversion, those new converts (but old church members) lived and died as Christians.

DESPAIR AND DEATH

Christians believed they had a responsibility to help others as a Christian duty, so during times of famine they shared their food; in times of sorrow they wept with the bereaved; and, in times of pestilence, they nursed the sick and dying. The non-Christians and the pagans took notice at such kindness, and at a time when other institutions were discredited and often dissolved, the Christian churches were enhanced. William McNeill wrote: "pagans fled from the sick and heartlessly abandoned them."[7] Christians stayed and served–and died.

After so much despair and death, a dullness set in. It seemed that people lost their fear of death and had really resigned themselves to death. Defoe wrote: "towards the latter end men's hearts were hardened, and death was so always before their eyes, that they did not so much concern themselves for the loss of their friends, expecting that themselves should be summoned the next hour."[8] They no longer asked people on the street (with whom they had to do business) how they were nor did they feel a need to inform others that they were not infected. The general attitude was: all were going to die. So now they went back to church and sat in hot, crowded pews without fear of the next person. It didn't matter. They were all among the walking dead.

Defoe, an outspoken Christian, made a cogent comment in this regard: "Indeed, the zeal which they showed in coming [to church], and the earnestness and affection they showed in their attention to what they heard, made it manifest what a value people would all put upon the worship of God if they thought every day they attended at the church that it would be their last."[9]

GLOOMY FANATICISM

When rumors reached a city that a pestilence was working its way to their area, the social fabric often ripped apart at the seams. To make matters worse, the authorities were often the first to flee to the countryside. Riots, thievery, killings, and plundering of homes were common. The approaching plague was cover for old hatreds and fears to spring to the surface.

One of the most flamboyant results of pestilence was also one of the most despicable, and it came out of religious excess. As I have mentioned, a time of dying was a time to look at one's self, and as is often true, some people became mentally or emotionally unbalanced. Such were the Flagellants or the Brotherhood of the Cross. Those confused, but sincere, people tore off their clothes and beat each other on their naked bodies with scourges, consisting of three lengths of leather with knots. In each knot were iron spikes, sharp as needles. The movement spread throughout Poland, Hungary, Bohemia, Germany, etc. The fanatics went from town to town spreading their fanaticism, and no doubt, the plague. One historian wrote of the Flagellants: "the gloomy fanaticism which gave rise to them infused a near poison into the despairing minds of the people. Thus, during the fourteenth century, the idea was spread that Jews had been responsible for spreading the pestilence by poisoning wells and infecting the air."[10] He was saying that a poisoned mind produced poisoned thinking and twisted actions, resulting in hatred of Jews and others.

CHRISTIANS DON'T KILL THE INNOCENT

In Mayence, 12,000 Jews were killed when the Flagellants entered the town. In Spain, the Muslims were the "culprits," so they were persecuted. In 1346, all the lepers in Languedoc were burned as suspected well poisoners, while gravediggers were persecuted in other cities. If the haters had opened their eyes, they would have seen that the Jews, Muslims, gravediggers, and others were dying of pestilence like everyone else. Some Jews saved their lives by accepting baptism (sprinkling by the Roman Catholic Church) but were later killed. When non-Catholic Christians tried to assist the helpless Jews, they too were executed.[11]

Church officials did not endorse most of this persecution. Pope Clement VI condemned the massacres and threatened to excommunicate those who harmed the Jews. It must be understood that Bible-believing (and practicing) Christians don't persecute anyone, but **church members** do. However, this does not mean that now and then a "flake" may become a genuine Christian, but he may remain a "flake." Christian converts are always changed but not totally remade (until eternity).

Someone needs to write a book about the "Christians" in Ireland and Lebanon. Usually, "Christian" simply means a specific part of the country, or a city, as in the case of Beirut. Real Christians don't kill innocent people, take hostages, and blow airplanes out of the sky. Nor do they finance such activities! Church members do, and all real Christians get the flak.

UNSOUND ASSUMPTIONS

The Flagellants were accepted in some cities and mocked in others, but the clergy rejected them almost everywhere because they saw their authority (often an iron grip) being superseded by the fanatics. The fanatics beat themselves and each other while others prayed, but the plague was not assuaged. This, among other things, caused the people to lose confidence in the Roman Catholic Church. The whole episode of the foolish Flagellants represented a reaction against the corruption and growing impotence of the Roman Church.

Some have made unsound assumptions, giving the plague credit for the Reformation. It has been argued that the Black Death led to religious fervor that eventually culminated in the Reformation, and the immediate result was the Inquisition. There was no doubt some connection, but there were many more factors that prompted the Reformation: the corruption of the Roman Catholic Church, the invention of printing, the general population's ability to read, etc.

The persecution of a minority, while never justified, is understandable. Death was stalking the streets. People were buried in mass graves. No one could be trusted, not politicians, priests, nor physicians. Terrified people looked for someone to blame and to hate, and they found them: Jews, Muslims, gravediggers, lepers, and others. Such action is a "scapegoat" response that is as old as man. They felt they had done **something** by placing blame and throwing stones.

SCAPEGOATS

During the sixth century, B.C., when a plague or famine lashed a Greek city, an ugly person would be chosen to take all the evils of the city upon himself. He was fed the best of food, then beaten seven times upon his genital organs while flutes played! Then he was burned on a pyre of trees, and his ashes cast into the sea.[12] Please note that this was during the "golden age" of Greece that some homosexuals talk so much about. Also during this "golden age," women were second class citizens; the most brilliant men did not know the function of the heart, liver, or brain nor did they know about the circulation of the blood. They believed the entrails of a chicken could predict the fate of a nation, and that the Greek "deities" really lived on Mt. Olympus! Golden age indeed!

When Marseilles was smacked by plague, a poor man would offer himself as a scapegoat! (He was not only poor, but dumb!) For a year he was fed the best food and kept in comfortable surroundings, but after the year he was led through the city while prayers were made asking the gods to put all the people's sins upon the well-fed dummy. He was then taken outside the city walls and stoned to death. At times the volunteer would only be cast out of the city.[13]

The Athenians always kept hapless souls at public expense, and during times of pestilence, famine or natural disaster, two of

219

them were sacrificed. Rome also resorted to scapegoats at times. (Isn't it interesting that all people have felt the need to have someone pay for their sins? Of course, Christ is our sin-bearer.)

TROUBLING TIMES

For thousands of years; mankind resorted to human sacrifices and with more enlightenment (and the teaching and preaching of the Bible), animals replaced humans. Whether human or animals, the sacrifice was to placate "the gods." Honest men know they are sinners and are in need of expiation, and being sinners they react to death's staring them in the face. Some will confess and repent, while other will become callous and rebellious. I am convinced that we will see the same division following more terror in the U.S.

I'm afraid people will act as they always have in times of major disasters. Will we see even more depravity, drunkenness, child abuse, robbery, and murder as terrorist deaths multiply? Will honesty, loyalty, kindness, honor, and compassion become obsolete and even suspect? Will those of us who profess normalcy exhibit major character flaws and not be true to our highest ideals? Will church members permit hatred, fear, and bigotry to take control instead of faith, hope, and love? Will real Christians get weary in the battle and surrender their long-held Bible principles to accommodate the soft, sinister purring of unbelieving liberals who tell us the Bible is antiquated and unreliable? Probably so! In times of distress, disease, and death, even good people often capitulate to evil to gain safety, succor, and success.

Consider that in A.D. 189, a great plague (thought to be smallpox) attacked the Roman Empire and 2,000 people died each day in Rome. Rome was in trouble at that time with internal strife, debased currency, encircling barbarians and demoralization of the populace. Those complex problems were made infinitely worse by 2,000 deaths daily. The labor supply was dwindling, military campaigns were stopped or hindered, day-to-day business operations were paralyzed, and production of food almost ceased. The weakened Empire was grinding to a halt.

MUSLIM ATTACK

How long would it take for any major city to be crippled if 2,000 people died each day? If there were a massive attack upon a major American city, could the hospitals care for the injured or infected? Who would handle all the paper work for their deaths? What would it do to the insurance companies? Are there enough funeral homes to handle the dead? Are there enough grave plots presently available? How long would it be before the labor force could no longer supply workers to replace the dead? Would there be enough experienced managers to train new workers, if workers could be found? What impact would those deaths have on the tax base? What would it do to the Social Security system?

What **would** follow a massive terrorist attack? Would law and order totally break down with looting and vandalism? Would stores close for the safety of the owners? If so, where would you get the supplies you need? If most stores closed, what would that do to our economy? Many financial advisors would tell you that a massive attack followed by a paralyzed economy would make the stock market plummet to the basement. What would that do to your retirement? Would the military take over police duties, and if so, how would that impact your daily life?

SOME QUESTIONS

There is no doubt that new, intrusive laws would be passed (or implemented) that would restrict our freedom of movement. There would be mandatory vaccination against smallpox and other infectious diseases. What if you think the shots would be far worse than the risk of getting the disease? What if you refused the shots? If a smallpox outbreak happens in your city, you will no doubt be quarantined. What about your travelling job? What about seeing your children in another city? Will you obey a law that restricts public meetings such as church services? If so, for how long?

Two of our major problems would be obtaining health care and eating. Where would the necessary nurses and physicians come from? What about hospital beds? How could we exist if only 30% of the farmers were no longer producing food? If politicians react as they have in the past to major disasters, they will freeze prices and wages and may even prohibit a person from changing jobs. Would you support a law that **requires** a man to stay in his present job? Well, what if he is a farmer, and if he doesn't farm, you won't eat? Would you support that law under that condition? How firm are your convictions when it affects the feeding of your family?

These questions must be faced now; however, our leaders

give no indication that they are being considered, and some will question my loyalty for asking the questions! Patriotic Americans will ask some questions and demand answers from the people whose salary they pay. Keep in mind that we are the masters, and the politicians and bureaucrats are the servants!

TROUBLE AHEAD

We are facing turbulent times while government officials are doing things to make us "feel good," such as providing military and "security" people at the airports. Airport security people are goosing little old ladies from Iowa, making grown men drop their pants, etc., while people frequently pass through security into planes with guns, knives, etc. That does **not** make me feel good, warm, or cozy.

Plagues have always influenced human lives in more ways than putting incompetent leaders in power, making certain jobs available, and impacting the economy. The constant threat of death, misery, fear, and pain changed people, not only conditions.

We can expect the divorce rate to soar even higher, as uninfected mates leave their infected spouses. To whom will judges give the children of those couples—the infected or uninfected mate? Euthanasia and suicide will become acceptable, even legal as the death rate climbs. Some political conservatives will notice the economic foundations cracking under the financial strain of millions of patients and will decide that it is a person's right to do what he wants with his or her body, without state interference. Euthanasia, suicide, and abortion (the unholy trinity) will become respectable and legal. Euthanasia and suicide will become more desirable for some people as the hope for a vaccine and cure becomes more and more distant. People will lose hope, and in despair will end their lives as the HIV-infected "couple" who tied themselves together with a silk rope and jumped to their deaths from the 35th floor of an office building. Similar events happened in every plague.

Since events of history have given us an indication how U.S. civilians, military, and politicians will react in a time of mass destruction, it is certain that Muslims will also pay a price as thoughtless and wicked people see them as "the enemy." Innocent and patriotic Muslims will be identified with the terrorists, and since they are available, when terrorists are not, a pound of flesh will be exacted from them. I expect a massive overreaction to the next terrorist attack upon the U.S. Every Muslim will have a target on his back; unprincipled politicians will declare them fair game to strike back at the enemy. That's another reason why Muslims should go to extremes to explain their disagreement, disapproval, disgust, and disassociation with all terrorist activity. It may help protect them later.

REACTION IN LONDON

People are basically the same everywhere in every age, so I want to close this chapter with how authorities reacted to the London plague.[14] It is most informative and interesting. It is worth noting that the London officials based their actions on law. When King James I came to the throne during a plague in 1603, the Parliament took action giving city officials authority to deal with the plague. When the plague sneaked into London in 1665, the officials of London took action. Will we see the same laws in America?

London officials appointed one or more "examiners" to inquire as to the status of every home in the parish. An examiner was to keep a list of the homes where plague victims lived, and those houses were to be "shut up" by the constable. If a man refused to become an "examiner" because of his family, job, fear, etc., he was to be imprisoned until he was convinced to do the work. "Watchmen" were to be appointed to watch every house where there was infection! There was to be a watchman for the day and one for the evening, and they were to keep anyone from entering or leaving the house. Any such person attempting to enter or leave was to be "severely punished."

"Searchers" were women who were appointed to identify the dead and ascertain whether they died of plague or some other disease. Such women were forbidden by law to "keep any shop or stall, or be employed as a laundress, or in any other common employment whatsoever." But what if she had to work or was fearful of examining the dead? Too bad. Since some of the searchers were not very effective and the disease continued to spread, "chirurgeons" were appointed to provide a more precise accounting. "Chirurgeon" is an archaic word for surgeon. Some of those surgeons worked in the "pest house" or hospital for those with contagious diseases, while others were independent physicians. They were to be paid from the personal effects of those they examined! If that did not prove profitable, the city would pay the cost.

Citizens were required to report to the examiner any member of the family who showed signs of infection, and it had to be done within two hours! Any infected person was to be sequestered for 30 days following the first signs of plague. All burials were to take place either before sunrise or after sunset, and no friend or neighbor could accompany the burial under threat of imprisonment. There could be no funeral in the church during this time, no matter what was the cause of death. Each house where a person was infected was to be marked with a 12 inch red cross in the middle of the door over which these words were to be written: "Lord, have mercy upon us." All those who came in contact with the dead were to carry, in public, a red rod at least 3 feet in length in their hands. Nor could they go into any house but their own except on official plague duties.

HOW WILL WE REACT?

If America experiences à massive biological attack, look for similar laws to be passed. There will be limitations on personal liberty, but hopefully lawmakers will think these issues through, debate them, and implement only those most necessary.

Reasonable people will argue that, in times of emergency, extreme measures must be taken for everyone's good; however, there is always a problem. When extreme measures are taken "for the present time," some of them persist after the danger is past. There are many examples of that in our history. So ask questions and expect answers from the authorities.

In 1878, a deadly plague started along the Gulf Coast of the U.S., almost wiping out some towns. It caused horror and fear wherever it hit. It slowly worked its way up the Mississippi River to New Orleans, killing the poor and prosperous, ignorant and intelligent, and city-folk and country-folk alike. Its name was whispered in awe: yellow fever.

New Orleans in 1878 was a prosperous, proud, and prissy city. Cotton was king, food was an obsession, dueling was common, and gambling was rampant. The wealthy lived in opulent, antebellum homes nestled along the Mississippi. Everyone knew that yellow fever was working its way north along the river, and everyone knew it was deadly; however, New Orleans officials and media told everyone not to worry. Things would be all right. They wanted to believe that but had no reason to believe it. When the fever hit New Orleans, it was the worst plague to lash across the face of the city in its history. More than half of the inhabitants were killed and in fact, the city lost its charter and was not an official city until 14 years later. Public officials dallied, dawdled, delayed, and denied the danger thinking they were too smart, sophisticated, and special for such a thing to happen to them. It happened. They refused to take the warning seriously and paid for it.

New Orleans may be a prototype of America when massive terrorism smacks us again. We know further attacks are coming and are reacting in ineffective, even silly ways. Federal officials are making plans for their survival, but there is little concern about the mass of citizens. We must realize that we are not too smart, sophisticated, and special that such a thing could never happen here. It already has, and plans are being made inside the Trojan Horse to see that further devastating attacks take place.

We must react as concerned, committed, and compassionate Christians, not as people have reacted in past times of distress, disease, and death.

1. Hans Zinsser, *Rats, Lice and History,* Boston: Brown and Co., 1935, p. 121.

2. Daniel Defoe, *A Journal of the Plague Years.* London, Everyman's Library, 1908, p. 7.

3. Ibid., pp. 29-30.

4. Ibid., 31.

5. Ibid., 32.

6. Ibid., 38.

7. William McNeill, *Plagues and People,* Garden City, NY: Anchor Press/ Doubleday, 1976, p.121.

8. Defoe, p.18.

9. Defoe, p. 198.

10. J. L. Cloudsley-Thompson, *Insects and History,* New York: St. Martin's Press, 1976, 68.

11. Ibid., 69.

12. Ibid., 25.

13. Ibid., 25.

14. Defoe, pp. 43-48.

Chapter Fourteen

The Message, I

A Watchdog That Will Bark and Bite!

A message must be sent to the terrorists worldwide, and the message must be clear, unambiguous, loud, and uncompromising: The U.S. will not be bullied or permit its citizens to be killed and others to be threatened into seclusion by any terrorist state, cultic religion, or extremist hate group.

The PLO, like al-Qaeda, Hamas, etc., is a terrorist organization and Arafat (not just another pretty face) is a forked-tongued terrorist. He and his followers are determined to force Israel into the sea. I think Arafat and the PLO should be "forced into the sea." The PLO and other extremist organizations have exploded bombs in Tel Aviv and Jerusalem killing many innocent civilians. The U.S. Government is funding both Israel (three billion per year!) **and** the PLO! We are idiots, fools, knaves, and dupes.

ISRAELI TERRORISTS

Terrorists are terrorists whatever their nationality, religion, race, or motives. There are no good terrorists and bad terrorists. They are all bad. How can anyone disagree with that statement? But people do, making exceptions for some. The present leader of Israel, Ariel Sharon, has a long history of terrorism going back to the early 1950s. Informed and indignant people around the world call him the "Butcher of Beirut." As a young man, he joined the underground military group known as "Haganah" in pre-state days and participated in many terrorist attacks killing many innocent people, including women and children.

It is a fact that the early leaders of Israel were dedicated terrorists: David Ben Gurion, Israel's first prime minister, personally

227

approved the terrorist bombing of the prestigious King David Hotel in Jerusalem on July 22, 1946, killing 92 Arab, British, and Jewish civilians. Fifty-eight were injured. Menachan Begin said that three warning phone calls were made just before the bomb exploded; however, he quoted a British official saying, "We don't take orders from Jews." Ben Gurion, Begin, and other Jewish leaders were terrorists, but it is not polite to say so. Yes, it is very true that one man's terrorist is another man's freedom fighter, but also keep in mind that the victors of war always write the histories. Question: Is one's support for Israel an excuse for dishonesty?

NEW SPEECH FOR BUSH

President Bush should make another speech (which he will not make) about terrorism, saying: "My fellow Americans, as of today, this nation will follow a new foreign policy that will solve the problem of terrorism. We will return to our roots and follow the wise advice of our Founding Fathers. We will no longer get entangled in foreign alliances. We will no longer meddle in the affairs of other nations nor consider ourselves the policeman of the world. We will always consider first our national interests. We will not presume that we know best for other countries. What may be "best" for us may not be best for them.

"Since we have been attacked, we have aggressively gone after those responsible. We will not try to topple governments and set up democracies; however, we will always encourage liberty everywhere. We will not carpet-bomb cities filled with innocent civilians. We do not believe 'total war' is morally right or militarily justified. But be assured those culpable individuals will be punished as a deterrent to others.

"Americans don't hate Muslims or anyone else since it is wrong and unproductive to hate; however, we will no longer plead with Muslims, at home and abroad, to 'love us.' We will no longer express guilt and self-loathing. Federal officials will no longer try to prove that Americans are not racists. It is up to Muslims to prove they are not terrorists!

"Furthermore, as of today, we have shut the welfare window. No more foreign aid to any nation. We may decide in the future that it **is** in our best interest to help some nation, but it will be as unusual as snow in July.

228

"We will also start bringing our troops home from all over the world. They will be sent to foreign nations only in event of declared war or in the interests of the U.S. This is not isolationism but it is an "America First" policy. Any other policy is insane.

"As to the Middle East, I and my advisors don't know what is best! The U.S. has vast disagreements with both the Israelis and the Palestinians. They both have good arguments for their positions, but they are both uncivilized, unreliable, and undemocratic. They must settle their own affairs, with or without the assistance of surrounding nations. Basically I am saying, 'You are both right and wrong.' I pray to the God of the Bible that they will solve their differences, but **they will do so without U.S. assistance.**

"As to our reliance on Middle East oil, we have already started drilling in Alaska, the Gulf of Mexico, and off the coast of California and will immediately expand the mining of our vast coal supplies. We will try to be sensitive to the environment; however, I believe that people are more precious than plants or bugs or snakes or fish or spotted owls. Our drilling equipment may cause a caribou here and there to abort her young or a bear may singe its rear end on our pipeline, but we will live with those tragedies. American oil will flow. And, of course, we will still buy oil from South America and even Middle East nations; however, we will not buy oil from states that support terrorists. They can pour their excess oil over their pancakes each morning for all I care. Or drink it! I will no longer pretend that terrorists are gracious gentlemen, nor will I shake their hands as I smile like an idiot.

"We will encourage American entrepreneurs by tax incentives and other measures to pursue the development of alternative fuels.

"We have some difficult days ahead that will require an adjustment by all of us. But I see a bright future after a few years of sacrifice. I promise to keep you informed since I work for you. You pay my salary as you do all Federal employees.

"I take my oath seriously; therefore, I promise that any further bill that crosses my desk will meet five criteria to qualify for my signature: It must be constitutional. It must be necessary. We must be able to afford the proposed law. It must not expand government and limit individual liberty. The last criterion is that it must not undermine the family, decency, and general morality. If a bill does not pass those five criteria, it will not get my signature.

"No doubt there are knees jerking all across America (left ones, of course) and those people can cast their vote against me and these policies in the next election. Until then, learn to live with it. I am your President, and I will do as I have promised. And may the God of the Bible bless America! Good night."

NO EXCUSE FOR TERROR

Yes, I think that might defuse Muslim terrorists throughout the world, and cause an epidemic of cardiac arrests among the entertainment industry, leftist politicians, and top honchos of the ACLU, Americans United for Separation of Church and State, etc. Muslim terrorists would have no justifiable reason to hate America. And it would be the right thing to do! Maybe President Bush would at least consider doing some of the above, if he received a few thousand notes or calls to this effect.

If decisive action is not taken soon by our public officials, I believe America's rivers and streets will run with blood. It is a fact: our government policies have influenced irrational people to do irrational things. (But that is no excuse for terror!)

On the day after Pearl Harbor, former President Herbert Hoover wrote to friends: "You and I know that this continuous putting pins in rattlesnakes finally got this country bitten." Friends, America has been bitten and while in the next years, we must "kill some rattlesnakes," we must also stop feeding the rattlesnakes.

Because the terrorist attacks on America have been so shocking, rendering us angry and helpless, some reputable, reasonable, and responsible people have made incredible statements. It seems "the end justifies the means," and "after all, you can't make an omelet without breaking some eggs." Much of the reaction to the September 11 attack has been irrational and at times, crazy. Even the liberals have lost their minds. *Newsweek* columnist Jonathan Alter wrote, "even a liberal can find his thoughts turning to...torture."[1] The column, titled "Time to Think About Torture," is breathtaking. It caused my knee to jerk incessantly. Right one of course. **Liberals** discussing the possibility of using torture to get information from suspects! Alter said that liberals approached him and whispered, "I agree with you." Alter said he did not agree with torture, but was only writing about it. I thought torture went out 50 years ago when cops in Chicago and New York had their rubber hoses (confession-makers) taken from them.

COMPASSIONATE CONSERVATIVES

But it gets worse. On the *CNN* program "Crossfire," neoconservative Tucker Carlson said: "Torture is bad. Keep in mind, some things are worse. And under certain circumstances, it may be the lesser of two evils. Because some evils are pretty evil." Now, even conservatives are suggesting torture! Has some nefarious secret weapon used against us fried all the brains?

Even the FBI, frustrated with suspects who have remained silent, has considered using truth drugs or sending suspects to countries that are not bound by such niceties as forbidding torture. So ship the suspects to Israel or the Philippines or Argentina where they are less principled in dealing with suspects. After all, the chains of the Constitution bind down American lawmen. "We're into this thing for 35 days and nobody is talking. Frustration has begun to appear," a senior FBI official told *The Washington Post.*

On Sept. 13, on *Fox* television channel, Bill O'Reilly said: "If the Taliban government of Afghanistan does not cooperate, then we will damage that government with air power, probably. All right? We will blast them, because..." Sam Husseini, Institute for Public Accuracy asked: "Who will you kill in the process?" O'Reilly: "Doesn't make any difference."

Senator Zell Miller: "I say, bomb the hell out of them. If there's collateral damage, so be it. They certainly found our civilians to be expendable."

Chris Weinkopf of the *Daily News*, in an article in *Frontpage*: "the tactical use of nuclear weapons could provide the key to such a victory [over radical Islam]."

Steve Dunleavy of the *New York Post* said, "As for cities or countries that host these worms, bomb them into basketball courts."

And here is *National Review* editor Rich Lowry: "If we flatten part of Damascus or Tehran or whatever it takes, that is part of the solution."

Or John Derbyshire, writing in *National Review Online*: "Justice must go by the board for a while, as it did when we firebombed German and Japanese cities, incinerating helpless babies and old folk who wished us no harm."

DOES WAR EXCUSE EVIL?

While Americans demand that terrorists be caught, convicted, then executed, we do not want to be the proponents of government terror. All Federal officials take an oath to support and defend the Constitution, and nowhere is it suggested that they can abrogate that oath because of the circumstances. "But," we are told, "don't you understand that we are at war. Thousands of Americans have been killed." True, but hundreds of thousands of Americans were killed defending our Constitutional rights to live free. Must we live with a **little** U.S. authorized terror to stop terrorism? How much terror can we justify? How much does the Constitution justify? And if the U.S. becomes tyrannical, how are we much different from the terrorists? Are you satisfied to be less evil than the enemy? Is our difference simply one of degree? Or of kind?

The sacrifice others have made in our history requires that we maintain a free nation where we can disagree without shooting each other. We don't have to like each other, but we can respect opinions of others and defend their right to have them. After all, it is not unconstitutional, unreasonable, or un-American to be wrong or even stupid! However, we will not remain free if we begin to act like the terrorists and terrorist-supporting nations we abhor!

It is about here that I should quote Benjamin Franklin's famous statement: "They that can give up essential liberty to obtain a little temporary safety deserve neither liberty or safety."[2] He was right on target. We are fools if we don't look at the big picture. At this point I think what Alexander Hamilton wrote is appropriate: "The violent destruction of life and property incident to war–the continual effort and alarm attendant on a state of continual danger–will compel nations most attached to liberty to resort, for repose and safety, to institutions which have a tendency to destroy their civil and political rights. To be more safe, they at length become willing to run the risk of being less free."[3] Hamilton's statement requires a second reading! It is as if he were looking at our present situation.

In late July of 2002, the media was full of Bush's plan to reorganize the Federal Government to make it more effective in the war on terror. This plan was in the feeble minds of those not chained to the Constitution for many months even before the Muslim attacks upon us. It means more power for an expanded government and it means less freedom for citizens. One of the most dangerous parts of the plan is to nullify the 1878 *posse comitatus* act that basically prohibits the military from exercising police powers over U.S. citizens. Let me remind you that the military has been trained to kill, not investigate, arrest, and detain.

SOME VERY DUMB THINGS

Our government has done some very dumb things since September 11. It is incredible that after the September 11 attack on America, our government permitted 14 Algerians, 14 Syrians, and 14 Iranians to enter the U.S for dubious purposes. The 14 Syrians and the 14 Algerians came for flight training in Texas! Need I remind you that Syria is on the U.S. list of recognized terrorist states and Algeria has been a hotbed for terrorists for more than 25 years?

Texas Immigration and Naturalization Service officials were concerned enough to contact the FBI, but the Feds decided not to pursue the matter! The Syrians and Algerians enrolled in flight schools in Tyler and Fort Worth. Some of the World Trade and Pentagon terrorists were trained in Florida schools. *WorldNetDaily* reported that six Iranian nationals also entered the U.S. at the Dallas-Fort Worth airport to attend a martial arts tournament, and eight Iranians were also admitted about this time to attend a building materials competition.[4]

You might think that these men will be observed very carefully and will be tracked by computers but not so. There is no system available to accomplish that task! Authorities don't know if the men are doing what they said they would do nor will they know if they overstay their visas! I think the world has gone mad or is it only incompetence by Federal officials? Or is it both?

Yes, all those young men may be completely innocent. They may even be lovers of America, but a reasonable, sane person would think that they **could** be terrorists. In the interests of our safety, don't you think that possibility should be considered? In fact, is it not dereliction of duty to fail in that regard?

MUSLIM ATTACKS

We know that Middle East terrorists have already attacked

the U.S. many times before and have admitted there will be further attacks, so why not take them at their word? After all, they may be dastardly killers, but that doesn't mean they can't occasionally tell the truth.

Following are some of the attacks Muslim terrorists have made upon our nation and our response:

- There was the 1993 World Trade Center bombing that killed six and injured about 1,000 people. You may remember that President Clinton promised that those responsible would be pursued into their darken dens and would be punished. It didn't happen.

- After the 1995 bombing in Saudi Arabia which killed five U.S. military personnel, Clinton promised that those responsible would be hunted down and punished. It didn't happen.

- Then there was the Khobar Towers bombing in 1996 in Saudi Arabia which killed 19 and injured 200 U.S. military personnel; Clinton again promised that those responsible would be hunted down and punished. It didn't happen. So are you beginning to see a pathetic pattern?

- In 1998, U.S. embassies in Africa were bombed, killing 224 and injuring about 5,000 people. Yet again, Clinton promised that those responsible would be punished. And yet again, it didn't happen. But it gets worse and worse.

- After the bombing of the USS Cole in 2000, which killed 17 and injured 39 U.S. sailors, Clinton promised that those terrorists would be pursued and prosecuted. And surprise, surprise, surprise, it didn't happen. By this time, the terrorists were convinced that the U.S. was a "paper tiger" without claws and fangs.

Some of us think that if those cases had been followed up and the killers brought to justice, we might not have lost over 3,000 innocent people on September 11. However, our government officials were busy doing other things.

The following statement and question, pregnant with truth, were on a Philadelphia radio call-in show: "There are two men, both extremely wealthy. One develops relatively cheap software and gives billions of dollars to charity. The other sponsors terrorism. That being the case, why is it that the Clinton Administration spent more money chasing down Bill Gates over the past eight years than Osama bin Laden?" That is a great question!

HOME GROWN TERRORISTS

Not only did the U.S. Government fail to follow up on Middle East terrorists, but our officials also have looked upon other terrorists as being a nuisance–but somewhat benign. We have had terrorists operating in the U.S. for many years. They are called animal rights and environmental terrorists. Wonder why they are being handled with kid gloves rather than an iron fist?

The Earth Liberation Front, the Animal Liberation Front, EarthFirst, etc., declared war against the free market system and individual businessmen. With their terrorism, they have cost many loggers their jobs and increased the cost of lumber. They painted a target on logging and tree farms, university laboratories, the fur business, and various corporations. Like Muslim terrorists they are from different nations, have no membership lists, and operate through small dedicated, fanatical cells. They give explicit instructions on how to terrorize their opposition (free enterprise) and have admitted committing arson, spiking trees, rioting, etc. These fanatics boast about the havoc they have wrought and the expense they have cost the "enemy."

Can someone tell me why almost no one has gone to prison for these crimes and why the media are silent about their crusade? Of course, it is because they are leftists. When Communism fell (or maybe stumbled), the Communists and socialists ended up in the green movement, or Watermelon Brigade: green on the outside and red on the inside. It is way past time to get serious about all terrorists, starting with the homegrown variety then to the Muslims.

CLOSE OUR BORDERS

There is now evidence that the Oklahoma City bombing had a Middle East connection but the Federal authorities have refused to pursue the connection. After all, **everyone** knows two right-wing, white boys carried off the bombing by themselves!

While we must never give solace to the terrorists nor provide them with any justification, they have been able to perpetrate their monstrous deeds because of the political climate in the U.S. It's time to close our borders and check out all Muslims living in our country. Many will be found to be patriotic Americans, so lawmen should apologize for any inconvenience or embarrassment, then proceed to those who are guilty. The Trojan Horse is full of them!

Now, I'm sure many are assuming that I hate people other than white Americans, but that is an assumption without any foundation. One of my precious daughters-in-law is Asian, so I have biracial grandchildren; however, she got here legally! She had to stand in lines, fill out forms, wait, stand in more lines, and wait some more! She recently received her U.S. citizenship and said, "I don't have to stand in any more lines." She has learned English and has melted into the melting pot.

I believe America should welcome people to our shores. It is a land of opportunity, freedom, etc. However, we are fools to permit the future to resemble the past and be flooded with further aliens. No nation is secure if its borders are porous. In recent years, the U.S. borders have leaked like a sieve.

COMMON SENSE

One of the most vacuous arguments I have heard in the last 25 years is that illegal aliens in the U.S. (up to 11 million, yes, eleven million!) have some protected rights in America: Taxpayers are responsible to educate them and their children! That they have a "right" to free medical treatment! That we must be very careful not to abuse or bruise their civil rights–even though they are lawbreakers! Such people, once it is proved that they are illegal, should be fingerprinted and returned to the border and told that if they return illegally, they will go to prison. No ifs, no ands, no buts.

Some of us can remember when President Eisenhower was elected in 1952 that he expelled all illegal aliens under a program known as Operation Wetback! There was very little objection; after all, those people had illegally entered our nation. Pat Buchanan opined in a column, "Imagine the reaction of the Washington establishment if, tomorrow, George W. Bush announced to the nation he was launching Operation Wetback II.[5] The politically correct fools will gasp and call for Pat and me to be drawn and quartered. It's interesting that liberals have more concern for the criminals than for those of us who try to obey the laws. It has nothing to do with their culture, color, education, religion, or politics. It has to do with law and common sense.

IMMIGRANT SENSITIVITY

Even so, I do believe strongly that if people are going to immigrate to America, they should be required to guarantee that they will not become dependent on taxpayers; they should learn our language, they should be assimilated into our society, at least by the second generation. After all, that's what the Germans, Irish, Italians, Jews, and others did. Of course each major city has its Chinatown, but those areas were formed by masses of people who came to do the "grunt" work for our first railroads. Upon their arrival they were without funds, friends, or family, and it was natural and desirable for them to congregate in one area. Future generations usually were absorbed into the melting pot. Few Muslims are "melting," and many are waiting for a time to strike.

New immigrants must understand that they are coming to America, and it is basically a "Christianized" nation. It has never been "Christian," since only a person can become a Christian through faith in Christ. They can not expect us to be supersensitive to their mores, customs, religion, etc. Since we made room for them, they should be sensitive to us and not antagonize us. And it would help if they showed a little gratitude.

Immigrants need to understand that our money screams our affirmation: "In God we trust." Now that is not some god of eastern religions nor is it the main god worshiped in Arabia during the sixth century known as Allah. It is the God of the Bible, whom our earliest settlers believed in and followed. This nation was built and defended by people who wanted it to remain "American" and "Christianized." Not African, Hispanic or Arabic nor Hindu, Buddhist, or Muslim.

PURPOSE FOR COMING

Just to set the record straight after so many years of distortion about religion and the church in American's past: America was founded upon the premise that its citizens would be Christians adhering to Biblical principles. Yes, I know, we have come a long way from that, but people look at me like a calf looking at a new gate when I speak about America's historic Christian roots.

In the *Mayflower Compact*, said to be America's birth certificate, it is clear that the original founders thought they were planting a "Christian" nation. They wrote, "Having undertaken for the Glory of God advancement of the Christian Faith and honor of our King and country...." Note that it was not some fuzzy, ambiguous god somewhere, but the God of the Christian faith.

This line of thinking continued in that first generation of leaders as expressed in the *New England Confederation* which affirmed: "We all came into these parts of America with one and the same end, namely, to advance the Kingdom of the Lord Jesus Christ." Can it be any clearer? After all, the people writing were first generation Americans. They should know their purpose for coming!

Even **after** the U.S. Constitution was passed, some states insisted that their lawmakers be Christian! In Maryland, the state constitution, as late as 1864, required office seekers to have a "belief in the Christian religion, or of the existence of God, and in a future state of rewards and punishments." In New Hampshire there was a requirement of senators and representatives as late as 1877 that they be of the "Protestant religion." Gasp!

PURPOSE OF FIRST AMENDMENT

We are told that the First Amendment forbids preferring one religion over another, but that is not true. Supreme Court Justice Joseph Story was a leading jurist who served on the U.S. Supreme Court from 1811 to 1845. Story was a Unitarian and he wrote in his *Commentaries on the Constitution:* "The real object of the (first) amendment was not to countenance, much less to advance, Mahometanism [Islam], or Judaism, or infidelity, by prostrating Christianity; but to exclude all rivalry among Christian sects, and to prevent any national ecclesiastical establishment which should give to a hierarchy the exclusive patronage of the national government." Story was saying that the purpose of the First Amendment was not to equate Christianity and other religions, but to exclude the establishment of a national church, i.e., Baptist, Methodist, Congregational, etc. Of course, the enemies of Christ and common sense have twisted that fact like a pretzel until it is now illegal to pray and to read the Bible in school, to place a nativity scene on public property, and other ridiculous prohibitions.

Justice Story further commented on this issue about equating all religions in 1833: "At the time of the adoption of the Constitution...[an] attempt to level all religions and to make it a matter of state policy to hold all in utter indifference, would have created... universal indignation."[6]

When foreigners visit national monuments, they can see numerous references to the God of the Bible and what our founders believed.

STRENGTH IN UNITY

Many states had laws that imprisoned atheists! No, I don't think that was right, and if I had been a legislator, I would have voted against it, even fought it, not because I'm an atheist, but because it is none of the government's business what one believes.

I do believe that some immigration is acceptable although I would stop it for a year or so, but people who want to blend with our culture should have priority. We want a cultural and national melting pot, not a salad bowl. However, there should be restrictions and requirements for immigrants. I think we should not permit anyone to become a citizen unless he or she can sing **in English** all the verses of "America, the Beautiful" and whistle the National Anthem at the same time–with a mouthful of saltine crackers! Well, maybe not quiet that extreme, but almost!

The proponents of the salad bowl theory tell us that one culture or religion is just as good as another. The 300-member, stone age culture with all its barbarism, brutality, and backwardness is just as viable as our modern, urbane, sophisticated society with elevators, airplanes, automobiles, hospitals, MRI machines, computers, etc. Likewise, the voodoo cultures practicing witchcraft, shamanism, demonism, pantheism, etc., are as acceptable and on par with Christianity! "After all," we are told, "there is strength in diversity." However, history proves the opposite: There is strength in unity!

IMMIGRANTS CAN LEAVE

Black Muslims, Sunni Muslims, Hindus, and others should take off their robes and turbans and assimilate as many are doing. We must stop calling people Arab-Americans, Afro-Americans, Jewish-Americans, etc. Why not simply be called "Americans"? It doesn't mean one cannot appreciate some of the good things that were left in the old country, but if one is in a new country, he should love it and never be ashamed to profess it.

Many Muslims have identified with the terrorists and have told journalists and pollsters that Americans are anti-Muslim! Well, for goodness sake, what did they expect? Are Americans expected to be pro-Muslim when they, for the most part, don't speak our language, dress in sixth-century, desert clothing, treat women like possessions, and seem to look for opportunities to criticize the nation that has opened its arms to them? They seem to be determined to change America to be like the country they left!

I am tired of immigrates who demand that we be so sensitive to their feelings when they don't give a flip about ours. We have our own language, lifestyle, culture, music (such as it is), and I am weary of foreigners who enjoy all the many benefits of our nation and are not sensitive to our feelings. In the name of multiculturalism and non-discrimination, we opened our collective arms and invited anyone and everyone to our shores with no questions asked and no obligations required. We have been fools and have watched our enemy drag a Trojan Horse into our nation.

If immigrants are offended when I sing patriotic songs, fly the American flag, and pray to Christ, then tough luck. This is a big world so they can find someplace else to live. There is plenty of empty space on the Arabian Desert!

NATIONAL IDENTITY

I think my grandchildren have a right to live in a nation similar to what I grew up in. I don't want to see our culture changed to that of the sixth or seventh-century Arabian Desert. It is not unreasonable to expect America to reflect the America I grew up in! I would like a return to the relative innocence of the 1950s; however, that won't happen. But we can have a return to Bible truth practiced by Christians, and impact society by walk and talk, not terror. If Christians are the salt and light Christ told us to be, we will make a difference. We will once again believe that there is a difference in right and wrong, and we have a moral responsibility to choose the right. We will discriminate in that we will make value judgments about cars, music, television shows, politics, and even religion.

With the massive increase in legal and illegal immigration, we are going to lose our national identity. Some think that is not bad. I'm **not** one of them. People from Europe immigrating to the

U.S. are much easier to assimilate than those from Latin American, African, and Middle Eastern nations. And as people come and hold loyalty to former homelands, it erodes our society. It weakens our sovereignty. If we have to assimilate a million new Americans here, do you think it would be easier to assimilate a million British or a million Zulus?

CUT OUT THE INFECTION

How can we win the war on terrorism when we don't police our borders, don't vigorously prosecute domestic terrorists, don't remove those visitors who overstay their visas, don't provide security for transported missiles or dangerous materiel, etc.?

Case in point of government failure: In November, the Energy Department's Inspector General disclosed that government records do not document the location of "substantial" amounts of plutonium and uranium that U.S. officials lent to universities, hospitals, and private companies! It is not known whether these dangerous materials were stolen or simply have been lost. Reading the Energy Department report is depressing! The bookkeeping was incredibly sloppy. Could we say criminal?[7]

President Bush could hire me to fire all the incompetent, inept, and inane bureaucrats in the Federal Government. All the whining, whimpering, and weeping of bleating hearts would not move me since I don't need the job and am not in a popularity contest.

I suggest that we put a moratorium on all immigration (see next chapter) for at least a year; multiply our efforts to stop illegal aliens at our borders; vigorously pursue foreigners with expired visas (then send them packing); and generally enforce the laws to protect America. At the same time, we must stop getting involved in every barroom brawl around the world, cut all foreign aid, and treat Jews and Muslims equally. After all we will never get rid of the symptoms (terror) unless we cut out the infection! Send out a message that this "watchdog" will not only bark but will bite the rear end off any that threaten our safety.

START PROFILING TODAY

Should we profile people in our efforts of apprehending terrorists? The liberal mantra is that we must never offend anyone, especially fanatics who want to kill us! And the leftists in the media and academia tell us to keep on strip-searching 80-year-old ladies, eight-year-old kids, and making congressmen and others take off their pants at airports! Not me. It will mean jail time for this Georgia cracker!

Let's think about profiling. If there were a string of killings done by a man that matches my description, should I be offended if I am stopped and checked out by police looking for the killer? No, I will answer their questions, prove my identity, and move on hoping they catch the killer.

If a black man robs a bank, killing three people, and drives off in a red Ferrari, it is not unjust, unfair, or unreasonable to stop every black man in a red Ferrari. It amazes me that any person can say otherwise, without bursting out in belly-bobbing laughter. Now, if the police stop all Blacks driving expensive cars, then I would come to their defense. In such a case, probable guilt is assumed against a whole race of people, and that is not right.

Young Middle Eastern men have committed horrendous terror so if those having the same profile are stopped and questioned, they should realize that is the price to pay. Airport officials should treat them kindly (as they should everyone), become satisfied that the men in question are innocent citizens, then apologize to them and even give them first class seats on their next flight if possible. That's profiling and it's good sense.

REMINDERS

Let me remind you that in 1979 when the U.S. embassy in Iran was taken over and our people were taken hostage, it was not done by Christian high school students from Dallas, Elvis and his buddies, or a senior citizens' group from Lakeland. It was done by Muslim male extremists, mostly between the ages of 17 and 40.

In 1983, when the U.S. Marine barracks in Beirut were blown up, it was not done by a pizza delivery boy; crazed feminists angry that their biological clock keeps ticking; or Geraldo Rivera making up for a slow news day. It was done by Muslim male extremists, mostly between the ages of 17 and 40.

In 1988, Pan Am Flight 103 was not bombed by the Tooth Fairy; Madonna, wearing only her underclothes; or Bobby Knight's basketball squad but by Muslim male extremists, mostly between the ages of 17 and 40.

In 1998, the U.S. embassies in Kenya and Tanzania were not bombed by Mr. Rogers; Jerry Falwell and his singing group from Liberty University; or the right-wingers at *Fox* television. It was done by Muslim male extremists, mostly between the ages of 17 and 40.

On September 11, the four airliners were not hijacked and destroyed by Bugs Bunny, Wiley E. Coyote, Daffy Duck, and Elmer Fudd; or Dr. James Dobson and his clan from Colorado Springs. It was done by Muslim male extremists, mostly between the ages of 17 and 40.

Now, let me write very slowly so television addicts can understand: do you see a pattern that is beginning to develop? Is it unreasonable to expect that the next terrorist attack will be carried out by Muslim male extremists, mostly between the ages of 17 and 40? So, do you think it reasonable to check out all men in that category? If not, why not?

Case in point: Suppose you were waiting to board a plane and at the last minute in walk two groups of three men. One group consists of Baptist preachers and the other group is made up of Middle Eastern men between the ages of 17 and 40. There is time to search only one group (a second time) so which group do you want searched? All but insane bigots will choose the Middle East men! How can I justify that when I would not support stopping all Blacks driving expensive cars after a bank robbery? Because all bank robbers are not black. We must stop playing "Let's stop the terrorists" game and get serious. Start the profiling today because lives are at stake.

NOT PROFILING COST LIVES

In fact, lives have already been lost because of reluctance to look realistically at the world of terror. There were witnesses who reported that the Washington area snipers were "dark skinned," "Hispanic," and a "black" man; so wouldn't most sensible people start looking for men who fit that general description? No, not in the world of super-sensitivity whenever race is involved. Montgomery County Police Chief Charles Moose didn't want to release a composite sketch of the suspects because he didn't want to "paint some group." So he painted all **white** men, but then we are also a group! The problem is we are not a recognized minority. On October 3 the two black snipers were stopped by Washington, D.C. police but were released because D.C. Police Chief Charles Ramsey said, "We were looking for a white van with white people." There was zero information to suggest that the snipers were white and at least three eyewitnesses who identified them as other than white! It is possible, even probable, that all deaths after October 3 could have been avoided had Moose used common sense and profiling to do his job. Did he think he was Public Relations Director for the NAACP instead of a law enforcement officer? If the two snipers had not basically surrendered (by boasting about the Alabama murder) Moose would still be looking for an angry white male. We do know that cops were told to search only vehicles driven by white males. Sounds like profiling to me.

Chief Moose has been praised profusely by almost everyone; however, a *WorldNetDaily* column (11-8-02), said praising Moose was rewarding and validating incompetence. That it does, whatever the color. I say to Moose, Ashcroft, Bush, et al., to stop assuming loyal Americans are the bad guys and go after the crooks and use common sense to put them away.

This is my idealistic message for our people and leaders. Some of these principles will be implemented, but most will not. They will not because politicians are not principled people and that is one reason we must never put our trust in politicians. Our confidence is in Christ alone, and when politicians make a decision that is principled, we thank God and move on. And, by the way, watch out for the Trojan Horse. It is full of the enemy!

1. Jonathan Alter, Newsweek magazine, 11-5-01.

2. Benjamin Franklin, *Historical Review of Pennsylvania, 1759.*

3. *Federalist,* number 8.

4. *WorldNetDaily,* 10-16-01.

5. Pat Buchanan, *WorldNetDaily,* 1-11-02.

6. *Constitutional History* (New York: Harper Torchbooks, 1965, p. 133.

7. Walter Pincus, *Washington Post,* 11-6-01.

Chapter Fifteen

The Message, II

America First, Last and Always

America, first, last and always! Liberals will scream bigotry but most sane, sensitive, and sincere Americans believe that we don't have to apologize for putting our national interests first and wanting to keep America, America! It does not mean that we think we are better or superior to anyone else, nor does it mean that we wish anyone else ill. It simply means that we like what we have here, although we would like to remove the crime, hatred, perversion, abortion, etc., but it would be abnormal if we did not want America to continue to be America. No one suggests that we are perfect or close to it, but I prefer America to any place I have been. What is wrong with that? Let me prompt your answer: nothing is wrong with it.

We identify with America as we identify with our family. I don't identify with your family but with mine. I don't wish you ill will or failure. I just identify with my family. Because, well, because it is my family. As with a family, so with a nation. If that were not true, then there would be no nations. But then, maybe that's exactly what the globalists want. One massive "family" in one big world with no boundary lines. And of course, all cultures would be equal.

KEEP AMERICA AMERICAN

President Calvin Coolidge obviously agreed with my position when he affirmed: "We cast no aspersions on any race or creed, but we must remember that every object of our institutions of society and government will fail unless America be kept American."[1] That's all I want.

Ernest Van den Haag suggested, "The feeling [love of country] needs no justification anymore than one's love and preference for oneself and one's own does. That the feeling has often been rationalized in rather foolish terms is as true as it is irrelevant. Even if I think silly your **belief** that your mother, or girlfriend, is the greatest thing God ever made, I do not condemn your **feeling** about them. It needs no justification."[2]

Theodore Roosevelt cast his vote for my position when he said: "There is no room in this country for hyphenated Americans....The one absolutely certain way of bringing this nation to ruin, of preventing all possibility of its continuing to be a nation at all, would be to permit it to become a tangle of squabbling nationalities." He also added, "a hyphenated American is not an American at all."[3] Right on the button, Teddy!

John Jay in *The Federalist Papers* wrote that Americans were "one united people, a people descended from the same ancestors, speaking the same language, professing the same religion, attached to the same principles of government, very similar in their manners and customs."[4]

Benjamin Franklin worried about German immigration in 1751: "Why should Pennsylvania, founded by the English, become a Colony of Aliens, who will shortly be so numerous as to Germanize us instead of our Anglifying them... ?" Was Franklin a bigot? Did he hate people? Or did he simply want to keep America, America?

GATECRASHERS

We are told that there are up to 11 million illegal aliens in the U.S.! Many or most of those people may be hard workers and love their families, but **they broke our laws to get here**. They pushed in line ahead of others who respected our laws, followed our procedures, filled out the paper work, paid the fee, and eventually qualified to be citizens of this great country. The 11 million thumbed their noses at our laws and decency and crawled across the Rio Grande (or whatever) to get here.

The fact that many or most of those people are now making a contribution to America does not change the facts. They broke the law and need to be removed. And I would remind you that if a field worker can slip into America, terrorists can do so just as easily. More easily. Of the 8 to 11 million illegal aliens in the U.S., how many are terrorists? Of course, the killers on September 11 were here legally!

Most Americans don't know that there are more than 115,000

246

illegal gatecrashers from Middle Eastern countries in America today! Furthermore, "More than 1,000 of them were smuggled through Mexico by convicted global crime ring leader George Tajirian. And some 6,000 Middle Eastern men who have defied deportation orders remain on the loose "[5]

A new report has been issued by the Pew Hispanic Center that admits, "the majority of the 7.8 million **illegal** residents in the United States come from Mexico," and "nearly half of America's farm workers...are illegal aliens." Most Americans think that the Mexican illegal aliens are only farm workers; they are wrong. The report reveals that illegal Mexicans are in garment-making, meat-packing, construction, and manufacturing.[6] Furthermore, **none** of those were checked for criminal records, contagious diseases, ability to provide a living, or if they had any Middle East connection with terrorists!

UNLIMITED IMMIGRATION?

May I suggest that authorities make a concerted effort to apprehend all those people and jail those who are known criminals and expel all others who are "only" gatecrashers? If we picked up only one terrorist in the group, it would be worthwhile. After all, he may be the one planning on dropping a bomb over your city or poisoning your water supply! But how could we remove them? Simply load the Mexican illegal aliens in a ship off the California coast, sail to the Mexican Coast, and dump them for Mexican officials to deal with. Then give each of the remaining illegal aliens a one way ticket to the country of their origin or to one of the nations whose leaders whine about the U.S. "pulling up the ladder!"

My critics whine that people are suffering all over the world, that many of the gatecrashers only want a better life, and that is true; however, does that mean that America must become the social welfare system for the world, as well as the policeman of the world? After all, is there not a limit to what one country can do? And most Americans don't realize that we take in over half of the immigrants of the world! Wait a minute, what about England, Spain, France, Australia, etc.? If immigration is good for America, then it would be good for other nations, so let's spread it around to all nations.

Pro-immigration voices will accuse me and others of wanting to pull up the ladder once we have climbed aboard the ship. Yes, all nations are nations of immigrants, but just because we have been generous in the past does not mean that we must have no restrictions in the future. After all, every ship has a limit as to the number of passengers it can carry. Pulling up one more passenger may sink the boat![7] I ask pro-immigration advocates: Should America permit an unlimited number of immigrants? No sane person believes in **unlimited** immigration, so we disagree on the number of immigrants we should accept.

AMERICA FIRST

When a country is young and in need of farmers, artisans, tradesmen, etc., then immigration is reasonable and desirable. When the U.S. frontier was the Alleghenies in the 1700s, we needed more people and had plenty of room for them, but our frontier has been pushed to the Pacific. Also when a nation is at war, there is a need to raise a fighting army. However, that is not the situation at this time in American history. It is time to call a halt before permitting further immigration, for a time of balance to be established.

The bleating hearts will almost always sob: "But what about the Statue of Liberty?" What about her? The statement on the base of the statue is compassionate but not constitutional. It is not in the Constitution or any other major American document. The words are commendable: "Give me your tired, your poor, your huddled masses yearning to breathe free, The wretched refuse of your teeming shore." The statue was not "given to us by France" but paid for by French and American citizens in honor of our centennial, and the full name is "The Statue of Liberty Enlightening the World." Emma Lazarus, a young Zionist, was reacting to the assassination of Czar Alexander II in 1881, and she wrote the words added to the base. Commendable thought but hardly a constitutional mandate.

When immigration is continued, it should be based on our needs, not the needs of others. There is nothing wrong with saying, "American first, last, and always." There is everything right in putting our interests first. We should accept immigrants who have skills to offer in the furtherance of strengthening America. It is interesting that Mexico requires **their** immigrants to have useful skills and a pension plan from their nation of origin! If the U.S. required that of Mexican immigrants, the Mexican officials would scream like a stuck pig! How do you say "hypocrites" in Spanish?

QUALITY NOT QUANTITY

In recent years, the U.S. has attracted a large percentage of low-skilled people from Mexico and South America. That is understandable since there is no large middle class in that area; it is only natural that they would look North where there is unlimited freedom and opportunity. So we get the lowest skilled workers from those areas. After all, why would a lawyer, physician, or highly successful person want to leave his homeland to take up life in a foreign, sometime hostile land?

In a high tech age, we may want to allow highly qualified people to immigrate since they have much to offer us. What should count is "not the quantity of people but their quality–and the quality of their ideas."[8] Selfish? No, it is a sane, sensible policy, one the U.S. is not following.

We must insist that those immigrants are not carrying diseases that could explode into our native and unprotected population. The *Washington Post* reported that Virginia State health authorities announced that "tuberculosis continues to rise" and that "immigration is fueling the spread." The Virginia State Health Department released figures showing an increase of almost 5 percent in TB cases in the state between 2000 and 2001. As the *Post* reported, "Health officials say the rise of TB....is largely a consequence of the migration of people from parts of the world where the disease is common. It is thought that two-thirds of the cases of TB brought into the United States originated in just three countries: Mexico, the Philippines and Vietnam."[9] Immigration officials are irresponsible if they don't inquire as to a person's health, and it is criminal to permit people to enter the U.S. if they are carriers of plague, AIDS, typhoid, and other contagious diseases.

AMERICA'S CHANGING FACE

It is irresponsible to suggest that a huge influx of low-skilled, under-educated, often hostile gatecrashers will not have a long term, adverse effect on America. Your nation is being changed as you sleep. Now if you don't mind that and your bleating heart demands that we open our borders to permit anyone access, then so be it. Don't whine to me when you can't get a job or when your taxes are double what they are now, when your kids can't be educated in an overcrowded public school (they shouldn't be there anyway), when you see signs in Spanish everywhere you look, when workers who are supposed to serve you don't speak clear English, etc.

Those of us who demand a balanced immigration policy (and unashamedly argue for an "America First" policy) are characterized as bigots, xenophobes, haters, etc., but those who would change the face of America do not give us any reason to think it is wise, compassionate, thoughtful, or economically prudent. I maintain that we don't have to debate the issue; I choose to keep America, American. I know there are people who would like to immigrate here and who would make good Americans, but the boat is full. One more person may sink the boat.

As previously stated, I want my grandchildren to experience the America I experienced. Of course, they will not since globalists have taken over the media, academia, and politics; however, there is still a semblance of America. But, if we are flooded with people of a different religion, culture, work ethic, language, race, etc., it will not be America. Let's keep America, American and apply some common sense to our future immigration policies.

IS WHITE PRIDE WRONG?

We have observed environmental fanatics, in collusion with the Federal government, who go to outrageous efforts to preserve the snail darter, spotted owl, and the yellow belly sap sucker, so is it unreasonable to preserve America as the land of the free and the home of the brave? Why is it commendable for Blacks, Hispanics, and others to loudly proclaim their ethnicity, but when a **white** person does so, everyone treats him like a bigot? This is an issue that no one wants to deal with. It is as if there is an elephant sitting in a formal living room that no one admits is sitting there! While I don't want to be identified with the white supremacist crowd, I do think it is not only right but also desirable to be proud of our heritage.

Hey, if immigration is good, then let other nations take in the immigrants who are "yearning to breathe free...." If it is noble, kind, and compassionate to take in an unlimited number of foreigners, then let the other advanced nations get the blessings of immigration. It is not racism to suggest that the complexion of America is being changed, and while some think that is good, I don't. Why must white people apologize for being white? Because we think being white is just as good as being black, brown, etc., is that *prima fascia* evidence that we hate other people?

Blacks, Latin Americans, etc., should be proud of their race, after all God made them that way. So would you mind if I believe the same thing about being white? And why make America into another Hispanic country? Aren't there enough of them south of America? There are far more nations populated by people of color than white nations. Why not have a mainly white nation here and there around the globe? Why do we need another Spanish-speaking nation? And those who immigrate to the U.S. should learn to speak English! That is the least they can do. Teddy Roosevelt suggested that any immigrant who did not learn English within five years of his arrival should be shipped back home!

NIGHTLY INVASION

President Bush has declared war on terrorism, but he is taking counter measures when he talks of massive amnesty for illegal aliens who broke our laws to enter the U.S. Remember that more than 115,000 people from Middle Eastern countries are in the U.S. illegally. More than 1,000 of them were smuggled through Mexico by convicted global crime ring leader George Tajirian. And some 6,000 Middle Eastern men who have defied deportation orders remain on the loose [10]

Southern border officials are quietly saying that illegal Mexican immigration has slowed, but there is a big increase in OTMs or Other Than Mexicans. In fact, about one in ten illegal aliens caught are from a Middle Eastern country such as Egypt or Yemen. While American troops are fighting terrorists in various parts of the world, aliens from terrorist nations are invading our own nation nightly from Mexico!

George Morgan is a rancher on the U.S.–Mexican border, and he related a frightening incident that took place on Thanksgiving Day of 1998. "I stepped outside my house and there were over a hundred 'crossers' in my yard. [Expletive deleted] bunch of illegals I ever saw. All of them were wearing black pants, white shirts and string ties. They left, with the Border Patrol in pursuit. A while later, an agent, Dan Green, let me know that they had caught them. He said that they were all Iranians."[11] Hmmm. Do you think they were interested in picking tomatoes? How about cotton?

The above source reported that thirteen Yemen citizens were caught on September 24, 2001, as they were about to cross the border into Arizona from the border town of Agua Prieta. U. S. immigration didn't think they were terrorists; however, the Agua Prieta newspaper, *El Ciarin,* seemed to scream a headline saying: "The Arab terrorists were here!" Mexican officials took them to a Mexico City detention camp where they were released. They returned to the same border town across from Douglas, Arizona, within days.

Then Carlos X Carrillo of the U.S. Border Patrol told *WorldNetDaily* that nine Yemenis were in a hotel in Agua Prieta, Sonora, Mexico, across the border from Douglas, Arizona. The FBI was informed. An anonymous Border Patrol agent confirmed that nine Yemenis were in the hotel, but "They can't get a coyote to transport them and they are offering $30,000 per person with no takers." A "coyote" is a criminal who transports illegal immigrants across the border for a fee.

On October 12, 2001, a Mexican national who had some dealings with the Agua Prieta hotel left Mexico and moved to Arizona to seek seclusion. He said, "There were 134 Arabs there [in the hotel] when I left. They were paying the coyotes 30 to 50,000 bucks, apiece, to transport them safely into the U.S. I became so frightened I left. They are genuinely bad hombres."

SOME SUGGESTIONS

An observation: Illegal farm workers don't pay $50,000.00 to come into the U.S. to pick tomatoes or strawberries! Terrorists do. It's time to plug the holes in our walls; however, the Trojan Horse is already here. Even though there are an unknown number of terrorists in the U.S. who want to wreak havoc upon us, it is possible to limit their success. Some suggestions:

- ♦ Recognize that the Trojan Horse is full of people who hate us and wish to destroy our way of life, even our very nation.

- ♦ Pull up the ladder. No more immigration for at least a year or two. Only exceptions would be if a military man marries a foreigner, then she would be accepted.

- ♦ Plug all holes in the borders even using the military.

- ♦ Assess large penalties to any employer who hires an

illegal alien.

- ♦ Recognize that non-citizens do not have the rights that Americans have. Deport all who are here illegally. Fingerprint and photograph them and imprison them if they return.

- ♦ Fingerprint and photograph all visitors who come to America from Islamic nations. Fine them heavily if they overstay their visas.

- ♦ Go on record that we are no longer the world's policeman. We will not get involved in every brawl. Nations will handle their own problems. Our stated purpose of U.S. foreign policy is to protect the freedoms of U.S. citizens.

- ♦ Also go on record that there will be no more national (or international) welfare. All foreign aid will stop.

- ♦ Take the position on the Middle East that we have no position! We have no animosity for Muslims or Jews. We wish them both well and expect them to settle their own problems.

- ♦ Reject multiculturalism as anti-American and anti-common sense. We will no longer have a guilt complex for being successful.

UNFAIR

The above suggestion to fingerprint and photograph all visitors from Muslim nations has caused left-wingers to scream like a stuck pig. Egyptian physician, Hany Fares, said that if it is done, it should be done to all visitors. He said, "Muslims and Middle Easterners don't have to be terrorists. This is an insult."[12] Hey, Hany, you are right–and wrong. Muslims don't **have** to be terrorists, but all the terrorists who have attacked America have been Muslims!

Others have said that such documenting of Muslim visitors is "unfair"! Can you believe that? We lost over 3,000 innocent Americans; children are orphans; spouses are alone; massive financial problems exist, and Muslims talk about **our** being unfair! That's like a skunk accusing a rabbit of having bad breath! It's not unfair, but it is unbelievable that we have not been documenting all visitors from nations that foment terror as a way of life.

253

We must be vigilant that we don't become haters of good and decent people who are different from most of us. Such a result of terror would mean that they have been successful in destroying America, and it would no longer be America.

We must also "hold public officials' feet to the fire" and chain them to the Constitution (notice how smoothly I go from one metaphor to another?). We must be careful not to become un-American in our desire to remain American! Questionable "anti-terrorist" legislation has already been passed with more to follow. Much of it is only "feel good" legislation with no positive results.

BIG, BAD BILL

One bill has being introduced in all 50 state legislatures, emanating from the inner sanctums of Washington, that would make Marx, Lenin, Stalin, and Company stand up and cheer. Castro would also add his two cents worth (and that's about its value). It is an overreaching, overreaction to terror that would vastly expand the power of the state. It could be the most dangerous threat to American freedoms in 100 years! It is called the Model State Health Powers Act. It gives each state governor unprecedented power over every citizen in his state. The catalyst for this monster, that should have been strangled in its crib, is the war on terror. What else?

After wading through this bill I discovered the following. If this bill becomes law in your state, the Governor could, without any further legal action:

- Medically examine and vaccinate you without any medical justification.

- Isolate or quarantine you and your family even if you have no contagious disease. You could be isolated for refusing to be examined and/or vaccinated!

- Confiscate your auto, truck, food, fuel, medicines, guns, etc.

- Destroy your home (church or business) without compensation!

- Force any health care provider to help in the vaccination of people, whatever their personal convictions.

- Refuse to compensate you if you or your property is

damaged.

♦ Conscript you into state service.

The bill defines "isolation" as "the physical separation and confinement of an individual or groups of individuals who are infected or **reasonably believed** to be infected...." (Emphasis added.) No proof is required, only "reasonably believed" is sufficient.

Quarantine is defined as "the physical separation and confinement of an individual or groups of individuals who are or **may have been exposed** to a contagious or possibly contagious disease and who do not show signs or symptoms of a contagious disease" from others who are unexposed to possible danger. (Emphasis added.) Again, no proof necessary.

Article III requires pharmacists to report any increase in prescriptions, unusual prescriptions, antibiotics, or over the counter drugs you may have purchased. Your friendly neighborhood pharmacist would become the equivalent of the Russian neighborhood spy.

Article V deals with facilities and gives the state authority to close any building **thought** to be contaminated. It authorizes the state to confiscate and "take immediate possession thereof" of any facilities or materials thought necessary by the local commissar. And what would that include? How about "communication devices, carriers, real estate, fuels, food, and clothing." Under (c), it gives authority for the state to "inspect, control, restrict, and regulate by rationing...transportation of food, fuel, clothing and other commodities...."

Under VI, the state can examine you or your family and if you refuse, you will be isolated or quarantined. And if you refuse to be vaccinated? You will be isolated or quarantined. Under VI, Sec. 608, (a) any health care provider can be forced to give any vaccination thought necessary.

NO HELP FROM LEGISLATORS

The act could be implemented without a massive terrorist attack. If the governor thinks it is necessary, that's all that is required. For whatever reason! Some may think that their state representatives would restrain the governor but not so. The state legislature can do nothing about it until 60 days have passed!

Seven states (and Washington, D.C.) have already passed this legislation and many others are considering it as you read these words. Only twelve states, California, Connecticut, Idaho, Illinois, Kansas, Kentucky, Mississippi, Nebraska, Oklahoma, Wyoming, Wisconsin, and Washington have rejected this monster. Since we now have the Department of Homeland Security, the above measures are deeply hidden in that **federal** legislation. Welcome to the world of Big Brother!

We don't need these laws since we have courts available that authorities can go to if needed to implement temporary measures for our protection. But then they would have to comply with all restrictions imposed on them to protect the citizens. The Bill of Rights would come into play if authorities had to use the judicial system, but our protection under the Bill of Rights is abrogated under this proposed act.

We don't need more oppressive laws but the enforcement of present laws. We don't need more bureaucracy but Federal officials such as the FBI, CIA, etc., acting in a responsible and competent manner to protect us and apprehend terrorists. Maybe someone should remind Washington officials that the American citizen is not the enemy. The enemy is Muslim terrorists.

This legislation will probably pass in most states because "we have to do something." Yes, but not the wrong "something." Edmund Burke made a prescient statement relating to freedom: "The people never give up their liberties but under some delusion." The "delusion" is that such a law would give us some protection. Thinking people will be concerned that there would be a loss of liberty after the emergency is over. Again, Burke wrote: "Bad laws are the worst sort of tyranny." Experience has proved that while most of the oppressive acts would probably be removed, some would stay long afterwards to be a curse to future generations.

Those government officials who would plead special authority because of serious offences against us must not seduce us. The Constitution does not give authority to suspend The Bill of Rights. The U.S. Supreme Court ruled: "The Constitution of the United States is a law for rulers and people, equally in war and in peace, and covers with the shield of its protection all classes of men, at all times, and under all circumstances. No doctrine, involving more pernicious consequences, was ever invented by the wit of man than that **any** of its provisions can be suspended during any of the great exigencies of government." –United States Supreme Court, in Ex Parte Milligan 71 U.S. 2 (1866)– (Emphasis added.)

NEUTRAL AMERICA

Finally, let's return to our roots and become a truly neutral nation like Switzerland. I have been to Switzerland many times and have a great appreciation for the Swiss. A Swiss writer expressed his nation's position very well: "Switzerland is a neutral country. It has made permanent armed neutrality, a concept of preventing war, the maxim of its foreign policy. By doing so Switzerland guarantees four permanent objectives. It will never begin a war, it will never enter a war on the side of a warring party, it will never one-sidedly support warring parties, but it will vigorously defend itself against any attacking party."[13] That is where America used to be. Switzerland goes a step further and requires each homeowner to possess and know how to use a gun. Every adult is expected to defend the nation if attacked by another. But why would any nation want to attack a nation that will defend itself and adheres to the above four principles of neutrality?

It is past time to start facing reality about terror. Ayn Rand reminded us that "You can evade reality, but you cannot evade the consequences of evading reality." American officials had better get serious about terror, beyond doing things to make us all feel warm and cozy. We must recognize the enemy as the enemy; remove him from our shores; restore our nation to a nation of free people living under a Constitution. It's late, and we must get started today!

1. Coolidge's Acceptance Speech at the Republican Presidential Nomination August 14, 1924.

2. *National Review*, 9-21-65.

3. Quoted by Philip Davis (ed.), *Immigration and Americanization,* Boston, Ginn and Company, 1920.

4. *Federalist Papers,* No. 2.

5. *Jewish World Review*, 3-22-02.

6. Chattanooga Times Free-Press, 3-22-02.

7. *National Review*, "Time to Rethink Immigration?" 6-22-92.

8. Ibid.

9. *Washington Post,* 3-18-02.

10. *Jewish World Review,* 3-22-02.

11. Donald McAlvany, *The McAlvany Intelligence Advisor,* Cited in *The Lion of Judah,* April 2002.

12. Marium Fam, Associated Press, "Arabs, Muslims angry over fingerprint plan," 6-6-02.

13. Matthias Erne, *Current Concerns,* "Reflections from Switzerland--Neutrality: Protection against Terror" Sept/Oct., 2001.

Epilogue

What Kind of America Do You Want?

There is no doubt that I have been misunderstood by many people reading these pages; however, that was not my intent. Yes, I have used sarcasm and have been forceful at times in presenting my position, but difficult times demand strong and decisive action. I repeat my question for those who think I have been too hard, harsh, or even hateful: What if terrorists drop a nuclear bomb over one of our major cities resulting in the deaths of 100,000 Americans from the blast with another 300,000 dying of radiation; plunging the stock market to the basement; devastating our economy for a generation; putting millions of people out of work; producing fear and anxiety up and down every street in the nation; would you still think me to be too harsh? Many national leaders think the above could happen, with millions being killed. Or major populations might be infected with a biological or chemical weapon! Government officials **have** distributed gas masks to Washington lawmakers in recent days!

I am firmly convinced (as I hope you are by now) that we are in a war. It is a clash of cultures and of religions, and even though we don't like religious wars, they do happen. We must remember that this war was not of our making. A large host of Muslims decided on this war. And war it is. It started even before September 11, 2001.

FORCES OF FREEDOM

If the U.S. and the "forces of freedom" are to win, then we must be dauntless, decisive, and determined. We must understand, if we have not already, that our world has changed forever. We will not be able to remove all Muslims from our country, and we should **not** remove those who are sincere, hardworking, assimilating Americans. But those who aid and abet terrorists are the enemy, even if they deplore extreme activities. Honest, kind, gracious Muslims must understand that if they are not for us, they are against us.

Muslim immigrants to the U.S. must be willing to melt into our society. No, they don't have to forget and reject everything from their home country, but they must love America if they choose to live here. Obviously they think America is better than their former home. If not, why come here? They should have a love affair with America. If not, they should go home. Theodore Roosevelt said: "The man who loves other countries as much as his own stands on a level with the man who loves other women as much as he loves his own wife."[1] So Muslims should be proud, appreciative, grateful Americans who happen to have been born in a foreign land, a land they have rejected when they stepped on our shores.

To the "moderate" Muslims out there who are trying to walk the fence, I would ask: What will you do if you must decide between the Koran and the U.S. Constitution? The great majority, even those who say they abhor terror, will choose the Koran. Informed people will say, "But you Christians believe that the Bible must be obeyed above everything else." That is correct, but we don't fly planes into buildings and walk into restaurants wearing body bombs! You see, we have proved over hundreds of years that we don't believe in violence, except in self-defense. Christians follow the Bible's command in II Timothy 2:24 that says: "And the servant of the Lord must not strive; but be gentle unto all men, apt to teach, patient." The Koran teaches anger, hatred, adultery, slavery, murder, oppression of women, etc., and while some professing Christians are guilty of some of those sins, they are disobedient to Christ and His Word. Nor do thinking Christians seek to defend professing Christians who disobey Christ.

WAR BETWEEN CHRIST AND MOHAMMED

In closing, I must make a major point: We have a Trojan Horse in America even if none of the terrorist attacks were done by Muslims! Assume there has been a massive mistake, conspiracy, whatever, and no Muslim was involved in the attacks on America. We still have a problem with our whole society being subjugated by a foreign religion that is determined to completely change our nation by coercion, if necessary. You must ask if that is what you want. What kind of America do you want for your children and grandchildren? It will be changed because the Trojan Horse in America is

260

Islam, and even a "peaceful" Islam is a threat to America's staying America!

I will be the first to demand that Muslims be treated kindly and with respect, even though they ridicule Christ and what we stand for. As Americans they have the right to do that. We don't have to like what they do and say, and they must not be intimidated, harmed, or harassed in any way unless they break the law. Then, like you and me, they must pay the penalty for lawbreaking.

Some Muslims have complained that they do not feel comfortable going to their mosques and about their everyday duties since September 11. Some of them have been cursed and intimidated by American thugs. I am ashamed of those Americans; however, it is interesting that few Muslims have demanded their former homeland guarantee religious freedom to Christians living there. And none of the heads of state in Muslim nations have called for religious freedom in those states.

Whether we like it or not and whether politicians recognize it or not, we are in a war between Christ and Mohammed. And Christ's cross will be victorious over the crescent moon. When men of the cross, with the mark of the cross, take the message of the cross (without making it a holy horseshoe), we will be "more than conquerors" through Christ.

Christians must win the Muslims to Christ as Muslims seek to win America to Islam! Maybe if we had been more aggressive in telling them the good news, we might not have the terror we have today. We must tell them that the bad news has a cure, and it is Christ. Everyone must hear the bad news, that all of us are sinners, but the good news is that there is a remedy for the bad news. It is faith in Christ. We will win them if we go after them in unreserved, unselfish, and unconditional love, telling them that repentance of sin and placing simple faith in Christ will produce the New Birth that Jesus said is the requirement to enter Heaven. Even those terrorists inside the Trojan Horse can have that life-changing, eternity-deciding experience. Let's get to it!

Jesus Christ is still the hope, the **only** hope for this world!

1.   "The Indomitable President," The American President web site.

Glossary

Abd: a male slave; a slave of God.

Abu: father of.

Adhan: a daily announcement from a mosque calling Muslims to prayer.

Ahl al-Bait: the people of the house.

Ahl al-Kitab: the "people of the Book."

Ahmad: another name for Mohammed.

Al-Akhirah: the after-life; the last day.

Allahu Akbar: Allah is the greatest.

Allah: the Islamic name for God although it was the pagan moon god of the Arabs. Claimed by Muslims to be the same as the God of the Jews and Christians.

'Amah: a female slave.

Amir: emir, a ruler, chief or nobleman.

'Aqeeda: belief in Allah, the one God; belief in angels; in Allah's revealed books; in Allah's judgment; in his messengers; in the day of Judgment; in fate.

Ashab al-A`raf: people who are not good enough to go to Paradise nor bad enough to be sent to hell. They will be sent someplace between the two.

Al-Asma al-Husna: the most exalted names of God that express all his attributes.

'Asr: late afternoon prayer said just before sunset. Also the name of Sura 103.

Assalamu 'Alaikum: One of the best known Islamic phrases meaning "peace be on you."

'Aurah: part of the human body that should not be exposed.

Bab Al-Raiyand: one of the gates of Heaven.

Badr: one of the first major battles won by Islam.

Bai'ah: a pledge given to a Muslim cleric to be faithful to his Islamic teaching.

Baitul Mal: treasury.

Bismillah Hir Rehman Nir Rahim: This is the first verse of Surah (Chapter 1) of the Koran. It is also a statement made by Muslims who are about to do something lawful, whether small or big. It means, "In the name of Allah, the Most Gracious, the Most Merciful."

Buhtan: a false accusation or slander.

Caliph: the head of a Muslim state.

Dar Al-Harb: the abode of war; territory not under Islam.

Dajjal: Anti-Christ.

Dar al-Kufr: domain of Unbelief; refers to the territory under the hegemony of the unbelievers.

Dawah: the spreading of Islam through word and action.

Dhihar: a kind of divorce that was common in pre-Islamic Arabia, but was made unlawful by Islam.

Dhimmi: a person in a non-Muslim religion tolerated upon payment of heavy taxes.

Dhu'l-Hijjah: the 12th month of the Islamic calendar. Also the month in which the pilgrimage to Mecca took place.

Din: the core meaning of din is obedience.

Diyah: blood money, paid by the guilty as a compensation for killing or harming a person.

Du'a: asking Allah for what one desires.

Duhr: second required prayer of the day, to be prayed any time between noon and mid-afternoon.

Eblis: Satan.

Eid Al-Adha: Literally means "the feast of the sacrifice." This feast is supposed to commemorate Abraham's obedience to Allah by being prepared to sacrifice his son Ishmael.

Emir: Muslim leader.

Fai: war booty gained without fighting.

Fajr: the time of the first required prayer that can be prayed between dawn and sunrise.

Faqeeh: an Islamic scholar who is qualified to give a legal opinion.

Faqih: a legal scholar of the sharia.

Fard 'Ain: any action which is required for every Muslim.

Fasad: corruption.

Fasiq: a transgressor, disobedient.

Fatwa: A legal opinion based upon the teaching of the Koran and the Hadith.

Fidya: Compensation for missing required acts of worship usually by donating money or sacrificing an animal.

Fiqh: Islamic jurisprudence.

Fi sabil Allah: A phrase used in the Koran meaning good actions that should be done only to please God.

Fisq: transgression against the command of God.

Gharar: This is selling something which you do not have such as selling eggs which have not yet been laid.

Ghayy: name of a pit in Hell.

Ghazwa: a battle for the cause of Allah in which Muhammad himself took part.

Gheebah: backbiting.

Ghusl: the full ritual of washing the body with water to be pure for prayer.

Gog and Magog: two wicked empires.

Hadi: a cow, sheep or a goat that is offered as a sacrifice by a pilgrim during the Hajj.

Hadith: narration and in Islam it means the collected sayings of Mohammed.

Hajar Al-Aswad: the black stone in a corner of the Kaaba that is kissed by pilgrims.

Hajj: the pilgrimage to Mecca.

Halal: legal as defined by Allah.

Hashr (Al): another name for the Day of Judgment.

265

Hawiyah: sixth level of Hell; the final home of Christians.

Hijra: Mohammed's flight from Mecca to Medina in 622.

Hukm: judgment or decision.

Iblis: chief promoter of evil; Satan.

Iftar: breaking of the fast immediately after sunset.

Ijma: consensus of Islamic scholars; comes next to the Koran and the Sunnah as source of doctrines.

Ijtihad: to exercise personal judgment based on the Koran and the Sunnah.

Imam: leader.

Insha Allah: "If Allah wills."

Intifada: uprising.

Iqamah: the call to prayer.

Islam: submission.

Isra: refers to Mohammed's alleged journey from Mecca to Jerusalem.

Ithm: indicates negligence; sin.

Jahanam: This is one of the seven levels of hell. There are seven levels of Hell.

1. Jaheem - this is the shallowest level of Hell reserved for those who believed in Allah and Mohammed but who ignored His commands.
2. Jahanam - a deeper level where the idol-worshippers are to be sent.
3. Sa'ir - is reserved for the worshippers of fire.
4. Saqar - this is where those who did not believe in Allah will be sent on the Day of Judgment.
5. Ladha - will be the home of the Jews.
6. Hawiyah - will be the eternal home of the Christians.
7. Hutama - the deepest level of Hellfire. This is where the religious hypocrites will spend eternity.

Jannah: a paradise created for those who believe in the Unity of Allah and his prophets and who follow them.

Jihad: striving; holy war; the obligation of all Muslims to combat unbelievers.

Jinn: creation of Allah who can choose between good and evil.

Jizyah: required tax upon non-Muslims for the privilege of living in an Islamic nation.

Jum'ah: Friday, the day that all Muslims must go to the mosque for prayers and a sermon.

Kaaba: a cube-shaped building in Mecca, allegedly built by Abraham and Ishmael; all Muslims pray toward it.

Kaffarah: atonement.

Kafir: this is a person who rejects Mohammed's message.

Khamrs: wine.

Khums: one-fifth of booty from battles that went to Mohammed.

Khutbah: sermon.

Koran: Islam's "holy" book; also spelled Quran.

Mahr: payment of husband to wife at time of their marriage.

Mahram: a person whom a woman can not marry because of close relationship.

Malaikah: angels.

Mansookha: replaced.

Midri: iron comb.

Mulla: a member of the ulama.

Mulhid: an atheist.

Munafiq: a hypocrite.

Murtad: an apostate.

Muslim: a person who accepts Islam as his or her way of life.

Nasara: Christians according to the Koran and Haditih.

Nifaq: hypocrisy.

Nikah: marriage.

Niqab: a type of veil that covers the entire face including the eyes.

P.B.U.H.: Peace be upon him and always used with the name of Mohammed.

Qabr: grave.

Quraish: the Arab tribe to which Mohammed belonged.

Ramadan: the ninth month of the Islamic calendar when fasting is required.

Rea': carrying out a religious act for worldly gains and not for Allah.

Sajdah: prostration.

Salah: prayers.

Sawm: fasting.

Shahid: martyr.

Sheikh: leader of a tribe; title of respect.

Shaheeds: martyrs.

Sharia: signifies the entire Islamic way of life, especially the Law of Islam.

Siwak: a piece of branch or root of a tree used as a toothbrush.

Sunna: the practice of Mohammed; the recording of the practice.

Tajweed: recitation of the Koran with exact articulation.

Takiya: peace made when one is weak to give time to gather strength so one can smash his enemy.

Tawaf: the circling of the Kaaba in sets of seven circuits.

Ulama: scholar of Islam.

Ummah: community, or nation.

'Umrah: pilgrimage that consists of a journey to the Kaaba, where Muslims circumambulate around the Kaaba.

Zanadiqa: atheist.

Zina: means illegal sexual intercourse.

INDEX

46, 48, 62, 68, 78, 81, 82, 83, 84, 85, 91, 92, 105, 120, 134, 137, 138, 153, 156, 158, 165, 167, 168, 171, 172, 175, 217, 218, 219, 228, 237, 241, 253, 263, 266

Jihad, 27, 28, 68, 74, 90, 158, 266

Josephus, 95, 153, 171, 176

Justinian, 199, 206, 207, 213, 214

Kaaba, 79, 83, 95, 96, 265, 266, 268

Kab, 81

Kabbani, Muhammad Hisham, 102

Kabbanii, Shaykh Hiham, 193

Kennedy, John, 180

Khadija, 78

Khaldun, Ibn, 104

Khalifa, Rashad, 128, 129

Khobar Towers, 234

Koran, 5, 16, 26, 27, 35, 39, 61, 68, 72, 76, 77, 79, 80, 85, 90, 97, 99, 100, 102, 105, 109, 111, 125, 127, 129, 130, 131, 132, 133, 134, 135, 136, 137, 139, 140, 142, 143, 144, 145, 148, 183, 260, 264, 265, 267

bin Laden, Osama, 28, 70, 152, 186, 235

Law, Cardinal, 156

Lebed, Alexander, 185

Lemnitzer, Lyman, 179, 181

Leo I, 154

Library of Congress, 2, 190

Limbaugh, David, 43

Little, Malcolm, 114

London, 6, 28, 30, 64, 65, 74, 94, 104, 145, 146, 148, 154, 177, 194, 200, 207, 210, 211, 214, 223, 225

Lowry, Rich, 231

Loyd, Anthony, 186, 195

Luther, Martin, 105, 162

malaria, 198, 202, 203, 205

Malcolm X, 5, 114, 115, 116, 117, 118, 119, 126

Malvo, Lee Boyd, 123

Manchester, William, 158, 176

Marcellinus, Ammianus, 198

Marshall, Thurgood, 117

Martel, Charles, 103

Mary, mother of Jesus, 119, 135, 137, 138, 171

Mason, George, 47

Mayflower Compact, 238

McCarthy, Senator Joe, 180

McClintock and Strong, 78

McVeigh, Tim, 21, 191

Mecca, 28, 37, 42, 58, 77, 79, 81, 82, 83, 95, 97, 112, 116, 127, 132, 133, 138, 143, 150, 152, 264, 265, 266

Meccans, 80, 82, 133

Medina, 79, 82, 103, 132, 143,

265

Printed in Canada